Martin Müller

Making Great Power Identities in Russia

Forum Politische Geographie

Herausgegeben von Paul Reuber

Schriftleitung: Günter Wolkersdorfer †

Band 4

www.politische-geographie.de

LIT

Martin Müller

Making Great Power Identities in Russia

An ethnographic discourse analysis of education at a Russian elite university

LIT

Umschlagbild: Ömer Alpaslan

D 30

Bibliographic information published by the Deutsche Nationalbibliothek
The Deutsche Nationalbibliothek lists this publication in the Deutsche Nationalbibliografie; detailed bibliographic data are available in the Internet at http://dnb.d-nb.de.

ISBN 978-3-643-90010-4
Zugl.: Frankfurt am Main, Goethe-Universität, Diss., 2008

A catalogue record for this book is available from the British Library

Dufourstr. 31
CH-8008 Zürich
Tel. +41 (0) 44-251 75 05
Fax +41 (0) 44-251 75 06
e-Mail: zuerich@lit-verlag.ch
http://www.lit-verlag.ch

LIT VERLAG Dr. W. Hopf
Berlin 2009
Fresnostr. 2
D-48159 Münster
Tel. +49 (0) 2 51-620 32 22
Fax +49 (0) 2 51-922 60 99
e-Mail: lit@lit-verlag.de
http://www.lit-verlag.de

Distribution:
In Germany: LIT Verlag Fresnostr. 2, D-48159 Münster
Tel. +49 (0) 2 51-620 32 22, Fax +49 (0) 2 51-922 60 99, e-Mail: vertrieb@lit-verlag.de

In Austria: Medienlogistik Pichler-ÖBZ GmbH & Co KG
IZ-NÖ, Süd, Straße 1, Objekt 34, A-2355 Wiener Neudorf
Tel. +43 (0) 22 36-63 53 52 90, Fax +43 (0) 22 36-63 53 52 43, e-Mail: mlo@medien-logistik.at

In Switzerland: B + M Buch- und Medienvertriebs AG
Hochstr. 357, CH-8200 Schaffhausen
Tel. +41 (0) 52-643 54 30, Fax +41 (0) 52-643 54 35, e-Mail: order@buch-medien.ch

Distributed in the UK by: Global Book Marketing, 99B Wallis Rd, London, E9 5LN
Phone: +44 (0) 20 8533 5800 – Fax: +44 (0) 1600 775 663
http://www.centralbooks.co.uk/html

Distributed in North America by:

Transaction Publishers
New Brunswick (U.S.A.) and London (U.K.)

Transaction Publishers
Rutgers University
35 Berrue Circle
Piscataway, NJ 08854

Phone: +1 (732) 445 - 2280
Fax: + 1 (732) 445 - 3138
for orders (U. S. only):
toll free (888) 999 - 6778
e-mail: orders@transactionpub.com

Abstract

This book examines how the geopolitical discourse of a strong Russia plays out at a Moscow cadre university. In so doing, it provides an inside perspective on the *geopolitical education of the future Russian elites* and thus, possibly, on the future directions of Russian foreign policy. The material for my research was gathered during nine months of *ethnographic research* as a guest student at the Moscow State Institute of International Relations (MGIMO). This institute is the pivotal Russian cadre university which trains students to serve in the Russian Foreign Ministry and to occupy influential positions in Russian society at large.

Conceptually, my project argues that the way identity has commonly been thought of in the fields of Political Geography and International Studies overlooks two crucial things: first, that social practice – what people *do* – is an important part of identity and, second, that identities are situated, i.e. they unfold in concrete contexts. To address these lacunae I draw on the *poststructuralist discourse theory* of Ernesto Laclau and Chantal Mouffe and ideas of Pierre Bourdieu and Michel Foucault. I combine this conceptual apparatus with ethnographic methodology to look at geopolitical discourses at MGIMO and how they come to position subjects in their identification.

With Foucault, MGIMO produces *'docile bodies'* and objectifies knowledge through various small disciplinary techniques. It is this disciplining effect which provides for the successful functioning of the hegemonic discourse of a strong Russia at MGIMO. This geopolitical identity of a strong Russia is articulated as a response to the crisis of identity following the dislocation after the collapse of the Soviet Union. Yet, antagonistic forces always *block the full realisation of a strong Russia.* What lies at the heart of this identity is a constitutive lack that makes for a fundamental ambiguity: articulations of a strong Russia are always intertwined with the imminent possibility of a weak Russia.

At MGIMO this ambiguous geopolitical identity of a strong Russia is paired with *banal patriotism.* This patriotism forms an almost natural element of students' everyday lives. Not only is it considered a central element of education and a pre-requisite for any good graduate and future diplomat but it also permeates quotidian practices of production and consumption. Through this banal patriotism the political is incorporated into the realm of the everyday and fashioned with the same objective qualities, thus naturalising the discourse of a strong Russia.

Contents

Index of tables

Index of figures

List of abbreviations

APEC	Asia-Pacific Economic Cooperation
CIS	Commonwealth of Independent States
CSTO	Collective Security Treaty Organisation (Military alliance of CIS states)
EurAsEC	Eurasian Economic Community (Economic association of CIS states)
EUR	Currency code of the euro
GDP	Gross Domestic Product
IJ	International Journalism (School at MGIMO)
IR	International Relations (School at MGIMO)
MGIMO	Moscow State Institute of International Relations
APEC	Asia-Pacific Economic Cooperation
MID	Ministry of Foreign Affairs of Russia
NATO	North Atlantic Treaty Organisation
OSCE	Organisation for Security and Co-operation in Europe
PS	Political Science (School at MGIMO)
RSFSR	Russian Soviet Federative Socialist Republic
RUB	Currency code of the Russian ruble
RUR	Currency code of the Russian ruble prior to the 1998 devaluation
USSR	Union of Soviet Socialist Republics

Technical preliminaries

Presentation of transcripts

Excerpts from interview transcripts are followed by information on the study year and the department of the interviewee as well as an index number. The relevant departments are International Relations (IR), Political Science (PS) and International Journalism (IJ). Students from other departments are marked as 'Other'. Student names have all been changed and fictitious first names are only used to distinguish individual students and indicate their gender. In order to be able to guarantee anonymity further information about students is not provided nor are names of lectures or lecturers.

Transliteration

Transliteration from the Cyrillic into the Latin alphabet follows scientific transliteration according to the International Scholarly System. Other transliterations of proper names were kept where they represented common use (e.g. *Yeltsin* instead of *El'cin*).

А, а	*A, a*	К, к	*K, k*	Х, х	*X, x*
Б, б	B, b	Л, л	L, l	Ц, ц	C, c
В, в	V, v	М, м	M, m	Ч, ч	Č, č
Г, г	G, g	Н, н	N, n	Ш, ш	Š, š
Д, д	D, d	О, о	O, o	Щ, щ	Šč, šč
Е, е	E, e	П, п	P, p	Ъ, ъ	"
Ё, ё	Ë, ë	Р, р	R, r	Ы, ы	Y, y
Ж, ж	Ž, ž	С, с	S, s	Ь, ь	'
З, з	Z, z	Т, т	T, t	Э, э	È, è
И, и	I, i	У, у	U, u	Ю, ю	Ju, ju
Й, й	J, j	Ф, ф	F, f	Я, я	Ja, ja

Preface

This study aims to present both conceptual advances in thinking about the discursive constitution of identities and new empirical insights on making great power identities in Russia. Beyond the theoretical discussion of discourse theory, it has been my concern to generate meaningful empirical material and draw out the political implications of my analysis. More than a purely idiographic study, I have sought to connect the insights of my ethnographic research to the larger debates on Russian foreign policy and geopolitical identity. This book is therefore relevant both for the academic world and for the professional expert who wants to understand Russian foreign policy from the inside.

Being the interdisciplinary project it is, this book is situated between the fields of human geography and international relations. Because of my own academic background in human geography, it builds on the body of literature that has become known as critical geopolitics and examines the social construction of global space. But it could just as well depart from the cognate fields of critical or poststructuralist international relations and the newly emergent international political sociology which have also informed my analysis.

The structure of the book follows the classic composition pattern: theory and critique – literature review – methodology – empirical analysis – discussion. Chapter nine constitutes the centrepiece of the work where theory and empirical material coalesce in a synthetic analysis. For those primarily interested in the empirical part I would recommend reading chapter three for a literature review of geopolitical orientations in Russia and chapters six to eight as well as ten for the presentation of geopolitical views at MGIMO and their larger implications for understanding Russian foreign policy.

A number of published and working papers have developed out of this project. I have tried to keep the overlap between the papers and the monograph as small as possible. Both are thus designed to complement each other and in the monograph I will occasionally refer to the papers for details of an argument. The publications in question can be found in the bibliography.

1

A different perspective on a strong Russia

> Russia is faced with an identity crisis: it must define what it means to be Russian without empire, where the boundaries of Russia should lie, and what role the country should play within the post-Cold-War world order. Above all, this search for place and meaning for Russians represents a crisis of homeland, of finding and negotiating a new role, border and identity for a country and its people (G. Smith 1999a: 49).

Ten years ago, Graham Smith was not the only one who saw Russia mired in a prolonged crisis of identity. Public and academic debate was rife with bleak assessments of Russia's state of the nation. For many, the desolate state of affairs was encapsulated in a nation-wide competition in 1996, endowed with a prize money of RUR 10 million (about EUR 1,500), to find a 'Russian, common-national idea' (*rossijskaja, obščenacional'naja ideja*). This was also the time when Boris Yeltsin appointed one of his presidential aides to investigate the 'problem' of Russia's absent national identity (Chinyaeva 1997). The crisis of identity was accompanied by a decline of Russia's perceived weight in world politics. At that time, the West considered Russia by and large a weak and troubled country, engrossed in a search of itself and fraught with domestic problems. World politics ran smoothly without it.

How different is the assessment today! In the aftermath of the war in South Ossetia in August 2008 Thomas Kleine-Brockhoff, Senior Director for Policy Programs at the German Marshall Fund of the United States, claims that the world witnesses

> the attempt of a country to return to the centre of world politics with force. The Russian occupation tanks in Georgia are a symbol for the attempt to re-establish old patterns of geopolitics. To create a belt of satellite states with limited sovereignty is Moscow's aim. ... Backed through an explosively rising oil price, Moscow has started a kind of rollback (Kleine-Brockhoff 2008: 2).

Writing in the *Washington Post* on 11 August 2008, neoconservative analyst Robert Kagan, member of the American Council on Foreign Relations and foreign policy advisor to then presidential candidate John McCain, detects

> a new geopolitical fault line that runs along the western and southwestern frontiers of Russia. From the Baltics in the north through Central Europe and the Balkans to the Caucasus and Central Asia, a geopolitical power struggle has emerged between a resurgent and revanchist Russia on one side and the European Union and the United States on the other (Kagan 2008: A15).

Kagan claims that Putin

> has reestablished a virtual czarist rule in Russia and is trying to restore the country to its once-dominant role in Eurasia and the world. Armed with wealth from oil and gas; holding a near-monopoly over the energy supply to Europe; with a million soldiers, thousands of nuclear warheads and the world's third-largest military budget, Vladimir Putin believes that now is the time to make his move (Kagan 2008: A15).

Making sense of Russian foreign policy behaviour, the rhetoric of geopolitical conflict and power politics experiences a renaissance. Reading these accounts, one cannot help but get the impression that world politics faces an evil empire redux. Times of crisis seem to be a thing of the past as Russia forcefully asserts its presence on the stage of world politics. Be it the open criticism of American unilateralism, the opposition to the American missile shield in Eastern Europe, the row with Britain over the extradition of criminals, the gas dispute with Ukraine or the military confrontation with Georgia – Russia's visibility and self-confidence in world politics appear to be higher than ever before. In the West, however, Russia's new assertiveness is accompanied by a sense of looming confrontation and threat. Commentators argue that with its newly gained power, Russia is growing ever more confident to enter into a rivalry with the West – perhaps precipitating a new Cold War, as Edward Lucas (2008) is not alone to suggest. Even more moderate analysts like Dmitrij Trenin (2006) write that 'Russia has begun acting like the great power it was in tsarist times', resuscitating imperialist ambitions.

It has been the mainstay of the field of *critical geopolitics* to expose such narratives of global confrontation and geopolitical power struggle as contingent social constructions. The purported objectivity of these analyses naturalises political action and partitions the complex, unruly landscapes of world politics into clear divisions: 'the West' is here and close, and 'Russia' is out there, threatening, and other. Russia is the revanchist, imperialist power and the

West has to stop it from becoming ever more aggressive. This division of world politics into Self and Other is the foundation for the emergence of geopolitical identities.

In the spirit of critical geopolitics, this book attempts a critical analysis of Russian great power identities – but from an uncommon perspective. Against the dominance of Western-centric, macro level studies of imaginations about Russia's place and role in world politics, it pits an in-depth, micro level analysis of the production of a 'strong Russia' from within Russia. The following pages present primary material from nine months of participant ethnographic research as a student at Moscow State Institute of International Relations (MGIMO), a cadre university for training future Russian elites. But in spite – or rather because – of its unique data, this book does not intend to reveal a new truth about Russia's 'real' place in world politics to complement or rival the old ones above. Instead, it shall attempt to present a *different perspective* in four distinct respects: conceptual, methodological, empirical and political.

In engaging with the making of great power identities in Russia through the *conceptual lens of discourse theory* this book positions itself as a response to three key challenges to discourse studies outlined by Torfing:

> (1) It [discourse studies] must demonstrate the analytical value of discourse theory in empirical studies that take us beyond the mere illustration of the arguments and concepts. …
>
> (2) It must address the core topics and areas within social and political science and not be content with specializing in allegedly 'soft' topics such as gender, ethnicity, and social movements. …
>
> (3) It must critically reflect upon the questions of method and research strategy (Torfing 2004: 25).

My study engages with the central but under-theorised concept of discourse in critical geopolitics by drawing on poststructuralist discourse theory in the interpretation by Ernesto Laclau and Chantal Mouffe (1985). In so doing, it argues for the centrality of social practices in the analysis of the discursive constitution of identities. The explicit attention to practice within the discourse concept urges to situate identities within specific institutional settings. By looking at practices in institutional settings we can get a more precise idea of the power of discourses to position subjects. In my study, the university plays a central role as the institutional locus for the situated production of geopolitical identities. The thoughts of social theorists Pierre Bourdieu (1996) and Michel Foucault (1979) are of particular relevance for understanding educational institutions as sites of subjectivation. With Bourdieu, MGIMO reproduces elites for Russian society through practices of consecration. With Foucault, MGIMO institutes a regime of discipline and truth that turns its subjects into 'docile bodies'.

The conceptual attention to discursive practices requires an adequate *methodological translation*. Ethnography suggests itself as the methodology of choice for this purpose. The long-term participation of the researcher in the contextualised meaning-making of a social group allows to collapse the analytical distance that is a feature of so much work in critical geopolitics and international relations (cf. Bigo and Walker 2007; Dowler and Sharp 2001; Megoran 2006). By distance I here mean a tendency to view world politics as a field of disembodied relations between states, sometimes even reduced to abstract statistical models. This analytical distance elides that people's experiences lie at the heart of every state and that writing them out of accounts of world politics produces a somewhat lop-sided scholarship. Ethnography's close observation of settings introduces a useful corrective in this respect; at the same time, however, I shall be careful not to reduce it to mere idiographic description. Making my ethnography relevant calls for connecting the local to the global and drawing out implications for understanding Russian geopolitical identity at large.

Empirically, critical analysis of Russian geopolitics has traditionally relied on quantitative methods or analysis of documents and media reports. In recent publications empirical instruments employed standardised surveys (e.g. O'Loughlin and Talbot 2005; O'Loughlin et al. 2004a, b, 2005; Rose and Munro 2008; Zimmerman 2002, 2005) or analysis of books, newspaper articles, government documents, speeches, foreign policy events etc. (e.g. Hopf 2002; Ingram 2001; Kolossov and Turovsky 2001; Mäkinen 2003; Neumann 1996; O'Loughlin 2001; O'Loughlin et al. 2004a, b; Prozorov 2006; G. Smith 1999a, b; Tsygankov 2003a, 2007). By presenting ethnographic material from inside an institution central to the teaching of Russian foreign policy my research adds a new empirical perspective to this field. Because MGIMO educates the future Russian elite, the university provides a window onto possible developments in Russian geopolitical orientation. If, as it is often assumed, Russia currently experiences a resurgence of a geopolitical identity as a great power, this will, to some extent, be reflected in young people that are to later occupy influential positions in the Russian state and in private companies.

What is more, in applying discourse theory to the analysis of my material, my study not only looks at *what* is articulated in discourses about Russia's place in world politics. More importantly, it looks at the functioning and structure of discourses – at *how* geopolitical identities are articulated.

Politically, this different perspective interprets discourse theory as a critical theory of hegemony. It is the task of the discourse theorist to map the closures and objectivities of hegemonic discourses and show where knowledge becomes naturalised. This task applies both to the empirical material and to the global production of knowledge about Russia as a great power. With regard to the empirical material, it calls to foreground the contingency of the subject positions with which students and lecturers at MGIMO identify. With regard to the global production of knowledge about Russian geopolitical orientations, it calls to challenge the hegemonic discourse of Russia as an imperialist, aggressive great power which seems to be almost *de rigueur* in Western writing about Russian foreign policy today. Although much critical scholarship rightly condemns human rights violations, xenophobic violence and democratic deficits in Russia, constructing Russia as an imperial Other in world politics is to be equally opposed as a hegemonic closure.

This different conceptual, methodological, empirical and political perspective is perhaps best summarised by Lorraine Dowler and Joanne Sharp, who sketch a vision of critical international studies that has inspired this book:

> A culturally informed but nevertheless still resolutely political take on ... international relations could consider the practices and institutional locales of international relations ... This would involve continued engagement with the discourses and narratives which structure these geographies ... but would go further to see how these discourses actually work in everyday life and how they make subjects of people: how they are articulated and performed in different contexts to make subjects of their identities and geopolitical visions (Dowler and Sharp 2001: 174).

2

Reframing critical geopolitics through poststructuralist discourse theory

2.1 Critical geopolitics: the social construction of global space

The analysis of the social construction of global space lies at the heart of the critical geopolitics project. Following Ó Tuathail, critical geopolitics departs from the basic assumption that

> [g]eography is about power. Although often assumed to be innocent, the geography of the world is not a product of nature but a product of histories of struggle between competing authorities over the power to organize, occupy and administer space (Ó Tuathail 1996: 1).

He continues to describe the field as concerned with 'the social inscription of global space by intellectuals of statecraft' (Ó Tuathail 1996: 61) and thus emphasises the focus on elites which is typical of much of critical geopolitics writing (Müller and Reuber 2008; Sharp 2000b). A key endeavour of critical geopolitics consists of uncovering the ways in which from privileged speaker positions a strategic construction of space takes place which inscribes hegemonic power relations. It seeks to

> (1) ... problematize the delimitation of the relationship between geography and politics to essential identities and domains;
>
> (2) ... document the strategies by which maps of global politics are produced by governmental sites; and
>
> (3) ... disrupt the infrastructural functioning of such maps (Ó Tuathail 1994a: 535).

Perhaps the most pivotal theoretical concept in critical geopolitics, discourse has been the conceptual centrepiece around which almost all critical geopolitics writing is arranged. '[T]o study geopolitics we must study discourse,' Ó Tuathail declares at the outset of *The Geopolitics Reader* (Ó Tuathail 2006: 1). Through the discourse concept critical geopolitics has managed to veer away from the mesmerised attention to supposedly 'real' actions and instead focus on discourses as the producers of meaning. The invasion of an army, the building-up of a navy become only meaningful through the workings of discourses, Ó Tuathail and Agnew argue (1992: 191). Through the discursive conceptual lens critical geopolitics comes to view geography as imbued with struggles for the power to command space (Ó Tuathail 1996: 1).

The social construction of global space and world politics is not innocent. But the fascination of geopolitics lies not only in the fusion of power and geography that serves to guide and legitimise global politics. Geopolitics as a politics which creates insides and outsides performs the basic function of providing identificatory potential. As Simon Dalby puts it:

> Geopolitics is about that ideological process of constructing spatial, political and cultural boundaries to demarcate the domestic space as separate from the threatening other (Dalby 1990b: 173).

The concept of identity employed here and in the majority of other critical geopolitics writing owes much to postcolonial and feminist theory. A first central commonality is the rejection of identity as an attribute of autonomous subjects. Subjects are not carriers of pre-existing, objective social or cultural traits but are rather made in the process of identification (Butler 1990; Minh-ha 1989). Identities are therefore far from objective but must be read as contingent upon their societal embeddedness. The second commonality can be found in the bipartite constitution of identity as Self and Other and the objectivation of identities through hegemonisation. For postcolonial theorists, identity claims are deeply political, because they rely on exclusions of what a certain identity is not. These exclusions are linked to the exercise of power, for whatever is relegated to the margins of a hegemonic identity is denied the right to speak (Spivak 1988).

From a sociological perspective, the production of identities through geopolitics fulfils the central function of providing group cohesion by creating in-groups and out-groups (Paasi 1996: 206). With its binary division of space, it provides orientation through geographical imaginations in a world which is characterised by frequent upheaval, insecurity and change. Mackinder's division into land and sea powers, heartland and rimland, established secular certainties and clearly fixed the geopolitical position of states: Britain – sea power, rimland; Russia – land power, heartland. At the dawn of the two World Wars the theories of Kjellén and Haushofer envisioned the geopolitical future, perhaps even destiny, of the state which lay beyond the war. Brzezińksi's and Kissinger's spatial metaphors have guided a global audience in making sense of the threatening opposition of the two super-powers during the Cold War and assembling the world order anew after 1991. The axis of evil and the coalition of the willing create binaries through geographical imaginations and make unambiguous identificatory proposals: you are either with us or you are against us in the war on terror. In this vein, geopolitics as the construction of identity rests constitutively on the exclusion of the Other (Ó Tuathail 1996: 14f.).

The broad appeal of geopolitics is profoundly social: it anchors the vicissitudes of the social in the purported objectivity of the geographical and territorial (cf. Clayton 2002: 814). Geopolitics performs the vital function of filling identificatory voids in times of crisis and uncertainty. It emerges 'to provide a sense of situation, a feeling of location, and an air of certainty about our place in the world' (Campbell 1996: 19). Taking over a stabilising function, geopolitical identities becomes unifying social forces which counteract processes of fragmentation and social uprooting (Redepenning 2006: 133-136) – such as in the wake of the collapse of the Soviet Union.

2.2 Four lacunae in critical geopolitics

The field of critical geopolitics has pioneered the critical analysis of constructions of global space and world politics. But while providing a powerful impetus to dissect the power enclosures of global politics, critical geopolitics has also developed its peculiar conceptual, methodological and empirical silences (see especially Dowler and Sharp 2001; Lossau 2000, 2002; Mattissek and Reuber 2004; Megoran 2006; Müller and Reuber 2008, Redepenning 2006; Sharp 2000b; N. Smith 2000; Thrift 2000). Tackling four of these silences from a poststructuralist vantage point is a central task of this book:

1) *Discursive constitution of identities in language and social practice*: a broader understanding of the concept of discourse and, consequently, of identities;

2) *Institutional context in micro settings*: tracing the authority of discourses to fashion identities and position subjects within institutions;

3) *Structural analysis of discourses*: moving from interpretive-explanatory analysis to an analysis of the structural configuration of discourses;

4) *Positionality*: recovering the interpreting subject for the analysis.

Discursive constitution of identities in language and social practice[1]

Critical geopolitics' focus on representations stems from a particular reading of poststructuralist writings which privileges the attention to texts and, in the wake of a general linguistic turn in geography, identifies the analysis of discourse primarily with the analysis of texts. Poststructuralist thought by thinkers such as Derrida is invoked, when Ó Tuathail (1996: 73) posits that there 'is nothing outside the text'. Metaphors such as 'writing global space', 'the scripting of places', 'geo-graphing' or 'reading discourse' point to this phenomenon. The concern with representations also becomes evident in much of the empirical work which has so far taken place under the label of critical geopolitics. For example, Dalby (1990a) draws on documents of the Committee on the Present Danger, Sharp (2000a) on articles from Reader's Digest, Dittmer (2005) on newspaper articles, Ackleson (2005) on elite speech acts and Dodds (1994) on government records. In the classic understanding of critical geopolitics therefore, representations constitute the main fibres in the fabric of discourses. As a consequence, analysing discourses almost always means analysing texts or images.

The fixation of critical geopolitics on representations has incited critique from different sides: Nick Megoran (2006), making a methodical argument, speaks of a repetition of existing patterns which erases people's experiences and everyday understandings of the phenomena under question and advocates a turn towards ethnography as a method complementary to discourse analysis. Similarly, Sturm (2008: 608) notes that 'there has been no sustained discussion ... on alternative methods of data acquisition outside of textual and media analysis'. Nigel Thrift (2000: 381), making a conceptual argument, critiques critical geopolitics for its 'mesmerized attention to texts and images' and spells out the case in favour of increased attention to practices in the everyday making

1 For the full argument see Müller (2008a, b). I shall restrict myself here to a brief rendition.

of geography. As Thrift further elaborates, this fixation he calls 'representationalism' critically hinges on an overly narrow conceptualisation of discourse as encompassing only linguistic phenomena, relegating practice to an extra-discursive realm.[2] As such, the prevailing concept of discourse in critical geopolitics appears to privilege linguistic aspects of the social over aspects of the social as practice.

If we perceive geopolitical identity only as codified, only as permanently inscribed in a place from which we need only retrieve it, don't we miss something important? Don't the practices of border control at the Polish-Russian border in Kaliningrad Oblast' tell us just as much or even more about geopolitical identity than official declarations on cross-border cooperation between the EU and Russia? Don't thousands of petty traders every day contest this identity by subjecting themselves to these arduous border controls in order to sell cigarettes and petrol in Poland? Do the everyday lives of people in the Ferghana Valley measure up with the positions on cross-border interaction of the national governments of Kyrgyzstan and Uzbekistan? Or do they perhaps tell us something completely different? These aspects of identity are what Anke Strüver refers to as 'performative acts of borderscaping' (Strüver 2005: 169) and what David Campbell means when writing of 'performative identity' (Campbell 1998: 25) more generally.

The concern with texts at the expense of practice all but vitiates a holistic conceptualisation of identity in its fullness, for identity 'functions within discourse, but in so doing, it transgresses and erases the discursive/extradiscursive distinction' (Campbell 1998: 25; see also Strüver 2005). The apparently limited ability of a representationalist discourse concept to fully grasp the social field translates into a methodological deficiency in the conceptualisation and analysis of identity. If we accept, with Campbell and Strüver, that identities are discursively constituted through language *and* social practice, then the adequate rendering of identity must lead via a broader *concept of discourse that incorporates social practice.*

Institutional context in micro settings

Classic geopolitics derives much of its thrust and fascination from the grand visions of world order it instils in people. It is predicated to a high degree on

---

2 In international relations, Iver Neumann (2002a) has argued to a similar effect.

the universal reach of its imaginations. This focus on the macro level is also a central characteristic of critical geopolitics. The most striking examples define critical geopolitics as dealing with the ways of 'how the geography of the international political economy has been "written and read" in the practices of foreign and economic policies during the different periods of geopolitical order' (Agnew and Corbridge 1995: 76) and their analysis stretches over centuries and covers the whole globe (Agnew 1998; Agnew and Corbridge 1995).

What results is a surveying over-view which tends to ignore the workings on and with geographical imaginations through such factors as class and gender or the influence of the local, regional or institutional context. It elides the fact that there is, to say the least, a reciprocal relationship between the national or global level and the local or organisational level, and it elides the fact that at these sub-levels the imaginations may be far more fiercely contested than becomes apparent from looking at codified sublimations only.

> Lives are constructed and reconstructed around political and patriarchal boundaries through discourses which apparently operate at the global and national scales. Attempts to understand the complex relations between the international and everyday demonstrate the importance of ensuring that small, mundane daily practices of everyday life are understood in relation to the reconstructions of the nation and the international (Dowler and Sharp 2001: 174).

Joanne Sharp (2000b: 362) alludes to the implicit elitism of critical geopolitics when she writes that ordinary people are reduced 'to culture industry drones, empty of agency and awaiting their regular injection of ideas'. Feminist work has been particularly head-on about this issue, arguing against a political geography that analyses a 'world without people' (Staeheli et al. 2004). In much the same vein, Thrift (2000: 384f.) asserts that identity and 'an accompanying geopolitical stance are inscribed through the smallest of details', referring to the 'constant hum of practices and their attendant territorializations within which geopower ferments and sometimes boils over'. An attentiveness to 'the details' makes it easier to see what is often overlooked: that visions of geopolitical identity are often contested and pluralised in places where we are conceptually blind.

This conceptual blindness is particularly evident in the case of critical geopolitics with its traditional focus on grand, sweeping theories and global politics. Partly foreshadowed in the work by Anssi Paasi (1996) and Eiki Berg (2000), Nick Megoran (2002, 2004, 2005, 2006) has recently taken a highly commendable step away both from the pre-occupation with elites and the media and from analyses proceeding at the level of the state by presenting a critical geopolitics ethnography within a micro setting. In his general plea for more ethnography in political geography he echoes Cook's and Crang's concern with understanding 'parts of the world as they are experienced and understood in the everyday lives of people who actually "live them out"' (Cook and Crang 1995: 4). While Megoran has framed his step theoretically as a departure from discourse theory, I would argue that it is rather the case of the discourse concept being too narrow which limits the path of research inquiry, the forms and settings of fieldwork and the kind of data critical geopolitics works with. In this sense, the call for ethnography in micro settings logically derives from the previous critique of both the discourse concept and the treatment of identities in critical geopolitics.

Linked to the empirical neglect of micro settings, critical geopolitics largely also fails to conceptually account for the sources of authority of geopolitical discourses. Geopolitical identities often appear to be free-floating entities, far removed from any institutional embeddedness. But how and why do subject positions become compelling points of identification? Whence do discourses acquire their power? An attentiveness to these questions would direct us towards examining institutions such as the military, political committees, foreign policy communities, schools, universities. '[T]he hidden and mundane acts of power that structure identities, interpellate citizen-subjects and therefore create and recreate political communities and agency' (Dowler and Sharp 2001: 166) continue to still be relatively understudied.

This lacuna appears particularly striking given critical geopolitics' stated affinity for Foucauldian thought. After all, Foucault pioneered the study of institutions as producing subjects through techniques of government and techniques of the Self (Foucault 1982). He dismisses the state as the primary, unified locus of power and in its place proposes to examine power regimes as distributed over social institutions: identities are constructed in social institutional contexts. This decentred study of power charts the micro practices within institutions that define, control and regulate processes of subjectivation (Foucault 1991). Thus, as Mark Bevir (1999: 353) notes, 'Foucault's approach encourages us ... to study the state and other political institutions not ... from the top down, but rather from the bottom up'. This postulate has yet to be fulfilled in critical geopolitics.

Structural analysis of discourses

Within critical geopolitics the idea of deconstruction, as we have seen, is taken to mean the exposure and displacement of the hidden assumptions, the closures, the seemingly objective realities geopolitical reasoning is based on (Ó Tuathail 1994a). Frequently, agency, intentionality and design play a salient role: discourses may be utilised as strategic resources by actors and interpretation then serves the purpose of unearthing the power effects of these discourses. While this idea of deconstruction is sometimes put admirably into practice (see especially Ó Tuathail 1996), more often than not it ends up turning into a mere reconstruction, a hermeneutic re-interpretation of texts. The pattern of analysis in this case is very similar: a descriptive content analysis and summary of the main arguments of the empirical material is followed by an attempt at explaining the intentions or motivations underlying the geopolitical positions expressed in the text and unearthing their silences. The critical component of this kind of research is often exhausted in a summary of geopolitical arguments and possible interests behind them. Power appears as the power of elites or the media to fashion discourses with authority so that they produce geopolitical realities for ordinary people.

In the critical analysis of Russian geopolitics such an approach is dominant. It is essentially limited to describing competing geopolitical imaginations of where in the world Russia is located. Different geopolitical imaginations, for example the classic Russian positions of Westernism and Slavophilism, are attributed to different politicians, parties or population groups who are deploying these imaginations to further their interests. The power of geopolitical storylines to shape spaces is gauged by their presence in the media or the percentage of population supporting them. Deconstruction takes place by pointing out the contingency of these imaginations and highlighting their arbitrariness as non-objective foundations of foreign policy.

From the viewpoint of discourse theory such an approach is problematic, because it focuses on the content, on the *what* of discourses, instead of examining their structural configuration, the *how* of discourses. Teun van Dijk, the editor of the journal *Discourse & Society,* argues that 'attention to "structure", "form", "organization", "order", or "patterns", is characteristic of virtually all contemporary approaches to discourse or conversation analysis. ... In other words, all comments on fragments of text/talk should be framed in terms of theoretically based categories of structure' (van Dijk 2008). He continues to point out that the 'majority of papers … do not go beyond repeating, paraphrasing, summarizing or (merely) commenting upon a fragment of text or talk'. Instead of reconstructing and comprehending meaning, discourse analysis concentrates on the structural features of the material to be analysed – it identifies recurring patterns and regularities in discourses. Such structural features may include hegemonic and antagonistic relationships, dislocations and their filling, contradictions and ambiguities, shifts and breaks. Distinguishing discourse analysis from hermeneutic interpretation, Martin Nonhoff (2006: 245) aptly remarks: 'the discourse analyst is not Hermes who interprets the reasoning of the gods for the recipients of his message'.

Positionality

Rendering the contingency of geopolitical arguments visible is one of the main aims of the deconstructionist enterprise of critical geopolitics. When students of critical geopolitics talk of deconstruction, what they usually mean is a method of 'critical interrogation' (Ó Tuathail 1994b: 329), of uncovering underlying assumptions of geopolitical representations and unravelling the God-trick of seeing everything from nowhere (Agnew 1998; Reuber 2000, Ó Tuathail 1996). Critical geopolitics claims to be able to do so because it deploys its arguments from a position outside of the discourses whose objectifying effects it critiques. In so doing, however, critical geopolitics becomes partly guilty of its own critique. Unravelling the geopolitical vision of seeing everything from nowhere is done by applying exactly this same vision:

> Critics stand at an ironic distance, constantly critiquing the representations with which they engage. The critics open up the spaces of representation in the text without having to disclose their own location (Dowler and Sharp 2001: 167).

This, of course, is the fundamental contradiction in which every form of deconstruction is caught: deconstruction can only take place through reapplying the very form of meaning construction that is deconstructed.

> Operating necessarily from the inside, borrowing all the strategic and economic resources of subversion from the old structure, borrowing them structurally, that is to say, without being able to isolate their elements and atoms, the enterprise of deconstruction always in a certain way falls prey to its own work (Derrida 1976: 24).

Feminist critics have forcefully argued that the subjectivity of the author is indelibly engraved into the accounts of geopolitical reasoning we render. A position as a white, male academics allows us to speak differently and with greater certainty. As researchers in the West we are positioned as subjects within discourses that we ourselves are not aware of, just as researchers in Russia are positioned in other discourses. A critical geopolitics therefore always and necessarily has to be situated and can only claim validity – if such a notion is appropriate at all – within its respective contexts. This calls for introducing positionality into the analysis and making explicit the researcher's own position as a speaker and product of discourses.

Much of critical geopolitics elides the positionality of the interpreting subject, thus merely supplanting one allegedly objective vision with another. Neil Smith (2000) applies this critique to one of the central texts in critical geopolitics, Ó Tuathail's *The Writing of Global Space*, when he asks, why 'certain arguments and fault lines get read into the interstices and out of the valences of his authors' texts when others never appear. ... How does a critical geopolitics choose the social fault lines it admits, and those it banishes?' (N. Smith 2000: 367). Smith does not hesitate to immediately give the answer to this question: the choice, of course, is made by the interpreting subject.

In order to be able to speak or write we need to have a position which is always necessarily inside a discourse (Hall 1997). Since the discourse researcher cannot claim a privileged access to truth, pretences at 'unravelling discourses' are limited to saying that other interpretations are possible, to uttering the unuttered so as to draw attention to what has been said by saying what has not been said. In so doing, the discourse researcher can construct a difference which exposes the silences of discourses, but at the same time this difference is predicated on the researcher's own discursive mooring. Foucault's famous dictum of a 'method of analysis purged of all anthropologism' (Foucault 1972: 28) must be seen as a purely programmatic statement that is impossible to implement.

2.3 Developing the discourse theory of Laclau and Mouffe

It is my contention in this book that many of the conceptual and methodological lacunae of critical geopolitics can be addressed through the prism of poststructuralist discourse theory and analysis. My own engagement with poststructuralist discourse theory and analysis in this chapter follows primarily the works of Ernesto Laclau and Chantal Mouffe. In their principal work *Hegemony and Socialist Strategy: Towards a Radical Democratic Politics* (1985) Laclau and Mouffe present a theory of discourse which seeks to square social radicalism with poststructuralism, developing their theory of discourse into a social theory of hegemony and the production of political identity. Analysis of discourse grounded in the framework of Laclau and Mouffe foregrounds the 'construction of social identity in and through hegemonic practices ... which partially fix ... the meaning of social identities by inscribing them in the differential system of certain discourses' (Torfing 1999: 41). Laclau and Mouffe's theory is 'interested in analysing *how* the structure, in the form of discourses, is constituted and changed. That is done by looking at how articulations constantly reproduce, challenge or transform discourses' (Jørgensen and Phillips 2002: 30).

Laclau and Mouffe's theory of discourse can be divided into three, operationally interdependent apparatuses: the *discourse apparatus*, the *identity apparatus* and the *politics apparatus*. Carrying an unmistakably poststructuralist mark, the *discourse apparatus* conceptualises the creation, transmutation and fixation of meaning through discourses within a hierarchical, relational and situationally contingent structure. The *identity apparatus* is primarily concerned with the construction of meaning of subjects and the identification with different subject positions. The *politics apparatus* accounts for the radical, post-Marxist edge of Laclau and Mouffe's discourse theory by introducing the concept of hegemony. Table 1 gives an overview of the central conceptual terms.

The discourse apparatus

Laclau and Mouffe's *discourse apparatus* conceives of meaning as arising from a system of differences (Laclau and Mouffe 1985: 106; for a concise summary of their approach see Laclau 2006). Their concept of discourse denies, however, the possibility of the complete totalisation of structure but argues instead that every closure is temporary and contingent, presupposing the unconditional openness of the social. Beyond linguistic channels of creating meaning Laclau and Mouffe explicitly open the discourse concept for the incorporation of social practices into the analysis of the constitution of meaning hegemonies:

> The practice of articulation, as fixation/dislocation of a system of differences, cannot consist of purely linguistic phenomena; but must instead pierce the entire material density of the multifarious institutions, rituals and practices (Laclau and Mouffe 1985: 109)

Table 1: Glossary of terminology in Laclau and Mouffe's discourse theory

Apparatus	Term	Concept
Discourse	Elements	Signifiers whose meanings are multiple and have not yet been fixed in a discourse
	Articulation	A practice through which a partial fixation of the meanings of elements is achieved
a relational ensemble of signifying practices creating meaning, which extends to the whole social space, both linguistic and extra-linguistic	Moments	Elements whose meaning has been partially fixated through articulation
	Closure	The fixation of the meaning of a signifier within a discourse
	Field of discursivity	The surplus of meaning which is outside discourse. A discourse is always constituted in relation to a field of discursivity. The field of discursivity harbours the potential for the contestation of a discourse.
	Nodal points	Privileged signifiers within discourses around which other moments are ordered in chains of equivalence
	Floating signifiers	Elements which are particularly open to different ascriptions of meaning and may form nodal points in different discourses
Identity	Subject positions	Different possibilities of the construction of meaning of a subject in different discourses
articulation of a subject position in a discourse which is always incomplete	Contingency	A given identity is possible but not necessary. There can never be one single discourse which exclusively structures the social.
	Split subject	The split subject is perpetually incomplete and constantly strives to become a whole.
Politics	Antagonism	Discursive exteriority which presents a threatening force for a hegemonic discourse
the organisation of society in a particular way that excludes other possible ways.	Hegemony	The fixation of meaning in an antagonistic terrain naturalising a particular articulation
	Objectivation	Discourses becoming seemingly natural and uncontested through hegemonic intervention
	Dislocation	A contingent event that cannot be symbolised or represented within a discourse and thus disrupts and destabilises orders of meaning
	Power	Constitutes identity by means of the exclusion of a constitutive outside

The central unit of analysis in Laclau and Mouffe's discourse apparatus is the signifier or, more precisely, signifying practices. In the following, I will use the term 'signifier' as a shorthand to refer to 'signifying practices'. There exist two different types of signifiers: 'moments' are signifiers whose meaning has been partially and temporarily fixated within relations of difference in a particular discourse, whereas 'elements' are signifiers which have retained their polysemy and thus have multiple potential meanings. A discourse is forged and promulgated by establishing relations of equivalence and difference among elements by which their polysemy is reduced and they become moments: '[a]ny discourse is constituted as an attempt ... to arrest the flow of differences' (Laclau and Mouffe 1985: 112). This crucial process of transforming elements into moments is called articulation.

Discursive closure, whether temporary or permanent, always is a reduction of meaning possibilities and thus implies an exclusion of alternative meanings of an element in the course of its articulation as a moment. This excluded 'surplus of meaning' (Laclau and Mouffe 1985: 111) is pooled in the *field of discursivity*, the totality of other meanings not articulated in a discourse. The field of discursivity is outside a particular discourse but not outside the discursive realm. Quite to the contrary, it embodies 'the discursive', the theoretical horizon for 'the constitution of the being of every object' (Laclau and Mouffe 1990: 105). The field of discursivity represents the impossibility of any discourse to achieve a final suture, since every discourse is constituted in relation to the field of discursivity, which holds the potential for disruption and subversion of the discursive meaning structures. Most importantly, the field of discursivity also symbolises the radical openness of the social which is a consequence of the 'constant overflowing of every discourse by the infinitude of the field of discursivity' (Laclau and Mouffe 1985: 113). This is how Laclau and Mouffe's discourse theory conceptually responds to the poststructuralist challenge, which rebuffs the notion of a centre and of the possibility of an ultimate fixation of meaning (Stäheli 1999).

The structuration of moments in a discourse takes place around nodal points, privileged signifiers around which moments are ordered in chains of equivalence. Before their articulation, nodal points were floating signifiers, elements which are not fixed to a particular signified and are therefore particularly open to differential ascriptions of meaning. Nodal points are thus privileged signifiers whose meaning within a discourse has already been established, whereas floating signifiers are potential nodal points whose meaning is still subject to struggle and contestation between different discourses (Torfing 1999: 98f; Žižek 1989: 88ff). Due to the virtual absence of a specific signified, floating signifiers can be inserted into a system of meaning differences and, turning into nodal points, derive their meaning from establishing equivalential relationships to other signifiers, as opposed to the system of differences which is otherwise characteristic. As such they can serve to unify a discourse, binding together initially disparate moments and representing the totality of the social field (Jørgensen and Phillips 2002: 26ff; Torfing 1999: 98).

The identity apparatus

The ability of nodal points to unify a given social field by including moments in a chain of equivalence is crucial for the functioning of the *identity apparatus*. As the chain of equivalence comes to encompass ever more moments, anything that remains excluded poses a potential threat to that particular discourse, for it pools the social antagonisms that would subvert the system of differences fixed in the discourse. However, besides being the condition of the impossibility of a discourse, the excluded elements at the same time also represent the condition of possibility of a discourse, since by determining its limits they constitute its identity – they serve as a constitutive outside (Laclau 1995; Torfing 1999). This logic also extends to the identity of subjects. The identity of subjects is equal to the identification with subject positions, i.e. different possibilities of the meaning of a subject that are constructed within discourses against a constitutive outside (Laclau and Mouffe 1985: 115). All identities are constituted by positing a difference that reinforces and challenges identity at the same time; the constitution of an 'us' is impossible without imagining a corresponding 'anti-us' or 'them' (Mouffe 1995).

Drawing on Lacan, Laclau supplements the theory developed with Mouffe with the notion of the *split subject*. The split subject refers to the fact that the subject is only partly structured by discourses but never in its totality. As a result of this failure to structure the subject completely, as a result of this 'lack in the structure' (Žižek 1989: 175), the subject is compelled to act (Howarth 2000). It is compelled to act in its attempt to fill this constitutive lack through identification with different subject positions and recreate a wholeness which is imaginary. Although imaginary, this wholeness is an indispensable horizon within which the Self is created and which makes for the driving force of the subject's actions (Stäheli 1999; Torfing 1999). Laclau speaks of the failed structural identity of subjects which grants them agency:

> I am condemned to be free, not because I have no structural identity as the existentialists assert, but because I have a failed structural identity. This means that the subject is partially self-determined. However, as this self-determination is not the expression of what the subject already is but the result of its lack of being instead, self-determination can only proceed through processes of identification. (Laclau 1990: 44).

Subjects' identity thus emerges from a structural lack and identification is crucial to filling this lack. This conclusion, Laclau argues, must refocus discourse theorists' attention: '*To understand social reality, then, is not to understand what society is, but what prevents it from being*' (Laclau 1990: 44; emphasis added).

The politics apparatus

The split subject marks the point where the concept of *politics* comes in. 'Politics as the filling of the empty place of identity has to be seen in relation to the blockages inherent in the actualization of the potential' (Bech Dyrberg 2004: 252). Politics constitutes a logical consequence of the split subject which is in perpetual search of a full realisation of its identity. Politics provides a hegemonic resolution to the identificatory blockages of the subject. The essential function of *hegemony* consists of reducing the undecidable level of total openness to a decidable level of discourse (Torfing 1999: 102), to bring about the articulation of one meaning of an element and exclude other meanings. More than merely providing an explication of hegemony, Laclau and Mouffe therefore also justify its necessity (Valentine 2001: 90). Hegemonic articulation is conditioned upon the failure of the discourse to establish a fully sutured space of representation, fully constituted identities (Torfing 1999: 118). Since all social objects display 'the traces of the acts of exclusion which govern their constitution' (Mouffe 2000: 21), they are all fundamentally political. The hegemonic filling of identificatory voids is a purely political act in that it organises society in a particular, contingent way which excludes other possible ways.

Through hegemonic intervention on an undecidable terrain an *objectivation* takes place: the hegemonic discourse is regarded as natural, its contingency is no longer obvious. A hegemonic articulation then turns into an ideology, veiling the undecidability of all social identity (A. M. Smith 1998; Torfing

2004). Such a situation may last for a variable length of time during which one discourse as *l'ordre dominant* structures the social. The striving for emancipation from hegemonic identities, which would involve a disruption of hegemony, can never lead to true emancipation in the sense of asserting a differential identity. As Laclau points out, such a disruption has ambiguous effects:

> I cannot assert a differential identity without distinguishing it from a context, and, in the process of making the distinction, I am asserting the context at the same time. And the opposite is also true: I cannot destroy a context without destroying at the same time the identity of the particular subject who carries out the destruction. It is a very well known historical fact that an oppositionist force whose identity is constructed within a certain system of power is ambiguous *vis-à-vis* that system, because the latter is what prevents the constitution of identity and it is, at the same time, its condition of existence. And any victory against the system also destabilizes the identity of the victorious force (Laclau 1996: 27).

Hegemonic discourses are displaced by *dislocation*, extra-discursive events which cannot be symbolised by an existing discourse and thus set free the disruptive potential of the field of discursivity. Dislocations are the central dynamic element in Laclau and Mouffe's discourse theory: they crack open discursive hegemonies, inciting new discursive struggles to articulate the dislocated elements.

According to Laclau and Mouffe, politics structures the social field by two different logics. In the *logic of equivalence* social forces are organised in terms of antagonisms between two chains of equivalence. This is the case when Russia is viewed as a Eurasian civilisation, entirely separate or even threatened by the West. Such a logic might articulate a chain of equivalence between Eurasia, Russian identity, economic prosperity, security and so on, whereas the antagonistic chain of equivalence might be articulated around signifiers like the West, imperialism, threat, oppression. The logic of equivalence is thus strictly a logic of 'you-against-us' which does not admit any differences. In contrast, the *logic of difference* structures the social field as a system of different subject positions which are not in an antagonistic relationship. Russia may be different from the West, but this difference is tolerated as legitimate and not constructed in terms of antagonistic opposition. Laclau and Mouffe claim that the two logics limit one another and the dominance of one logic always provokes the resistance of the other logic. It is a characteristic of the social field that it can never be structured completely by one logic (Laclau and Mouffe 1985: 129f.).

A discourse analysis?

Laclau and Mouffe provide few hints beyond their social theory as to the concrete implementation and application of their concepts in empirical studies (cf. Howarth 2000: 133ff.; Keller 2004: 54; Torfing 1999: 291f.). In their writings they have predominantly concentrated on specifying the epistemological framework within which a variety of methods can find application. Jacob Torfing issues a caveat concerning the

> quest for a methodology able to utilize discourse theory in the concrete study of the construction of identity. Such a recipe does not exist and should not be developed. For, whereas there is a great need to develop our critical reflections on how to apply discourse theory in concrete studies, we should not aim to solve the methodological question once and for all. Discourse theorists must remain methodological bricoleurs and refrain from developing an all-purpose technique for discourse analysis (Torfing 1999: 292).

Similarly, Howarth maintains that

> [m]ethod is not synonymous with a free-standing and neutral set of rules and techniques that can be applied mechanically to all empirical objects. Instead, while discourse theorists ought to reflect upon and theorize the ways they conduct research, these questions are always understood within a wider set of ontological and epistemological postulates, and in relation to particular problems (Howarth 2004: 317)

This does not mean that Laclau and Mouffe's project as such is hostile to methodologisation (see Howarth 2004), but adapting their concept for concrete analyses of data requires further specification of methods (see, for example, Howarth and Torfing 2004; Howarth et al. 2000). The discourse analyst is therefore called on to be especially candid about the process of constructing a methodology, all the more so in view of the relative reticence on methodology that can be observed in many empirical studies which draw on Laclau and Mouffe. The transition from discourse theory to discourse analysis is achieved when the bricoleur has adapted the discourse theoretical framework to the empirical phenomena in question. As Torfing (1999: 292) avers, this bricolage must be assembled in close concordance with the empirical data, otherwise it runs the danger of losing its analytical power.

How have others approached this challenge? In the methodological construction of a discourse analysis, what aspects have empirical studies foregrounded in the work of Laclau and Mouffe? Exhibiting an unmistakably radical orientation, the majority of studies investigate hegemonic processes and the constitution of meaning hegemonies.

> It is one of the tasks of hegemony analysis to examine why some signifiers come to represent the whole and why others do not. The analysis of hegemony cannot stop at the identification of a successful hegemony, but must also examine which alternatives have been excluded for the present hegemony to be possible (Thomassen 2005).

Hegemony analysis has been the mainstay of discourse analysis by Laclau and Mouffe. Of all studies that analyse hegemony, Nonhoff's (2006) monograph on the project of a social market economy in Germany is probably the most detailed in terms of methodology. In it he aims to trace how the model of the social market economy became hegemonic in post-war Germany and garnered wide-spread support in a society which came to see it as a superior form of organisation of the economy. Nonhoff introduces the concept of hegemonic strategy as a hinge between discourse theory and empirical analysis. Hegemonic strategy is a means of arranging discursive elements with the help of strategemes. Nonhoff develops nine different strategemes which can establish different relations between signifiers and thus weave together the discursive fabric. Using documents from the late 1940s and the 1950s from economists, political parties and interest groups he shows how the lacking universal – Germany's economic prosperity – engendered a host of demands and analyses the type of relations established between these demands, the nodal point around which they were articulated and the lacking particulars to which they were a response. In so doing, Nonhoff is able to move beyond a mere content analysis and to explain the mechanisms of the emergence of hegemony by highlighting the structural relationships between signifiers.

Other studies home in on the identification of empty signifiers and the shifts and changes in meaning fixations over time. Glasze (2007a, b) investigates how Francophonia has historically been constituted through varying nodal points as a world-spanning region or geocultural space. Conjoining methods from lexicometry and narratology, he seeks to triangulate his analysis by exploiting the specificities of each method. Working with large digital text corpora that extend over several decades, he endorses a lexicometric approach, which analyses the relations between lexical elements in a quantitative fashion, for its aptitude to reflect the regularity of relations between signifiers and to chart the frequency and co-occurence of signifiers from a diachronic perspective. Where lexicometric analysis falls short of analysing the exact qualities of relations between signifiers, it is supplemented by narrative analysis, which embeds signifiers into the corresponding relations of difference or equivalence and is able to mark the emergence of antagonistic frontiers and dislocations.

Although showing some similarities with these approaches, my own project is more microscopic in its endeavour. It seeks to map the discursive structures of the social field and trace processes of identity production in the articulation and contestation of meaning in everyday life. This focus emphasises that discursive fixations are always contingent and situated in specific contexts from which they draw their authority (Shapiro 1992: 38). Instead of deconstructing hegemony or tracing shifts in discourses over time, I attempt to 'locate and analyse the mechanisms by which meaning is produced, fixed, contested, and subverted' (Howarth 2004: 341). In order to tease out those mechanisms reactive forms of data collection such as interviews or participant observation are employed, which afford a more comprehensive view on the context of identity formation than texts gleaned from documents.Yet, while gaining purchase on the lifeworlds of subjects is critical, such an approach must resist the temptation of succumbing to mere hermeneutic interpretation and losing the wider structural anchors and relations between signifiers out of sight (Pouliot 2007).

In my understanding, discourse analysis, then, is not a novel method of data analysis to replace or supplement conventional methods of text or ethnographic analysis. It is rather the identification of theoretical concepts within empirical material – the application of a discourse theory to data. In Laclau and Mouffe's theory, meaning and its contestation arise out of relational structures which can be seen as authorised by institutional practices. Mapping concepts of the authorisation, structural organisation and contestation of discourse onto the empirical material is the main task of the discourse analysis in this book.

2.4 Rethinking institutional practices: Butler and Foucault

Judith Butler and the idea of performativity

By conceptualising social practices as an inalienable part of discourse, Laclau and Mouffe transcend the fixation on language which is so characteristic of many discourse concepts. With this conceptual move they open up a whole new empirical field for discourse theory. What is largely missing in their work, however, is an extended elaboration of the implications of this idea. How can we think the connection of language, practice and identity? How does the production of identities take place? The work of Judith Butler, and especially her concept of performativity, promises to fill this lack and shows a remarkable convergence with the ideas of Laclau and Žižek (see, for example, the joint volume Butler et al. 2000).

Judith Butler (1990, 1993) operates within a broadly poststructuralist conception of discourse, which unites language and practice as forms of discursive signification and the creation of meaning (Stäheli 2000: 63ff.). Central to her ideas is the concept she terms performativity, 'the reiterative and citational practice through which discourse produces the effects that it names' (Butler 1993: 2). Initially, Butler's thoughts for combining language and performance in one theoretical approach departed from speech act theory (Austin 1962). Speech act theory holds that there are situations where in uttering something, we are also performing a certain action – situations in which language not merely represents but actually does something. The classic example would be the marriage ceremony in which the priest says 'I now pronounce you husband and wife' and in so doing produces the effect that this utterance names. This performance is only successful, however, if it can tie into a discourse which fashions it with authority. The priest needs to be a priest and not any other person, it needs to be performed in a chapel and so on.

Considerably broadening the basic ideas of speech act theory, Butler applies them to the process of signification in general: things we do can create meaning, yet only if we do the right things in the right context – if we cite certain discourses. More so, these performances are not voluntaristic but constitutively make up our identities. Probably her most famous works, *Gender Trouble* (1990) and *Bodies That Matter* (1993) argue that gender, sex and heterosexuality are not natural givens but arise out of performance. What makes a woman a woman is not biological determination but the performative citation of a female discourse. This can be certain ways of dressing, ways of walking, ways of talking and so on. Gender, thus, cannot be true or false but is rather produced 'as the truth effects of a discourse of primary and stable identity' through a stylised repetition of acts (Butler 1990: 140f.). What is important for Butler is that there is not an intentional act behind becoming 'woman', but that those performances recite already established bodies of knowledge through which subjectivity is created in the first place. If performance was merely free play 'that could mean that I thought one woke in the morning, perused the closet or some more open space for the gender of choice, donned that gender for the day, and then restored the garment to its place at night' (Butler 1993: x). Such an assumption would collapse the crucial distinction between performance and performativity. As Gregson and Rose (2000) put it, subjects have to act in order to exist and not vice versa. Performance – what subjects do, say, enact and what Laclau and Mouffe call practices – is therefore invariably connected to performativity, the citational practices which articulate discourse and bring subjects into being. Identity is thus constituted by the very acts that are said to be its results (Butler 1990). Butler

> understands discourse as multiple and contradictory but always productive; it has specific effects, and this is where its power lies. Discourse in Butler's account thus disciplines its subjects even as it produces them (Gregson and Rose 2000: 436f.).

She suggests that identificatory practices are neither structurally determined nor autonomously chosen but rather the articulation of a sedimented, naturalised discourse.

This is to say that performance has power effects through performativity: it positions subjects in their identification. This idea has been read by some as leaning towards discursive determinism (e.g. Livia and Hall 1997; Hall 2003), since it would seem to preclude a stance that allows for a contestation or subversion of discourse. Such a critique, however, misses the distinction between determination and constitution: while a determined subject would have a stable, a-priority identity, discursive constitution through repeated recitation is the very pre-condition for agency. Because identification is

> a repeated process, an iterable process, [it] is precisely the condition of agency within discourse. If a subject were constituted once and for all, there would be no possibility of a reiteration of those constituting conventions or norms. That the subject is that which must be constituted again and again implies that it is open to formations that are not fully constrained in advance. Hence, the insistence of finding agency as resignification (Butler 1995: 135).

Far from succumbing to a structuralist view, Butler (1990) thus argues that it is precisely the need for the constant reiteration of performative acts which offers the potential for slippage and disruption. Identities are neither based on foundational, pre-discursive grounds nor are they fully sutured products of discourse. In positing this, she echoes the poststructuralist conception of identity in the theory of Laclau and Mouffe where subjects can never have a fully constituted identity but are always penetrated by a constitutive lack. What is excluded from these identities always threatens to disrupt them and contains the potential for change.

The gist of Butler's argument, which I would like to carry forward from all this, is the connection she draws between practice, discourse and identity – or performance and performativity, as she terms it. What individuals do and say constitutes their identity and is necessarily always a recitation of discourse. They cannot act otherwise because reciting this discourse is essential for becoming subjects with identities. This is also how discourse becomes powerful, for it is only *qua* discourse that subjectivation can occur. Butler's compelling theoretical sketch thus helps us to rethink the link between language and practice and to refocus on practice as constitutive for the production of identities.

Michel Foucault and the institutional setting of discourses: producing docile bodies

Social context is crucial in the performance of discourses and the articulation of meaning. For Butler, performance acquires its citational quality only in certain contexts that are delimited by discourses. Laclau and Mouffe describe these contexts as naturalised discourses, as institutions that have a high degree of stability making them relatively permanent and durable. Mouzelis (1988, 1990), however, critiqued Laclau and Mouffe's analysis of articulatory practices for taking place in an 'institutional vacuum' (Mouzelis 1988: 115). Similarly, Howarth (2000: 119f.) highlights the lack of discourse analytical studies on what he calls organisations.[3] He underscores that '[c]onducting research into these precise organizational outcomes and logics, and pinpointing the constraints they exert on social actors and agencies, is precisely the sort of "ontical research" that discourse theorists must conduct'. As my own research crucially involves the study of discourse within a particular institutional context, which itself is nothing but a sedimented discourse, this point is of particular importance to my project.

In conceptualising the role of institutions for subject formation, Michel Foucault can help think the disciplining power of educational institutions (Ball 1990; McNicol Jardine 2005). While institutions such as the prison or the

3 I use the terms institutions and organisations interchangeably here.

hospital figure prominently in Foucault's writing, the implications of his work for educational settings are far more dispersed. Deacon (2006: 178) remarks that it is only in two, relatively short texts – an interview and a public discussion – that Foucault ponders on education (Foucault 1971, 1977). Nevertheless, many of Foucault's ideas on truth and discipline, especially in *Discipline and Punish*, his history of the Western penal system, can be usefully harnessed for an analysis of educational institutions.

For Foucault, educational institutions such as schools and universities do not only impart formal academic knowledge but rather maintain a common social environment (Cladis 1999). They provide an initiation into society by teaching 'not only punctuation, but also punctuality, and not only reading, but also hygiene' (Deacon 2005: 97) – a process that Deacon calls 'moral orthopedics'. As institutions of normalisation, schools and universities functions as places of subjectivation:

> the judges of normality are present everywhere. We are in the society of the teacher-judge, the doctor-judge, the educator-judge ...; it is on them that the universal reign of the normative is based; and each individual ... subjects to it his body, his gestures, his behaviour, his aptitudes, his achievements (Foucault 1979: 304).

University campuses then represent nodes in which economic, political, judicial relations of power amalgamate in the formation of subjects. They are enclaves where students are instilled with modes of behaviour and knowledge for the reproduction of societal relations (Deacon 2006). Education is thus a form of governmentality – a set of organised practices through which subjects are governed.

If we are to follow Foucault, then knowledge plays a crucial role in processes of subjectivation. In the classic philosophy of the Enlightenment, schools and universities are critical to human emancipation. Acquiring knowledge is regarded as a necessary precondition for developing and applying the power to reason and by virtue of this very power, to transform nature and society for the better. Through teaching to acquire and apply knowledge, educational institutions serve as lighthouses, as catalysts of social development towards individual political maturity. Foucault takes an almost opposed tack on knowledge. For him it does not contribute to the emergence of freely thinking individuals, but it rather is complicit in the establishment of power relations.

> Power produces knowledge (and not simply by encouraging it because it serves power or by applying it because it is useful) ... power and knowledge directly imply

> one another. .. There is no power relation without the correlative constitution of a field of knowledge, nor any knowledge that does not presuppose and constitute at the same time power relations (Foucault 1979: 27)

In this understanding of power, Foucault is not concerned with its oppressive effects but with the power to create subject positions. Through internalising knowledge created at schools and universities we are internalising a whole system of meanings – a discourse that regulates subjectivities. This regulation is upheld through institutional practices that students and teachers engage in and that constitute a commonly accepted truth. The objectivation of knowledge – its creation as an external object of truth as it happens in educational institutions – disguises the positioning power of discourse.

The Foucauldian term 'discipline'[4] has been used to describe how educational institutions, not unlike hospitals or prisons, produce

> subjected and practised bodies, "docile" bodies. Discipline increases the forces of the body (in economic terms of utility) and diminishes these same forces (in political terms of obedience). ... [D]isciplinary coercion establishes in the body the constricted link between an increased aptitude and an increased domination (Foucault 1979: 138).

Discipline/surveillance requires that those bodies are constantly observed and recorded to ensure the internalisation of institutional practices. Educational institutions have developed quite a refined arrangement of observation and control that guarantees discipline.

> The activity which ensures apprenticeship and the acquisition of aptitudes or types of behavior is developed there [in education] by means of a whole ensemble of regulated communications (lessons, questions and answers, orders, exhortations, coded signs of obedience, differentiation marks of the 'value' of each person and of the levels of knowledge) and by the means of a whole series of power processes (enclosure, surveillance, reward and punishment, the pyramidal hierarchy). (Foucault 1982: 218-219)

The disciplining technique most germane to educational institutions, according to Foucault, is the examination. More than merely written or oral exams, the examination is a technique by which the quest for truth is institutionalised. In so far as it also establishes moral authority, it includes reprimands or exhortations by teachers as well as formal methods of assessing knowledge. The

---

4 'Surveiller' is the original French term which might be more adequately translated as 'surveillance', retaining the central notions of observation and control.

examination casts a 'normalizing gaze, a surveillance that makes it possible to qualify, to classify and to punish. It establishes over individuals a visibility through which one differentiates them and judges them' (Foucault 1979: 184). The classification of students according to marks or, more generally, according to performance, not only authenticates the acquisition of knowledge but also subjects them to the whole educational apparatus (Deacon and Parker 1995). It renders every student clearly visible and assessable and permits to rank them by the logic of the institution. In so doing, it makes individual performance comparable and locates students within a quantifiable norm (Roth 1992). Beyond surveillance therefore the production of docile bodies is also based on normalisation.

It would be wrong, however, to conceive power relationships between teachers and students at educational institutions as 'unequal' or describe them as an 'uneven hierarchy', as Foucault's work is sometimes read. Teachers do not have power over students but are themselves caught up in the educational apparatus which they neither control nor dominate. The disciplining power of the educational discourse applies equally to them. When teachers give lectures or seminars, they do not create autonomous knowledge but are subject to the same disciplining techniques of examination and surveillance which they cannot manipulate but merely enact. At the same time, the subjectivation of students relies not purely on coercion but also on a measure of self-discipline which recognises the necessity of the disciplining techniques at educational institutions. Individuals are constituted then as objectified selves that consent to the disciplining techniques by self-governing their bodies (Roth 1992).

Foucault (1971: 199f.) referred in somewhat greater detail to two distinct forms of instruction that are also the mainstay of higher education in Russia: the lecture and the seminar. At first glance, the lecture might seem as the archetypical disciplining technique, since it involves non-reciprocal relationships between lecturers and students in which knowledge is lectured *ex catedra*. The specific arrangement of the lecture would seem to contribute to objectifying knowledge and instituting it as the undisputed truth. Foucault, however, claims that the ostensible freedom and reciprocity of the seminar may be more devious, since it disguises the power relations inherent in it. It is especially in seminars that students may be absorbing as objective knowledge what seems to arise out of equal scholarly discussion between teacher and students. Due to this disguised objectivity, seminar knowledge is also more difficult to resist, since its normalising component is not as obvious as in the case of lectures.

The production of subjects through institutional practices of education marks the conceptual confluence of Butler's and Foucault's thoughts. Butler tells us how practices become powerful through performativity and constitute identities – and Foucault elaborates this more specifically for the production of docile bodies at educational institutions. While providing some sweeping ideas about the subjectivating effects of educational institutions, Foucault especially calls on the researcher to examine the small techniques and details that are put to work in disciplining subjects. This implies not only looking at what knowledge is taught at universities but also at how it is taught, how a university becomes successful as a disciplining institution that constitutes subjectivities through particular institutional practices.

2.5 Conceptual reflection: filling the holes of critical geopolitics

The common definition of identities in critical geopolitics as being 'about that ideological process of constructing spatial, political and cultural boundaries to demarcate the domestic space as separate from the threatening other' (Dalby 1990b: 173) resonates with Laclau and Mouffe's idea of identity. The two political theorists in particular focus on the production and contestation of identity in discourses through hegemonic practices and antagonisms. If, with Laclau and Mouffe, geopolitics is about the construction of identity through the temporary closure of a subject position within a geopolitical discourse, then critical geopolitics must treat this identity as given within a naturalised discourse in which temporal closure has been achieved by hegemonic articulations.

Critical geopolitics creates awareness as to the contingency and ambiguity of these hegemonic articulations and highlights the antagonisms which embody this ambiguity. It recognises the split constitution of the subject through a perpetual lack which it seeks to fill by processes of identification. It alerts us to dislocatory events and their transformative impacts on discursive hegemony and geopolitical identities. It traces the role of chains of equivalence in establishing hegemonies and charts the logics of equivalence and difference in the constitution of geopolitical identities. In particular, critical geopolitics recognises the fundamentally open character of any identity which may be concealed, however, through objectivation. In this sense, critical geopolitics does not *work* with discourse analysis as an instrument but it rather *is* discourse analysis itself.

This chapter has pointed out four conceptual and methodological lacunae of critical geopolitics. The understanding of poststructuralist discourse theory I have developed on the preceding pages helps us address three crucial ones. First, the *discursive constitution of identities in language and social practice*. Laclau and Mouffe's concept of discourse is explicitly a theory of identity. It links the constitution of meaning and meaning hegemonies to the formation of the subject. More important still, it transcends the discursive/extra-discursive divide that characterises much discourse scholarship. In so doing, it recognises that identities are not limited to the linguistic realm but cut across different systems of signification including social practices. By foregrounding the contingency of the social, Laclau and Mouffe's theory advocates an explicitly political stance by developing a wide-ranging critique of hegemony. While Laclau and Mouffe are somewhat reticent on the relationship between discourse and practice, the work of Judith Butler and her concept of performativity can help us think practices as recitations of discourse and how performative repetitions fixate identities.

The ideas of Foucault become useful when addressing the second lacuna of critical geopolitics: a neglect of the *institutional context in micro settings*. In order to account for the power of discourses to position subjects, the institutional context plays an important role. Geopolitical identities do not emerge devoid of a context but are always situated productions. Educational institutions have particular disciplining practices that transform subjects into 'docile bodies'. The transfer of geopolitical knowledge, the articulation of geopolitical signifiers, must be analysed as embedded in the particular institutional practices of micro settings, which may include foreign policy communities just as well as local border residents. Such a perspective does not treat subjects as lifeless drones but interrogates their very corporeal acting and making. For my own research, an attentiveness to institutional practices calls for minding not only about what geopolitical knowledge is produced and reproduced at MGIMO, but also about the practices that underpin subjectivation processes at that university.

Finally, the theory of Laclau and Mouffe provides clues as to what I have called a *structural analysis of discourses*. This form of analysis does not stop at merely interpreting discourses by summing up their content or offering critical commentary on them. Instead, it attempts to identify patterns and regularities in the construction and alteration of discourses. Such patterns have been identified in the conceptual vocabulary of Laclau and Mouffe, describing hegemony and antagonism, dislocation and filling, the logics of difference and equivalence, nodal points and moments, the split subject and identification. Applying such a framework to the analysis of empirical material points discourse analysis beyond the traditional critical interpretation of texts and towards the theory-based identification of features structuring identities and their contestation.

3

Geopolitical orientations in post-Soviet Russia

> Across the centuries Russians have articulated, through a process that may be called the interpretation or construction of geographical space, a variety of highly contrasting geographical or geopolitical self-images: visions, in effect, of Russia as a particular sort of geographical entity. Although they were based on the same a priori convictions and interests that conditioned views on other aspects of Russia's identity, once created they nevertheless carried a certain aura of objectivity and so appeared to be incontestable in a way that no other factor could be (Bassin 1991: 2).

The central question of geopolitical identities seems to be simple: *Where in the world does Russia belong? What is Russia's place in world politics?* This chapter shows that answers to this question have taken multiple forms in multiple contexts and are not so simple at all. Perhaps more than with any other country, foreign policy scholars have pondered on Russia's geopolitical orientation. In order to establish the empirical background against which my research is situated, this chapter presents primarily a review of the pertinent literature on Russian geopolitics and geopolitical identities and provides an overview of important debates around Russian foreign policy (see also Figure 1). Knowledge of the current events and discussions surrounding Russia's role in world politics is quintessential for understanding material from interviews and lectures in the empirical part.

3.1 The Russian crisis of identity and the emergence of geopolitics

Geopolitical discourses perform the vital function of filling identificatory voids in times of crisis and uncertainty. This became especially visible in Russia after 1991, the year which marks the end of the Soviet Union. The collapse of communism in Eastern Europe is often viewed as one of the most incisive dislocations of the present (Bassin and Aksenov 2006; Torfing 1999). It plunged hundreds of millions of people into disorientation in manifold ways: economic, social, political, ethnic and certainly also geopolitical.

Graham Smith (1999a: 49), like a number of other authors, argues that the demise of the Soviet Union triggered an identity crisis: within a comparatively short period of time Russia's position changed from being the nucleus of a superpower to that of a comparatively peripheral state in world politics. Smith (1999a) writes that many ordinary people took pride in the Soviet position as one of two superpowers in the international system. The collapse of the old identity without the immediate availability of a hegemonic new one to replace it left many Russians bereft of an identificatory core, while people were suddenly confronted with the need to take care of the immediate material necessities of life as combines closed down, family incomes dropped and food prices rose. Although the day-to-day imperative of the majority of ordinary people in the 1990s was less to come to terms with their geopolitical identity than with making ends meet, the unprecedented social uprooting certainly provided fertile ground for the articulation of identities that could provide stability and orientation in times of constant upheavals.

According to Smith (1999a: 49), the Russian identity crisis is characterised by a salient territorial component which has led to the formation of a multitude of geographical imaginations of Russia and Russianness. Concomitantly, geopolitical thinking has undergone a stunning revival in post-Soviet Russia. In Soviet times geopolitics was denounced as a false science or *lženauka* (Bassin and Aksenov 2006). The demise of the Soviet Union, however, created circumstances which were propitious for the emergence of geopolitical reasoning, since it provided seemingly objective and easy answers to the host of political and identity questions Russia and Russians were suddenly confronted with. In the first month of post-Soviet Russia's existence, foreign minister Kozyrev declared:

> Shifting away from messianism (*messianstvo*) we set course towards pragmatism. ... The place of ideology is now occupied by geopolitics, that is the normal perspective of natural interests (*Rossijskaja Gazeta, 21 January 1992*).

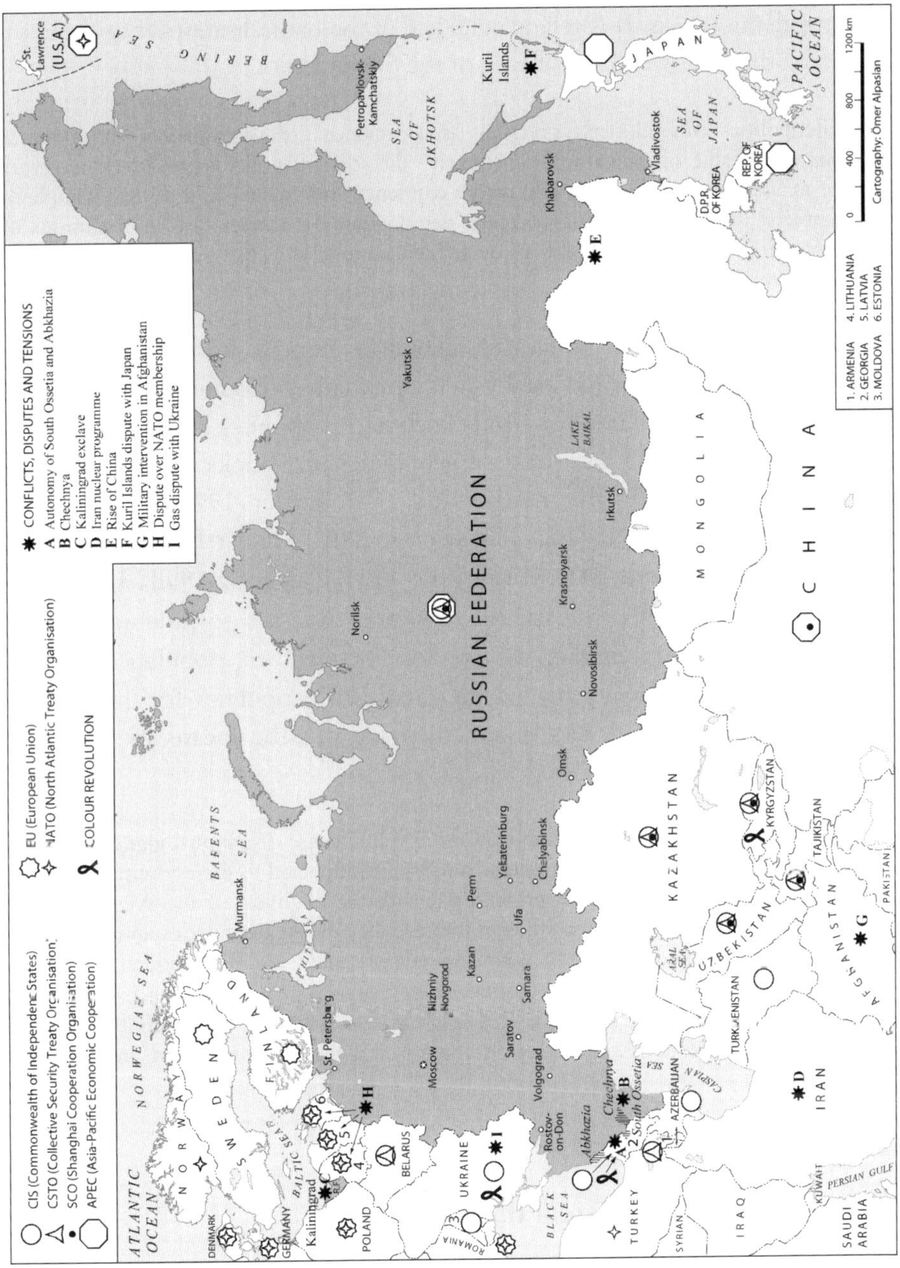

Figure 1: Map of Russia's geopolitical environment

This statement shows to what degree geopolitics was perceived as a rational, objective answer to the ideological distortions of Soviet foreign policy and the ensuing identity crisis. It is telling evidence of the naturalisation of geopolitical reasoning that followed the collapse of the Soviet Union.

> [G]eopolitics offered itself precisely as a "science" of geographical and political analysis capable of indicating "objectively" the sorts of policy imperatives necessary for maintaining or regaining a country's eminence and vitality. And as the example of *Geopolitik* in interwar Germany vividly demonstrates, it thrives best in conditions of dislocation and *Angst* brought on by sudden national collapse or defeat (Bassin and Aksenov 2006: 100f.)

Nowadays, geopolitics is an almost ubiquitous term in Russian political debate. The Russian Duma has established a permanent 'Committee for Geopolitical Analysis', the military has firmly anchored geopolitics in the syllabi of its officer academies and a vast array of geopolitics text books or programmatic declarations penetrates the market (e.g. Cymburskij 1993; Dugin 2000; Gadžiev 2003; Kolossov and Mironenko 2001; Min'jar-Beloručev 2006; Nartov 2004; Vasilenko 2007; Žirinovskij 1993; Zjuganov 1998). For Bassin and Aksenov (2006) it is the sudden erosion of Russia's position as a *velikaja deržava* (great power), marked by the loss of territory, population and its sphere of influence, which fuelled the revival of geopolitics for imagining a vision for a regenerated Russia and mapping out the means by which to achieve such a status.

> Since at least the early eighteenth century, a secure sense of national identity and historical destiny was for many Russians intimately connected to their country's potency as a military and political power on a par with the mightiest of the Western states, capable at once of projecting Russian interests beyond its boundaries and of defending its territory and population against predatory incursion. The sudden erosion of *derzhava* status, which appears to undermine Russia's ability to contend with and resist the strategic and civilisational challenges it faces from the surrounding world, stirs deep feelings of unease mixed with chagrin and resentment (Bassin and Aksenov 2006: 101).

3.2 Schools of geopolitical thought

Geopolitical narratives and orientations in post-Soviet Russia have drawn considerable scholarly attention in the past 10 to 15 years. A host of studies have sought to identify and describe the most salient geopolitical schools of thought. Although most studies find very similar geopolitical orientations, names and categories differ between authors. Tsygankov (1997) lists International Institutionalism, Realism and Revolutionary Expansionism; Trenin (2002) identifies an Anti-Western, a Great-Russian and a European discourse; Kerr (1995) names Westernisers, Moderate Liberals and Moderate Conservatives; Hopf (2005) speaks of Liberals, Centrists and Conservatives; O'Loughlin and Talbot (2005) enumerate moderate Eurasianism, extreme Eurasianism and Westernism, whereas O'Loughlin et al. (2004b) discern different reactions to 9/11 along a common-enemy storyline, a skeptical storyline and a American-imperialism storyline; Sergunin (2004), finally, has Atlanticists, Eurasianists, Realists, Liberalists, Neo-Marxists and Post-Modernists. Due to the overlaps and similarities of many of these categories I shall restrict myself to presenting what are probably the three most established typologies, suggested by Graham Smith (1999a) and Andrei Tsygankov (2003a, 2007).

Geopolitical schools of thought according to Graham Smith

The typology by the late Graham Smith (1999a: 55), derived from analysing different images of Eurasia, has guided the discussion on Russian geopolitics in human geography. In his typology Smith distinguishes between liberal-Westernist, neo-nationalist, neo-Soviet and democratic statist images of Eurasia (see Table 2).

The *liberal-Westernist* geopolitical discourse was particularly prominent in the early 1990s when Russian foreign policy was essentially defined vis-à-vis the West. It is based on a notion of Russian geopolitical identity as European. According to the liberal-Westernist discourse, Russia must strive to return to the path of Europe from which it deviated in 1917 and align itself with the successful Western model of development. This would require the country to focus largely on its internal problems and the restructuring of economy and society instead of thinking in terms of spheres of influence and national interests. The interests of Russia are considered to be identical to those of other Western countries and consequently its foreign policy should be conducted in concordance with the Western community. Russia's geopolitical future lies thus in adopting an avowedly Western strategy of partnership and coexistence (G. Smith 1999a: 54-56).

Table 2: Russian geopolitical schools of thought according to Smith (1999a, adapted)

	Liberal-Westernist	**Neo-nationalist**	**Neo-Soviet**	**Democratic statist**
	European/Western	Eurasian, non-Western	Eurasian, non-Western; capitalism is foreign to Russian culture and way of life	Eurasian, non-Western; accepts that it has something to learn from both West and East
Geopolitical borders	Fixed	Slavic lands or Russian empire	USSR	Fixed
Cultural identity	Pluralist	Russian (*Russkij*)	Pluralist but Russia as 'first among equals'	Slavic-Turkic
Type of state	Federation	Empire	Confederation of Soviet states	Confederation
Attitude towards Russians in the Near Abroad	Encourage them to become citizens of country of residence	Incorporate the lands settled by ethnic Russians into Russia		Dual citizenship
Attitude towards the post-Soviet states	Non-threatening	Threatening until they are reintegrated into a larger Russia	Threatening because they are increasingly influenced by capitalist geopolitical powers	Some are threatening to Russia because of internal military and ethnic conflicts
Attitude towards the West	Friendly, in favour of cooperation	Openly hostile towards USA but less so towards Europe	Openly hostile: the West is a foreign culture	Neutral or implicitly hostile; can co-operate on some issues
Attitude towards East Asia	Generally friendly but cool: Russia's interests are in the West	Generally hostile	Generally suspicious and hostile, especially towards China	Neutral: Russia has special interests in developing better relations with East Asia

Neo-nationalist discourse differs from liberalist-Western discourse in repudiating an integration with the West. Neo-nationalists argue that Russia is a unique civilisation which has to pursue its own distinct path in international relations and occupy a special place in Eurasia. Following this path necessarily involves the restoration of Russia as an empire or *velikaja deržava* (great power). Integration or even coexistence with the West are rejected, as is Western-style capitalism. Neo-nationalist discourse is often associated with pan-Slavic notions of integrating all Slavic people into one confederation or union. The most prominent advocate of pan-Slavism, nobel laureate Aleksandr Solženicyn held that reuniting with the Slavic brethren in Belarus and Ukraine would be the path towards the spiritual and bodily salvation of the Russian people. Spheres-of-influence thinking is a characteristic feature of this discourse: the world is divided up in different natural regions which are dominated by different states. Accordingly, the Eurasian region has Russia as a natural hegemon. While advocating the reassertion of Russian power, only in the most extreme cases does neo-nationalist discourse imply territorial expansion (G. Smith 1999a: 56-60).

From a geopolitical perspective, neo-nationalism shares the eminent drive towards asserting Russian hegemony with *neo-Soviet* discourse. The neo-Soviet stance, however, highlights the socialist component as a marker of cultural difference or even opposition to the capitalist-bourgeois West, which must result in adequate geopolitical measures to guarantee territorial security. The nostalgic reference point for neo-Sovietism are the values and ideas embodied in the Soviet Union, which is identified as the Russian 'homeland'. Paired with nationalist sentiments, the neo-Soviet discourse supports the resurrection of a communist Russia which restores its lost positions in Eurasia and is able to counter Western plots to undermine Russian geopolitical authority (G. Smith 1999a: 61-62).

Finally, *democratic statism* constitutes a hybrid of liberal-Westernist and neo-nationalist discourse: on the one hand democratic statist discourse re-affirms Russia's distinctiveness from the West both in terms of its cultural values and geopolitical interests; on the other hand it applies pragmatism in building relations with the West, recognising that cooperation in some issues may be more conducive to further Russia's interest than outright opposition. Democratic statism views Russia as a great power with vested interests in Eurasia which need to be defended and pursued. Besides 'Eurasia' and 'great power', the signifiers of the 'Near Abroad' (i.e. the states of the Former Soviet

Union), 'Russian interests' and 'sphere of influence' play central roles in democratic statist discourse. In 1999, Smith perceived democratic statism to be the most influential discourse in Russia and the one leaving the biggest scope for pragmatic manoeuvring (G. Smith 1999a: 63-64). O'Loughlin et al. (2004a: 14f.; 2005) additionally stress the geoeconomic aspects of democratic statism which views a weak economy as the biggest threat to national security. Accordingly, Russian foreign policy must ensure favourable conditions for economic growth and be guided by economic interests – precepts which have gained in validity since Putin's inauguration.

Geopolitical schools of thought according to Andrei Tsygankov

A professor at the University of California at San Francisco, Andrei Tsygankov is probably the most prolific writer on geopolitical orientations in Russia (e.g. Tsygankov 1997, 2001, 2002a, b, 2003a, b, 2006a, b, 2007; Tsygankov and Tsygankov 1999, 2004). Tsygankov (2003a) lists five schools of geopolitical thought of which each corresponds to a monograph on geopolitics by Russian authors (see Table 3): Expansionists, Civilisationists, Stabilisers, Geoeconomists and Westernisers.

Expansionists are ideationally linked to the textbook by Aleksandr Dugin (2000). Dugin has managed to establish himself as *the* geopolitical expert in post-Soviet Russia, appearing frequently on TV and writing amply on Russian geopolitics. Delivered as a philosophical geopolitics of sorts resuscitating Mackinder and Haushofer, Dugin's Eurasianism argues to the effect that the Eurasian continent is the heartland of the world and Russia is in a strategic position to seize control of it. In order to do so he advocates the territorial expansion of Russia beyond the boundaries of the Former Soviet Union:

> This Empire, following a geopolitical logic, must strategically and spatially exceed the boundaries of the previous variant (USSR). Consequently, the New Empire must be Eurasian, reach over the entire continent and, in perspective, over the entire world (Dugin 2000: 213).

Table 3: Russian geopolitical schools of thought according to Tsygankov (2003a, adapted)

	Expansionists	Civilisationists	Stabilisers	Geoeconomists	Westernisers
Image of Eurasia	'Continental empire'	'Civilisation'	'Intersection' of economic and cultural elements		A spatial non-entity
Security goals in Eurasia	Power	Survival	Stability	Development	Adjustment, democracy
Political borders in Eurasia	Beyond the former Soviet Union	Former Soviet Union	Contemporary post-Soviet borders		
Security strategy in Eurasia	Unlimited politico-military expansion and alliances	Moderate politico-military expansion and geoeconomic autarchy	Politico-military balancing and state-led geoeconomic projects	Transregional economic developments through state and private initiatives	Adjustment to Western dominance
Main partners	Germany, Japan, Iran	China, India and other Eurasian states	No main partners ('multi-vector' foreign policy)		The West (US and Europe)
External threats	Atlanticism or 'trade civilisation'	Geopolitical and geo-economic pressures from the West and the East			West-hostile states
Political orientation	Conservative revolution	Old conservativism	Conservative-liberal synthesis		Old liberalism
Intellectual roots	Old European and Russian geopolitics	Old Russian Eurasianism	A synthesis of Western transnationalism, critical geography (sic!), and Russian geopolitics		Western liberal philosophy
Socio-economic support	Hard-line military	Military industrialists	State bureaucrats, nationally- and regionally-oriented private sector		West-oriented private sector

According to Dugin, Russia has a unique cultural, historical and spiritual Eurasian geopolitical identity, being neither East nor West but something special in-between. In his widely-read work, Dugin operates with pervasive bipolar oppositions. He essentialises the eternal conflict between the land-based, Eurasianist powers of Russia, Germany and Iran and the sea-based, Atlanticist powers of Great Britain and the US and draws up a number of similar oppositions: tradition versus modernity, space versus time, Rome versus Carthage and so on. 'Under Dugin's geopolitical gaze, vast complex landscapes are reduced to homogenous spaces, allotted to one or another zone, and 'decomposed' or 'integrated' at will' (Ingram 2001: 1036). In so doing, he conjures up binary and highly apodictic visions of Russia's geopolitical destiny and has fuelled the rising popularity of traditional geopolitics both within elite circles and among ordinary Russians (Höllwerth 2007; Ingram 2001). His textbook was adopted as the standard work for instruction in military academies, for instance, and in 2002 he launched a geopolitical Eurasian movement (Bassin and Aksenov 2006: 105f.) which is especially active in recruiting young people to the so-called Eurasian Youth Association (*Evrazijskij Sojuz Molodëži*).

The *civilisationist* perspective is linked to the books by Nartov (2004) and Zjuganov (1998), both of whom lay claim to producing objective, scientific knowledge with their analyses of geopolitics, not just 'another ideology'. According to Tsygankov, civilisationalists argue that Russia is a unique economic, cultural and political entity in Eurasia – a unique civilisation. In this constitution it is fundamentally incompatible with the European or Western civilisation and must be isolated from it to retain its distinctiveness. Cooperating with the West would only further global Western dominance and constitute a threat to Russian culture. The former Soviet empire reflects the natural geopolitical form of Russia, whereas Russia's current boundaries are the result of Western ploys to keep Russia down. Civilisationists put an emphasis on military power for preserving and extending Russian influence in Eurasia and lining up a bulwark against the West (Tsygankov 2003a: 120-123).

Stabilisers and *Geoeconomists*, associated respectively with the work of Gadžiev (2003) and of Kolossov and Mironenko (2001), have a number of commonalities in their geopolitical views. Both regard Russia as a distinct geopolitical culture and as a key state on the Eurasian continent. Russia would be well-advised to develop a special Eurasian strategy as part of its multi-vector policy to establish a multipolar world order within which the country should play an important role. Stabilisers and geoeconomists are somewhat divided, however, over the strategy how to realise Russia's geopolitical aims. Stabilisers contend that Russia should play a leading political role in the post-Soviet space, trying to stabilise this region by integration. Coordinating the efforts for enhanced security in Eurasia, Russia is faced with the principal mission of maintaining a secure international environment and balancing a delicate geopolitical equilibrium.

Geoeconomists on the other hand consider Eurasia the heart of geoeconomic flows and deduce from this the need to actively develop Russia's position in the global economy so that it can benefit from this central location and withstand external economic pressures. At the same time, Russia is called on to integrate the other post-Soviet countries in Eurasia into this geoeconomic space of cooperation. Kolossov and Mironenko (2001) argue that traditional geopolitics has become obsolete and what we are witnessing at the moment is a rise of geoeconomic strategies of controlling global patterns of production and flows of resources. They assert that Russia's propitious location in Eurasia positions it at the nexus of global economic flows and what is needed to take advantage of this location is a geopolitics of cooperation with the West, China and the Asia-Pacific. More than that, Russia also needs to develop a Eurasian strategy which should be aimed at transforming Russia into the centre of economic activities in the post-Soviet space and in so doing would guarantee security and stability in the Near Abroad (Tsygankov 2003a: 115-120).

The *Westernist* position finally, represented by the book by Trenin (2005), shares many features with Westernism as it is described by Graham Smith. It advocates a modernisation and integration of Russia with Europe instead of a retreat into Eurasia. This choice is addressed as the choice between a post-modern, European and a modern, Eurasian alternative. In a globalised world, Russia cannot but sing along with the Western majority, lest it become marginalised in global politics. According to the Westernist position, such a choice would also spell out the necessity to withdraw from Eurasia and renounce both outmoded great power ambitions and obsessions with Russia's territorial reconstitution as an important foreign policy goal. Since there is no fundamental difference between Russia's geopolitical identity and the West, Westernists see Russian integration with the West not as submissive but as a natural process.

While the empirical richness of Tsygankov's work on Russian geopolitics is largely unparalleled, the conceptual value for a critical interrogation of Russian geopolitics is rather negligible. In almost all of his publications, Tsygankov espouses a conceptually thin and often contradictory version of constructivism: while subscribing to the view that identities, space or world politics are socially constructed, this theoretical commitment mostly remains formulaic rhetoric and is only tenuously reflected in his analysis or in the conclusions he draws. His treatment of critical geopolitics, which he confusingly calls 'new geopolitics', is very telling in this respect. He criticises practitioners of traditional geopolitics for doing 'a disservice to their respective countries' and, somewhat mistakenly, views this 'new geopolitics' as a way of creatively re-shaping political space for the 'common human interest' (Tsygankov 2003a: 105). From this he proceeds to judge Russian geopolitical schools according to the presence or 'lack of geopolitical imagination' they display (Tsygankov 2003a: 123). Viewing critical geopolitics as a positivist enterprise that advocates a different, possibly more humane geopolitics, he is unable to escape the trap of realism. It is only consequent then that he evaluates the geopolitical schools of thought in his analysis for the potential they offer for 'addressing the variety of security threats in Eurasia' and for dealing with 'the new reality' in geopolitics after the collapse of the Soviet Union (Tsygankov 2003a: 126).

The geopolitical orientation of foreign policy in post-Soviet Russia

Since the historical development and principles of Russian foreign policy are frequently dealt with at MGIMO, a brief review of the geopolitical orientations and assumptions underpinning Russian foreign policy in the post-Soviet era provides useful context for the empirical section. The vacillations in Russian foreign policy from 1991 onwards and the emergence of different hegemonic discourses reflects the twists and turns of the search of a geopolitical identity at the macro level particularly well. In the majority of analyses, Russia's foreign policy is split into three periods: an early Westernist period under foreign minister Andrej Kozyrev from 1991 until about 1995; a Eurasianist period under Evgenij Primakov from about 1995 to 1999; and a great power period under Putin from 2000 to 2008.

Immediately after the Soviet disintegration, under Andrej Kozyrev Russian foreign policy was oriented strongly towards the West, especially the United States. The dominant order of the day was integration with the West, extensive cooperation and alignment with the democratic-capitalist model of the United States. Russia was inundated with Western experts on democratic and market reforms and declared as a state in 'transition' from authoritarian communism to democratic market capitalism (Åslund 2002, 2007; Wedel 2001). During the first half of the 1990s the West functioned as a role model and nodal point of identification in the dominant elite discourse of geopolitical identity (Baev 1997; Dunlop 1997; Tsygankov 2007).

Kozyrev, however, was increasingly criticised for what many believed was an unacceptable selling-off of Russia's foreign policy clout to the West. The appointment of Evgenij Primakov as foreign minister in early 1996 saw a significant valorisation of the Eurasian vector in Russian foreign policy and a strive to resurrect Russia as a great power and Russian influence in the post-Soviet republics. The 'Near Abroad' as a 'natural sphere of influence' of Russia began to play a more important role as key signifiers in Russian foreign policy considerations (Baev 1997). Similarly, nurturing foreign relations with 'the East', in particular China and India enjoyed a privileged position to achieve the strategic goal of moving towards a multipolar world order. A key justification of Primakov's new Eurasian direction in foreign policy was provided by traditional geopolitics through invoking Russia's physical geographical location between Europe and Asia as a key factor begging attention (Dijkink 1996; Kolossov and Turovsky 2001). Russian geopolitical identity increasingly began to be formulated not as equal to the West but as distinct and unique. In the Primakov years the gradual emergence of great-power thinking and orientation towards Eurasia introduced alternative points of identification replacing the West (Neumann 1997; Tsygankov 2007).

Since 2000, Putin's presidency has meant the stabilisation of geopolitical identities (O'Loughlin and Talbot 2005). For Neumann (2008), this time saw the concentration of geopolitical discourse around the ideas of Russia as a great power, with an ambiguous status as a Eurasian state – but as a great power which wanted to be recognised as a market economy and democracy. Visions of Russia as a great power also include Russia as a strong state which guards its role as an independent player on the world stage (Morozov 2008). The concepts of 'sovereign democracy' and 'sovereign economy', coined and propagated in the Putin period, have been read as signs of autonomy becoming an end in itself. Although events such as 9/11 and the ensuing war on terror have brought Russian geopolitical discourse temporarily closer to the West and to Europe, the dominant position still insists on preserving Russia's distinctiveness and great power status. This is why Tsygankov (2007) calls the geopolitical idea of the Putin period 'Euro-East': Russia as a distinct great power in the European East which does not completely disconnect from Europe but at the same time pursues its independent, 'Eastern' policy line.

Just as interesting as the overarching discourses are the different closures of moments in discourses. A signifier like 'Eurasia' can be imbued with highly contrasting meanings, ranging from its virtual marginalisation to its articulation as 'a space Russia is destined to occupy in its realisation of great power status'. A focus on the signifiers also serves to remind us that meaning is not pre-determined but fundamentally open and therefore a political product of discursive articulation and hegemonies, a central pillar of Laclau and Mouffe's theory. It is to a closer examination of the articulations of several central signifiers in Russian geopolitical discourses that I will turn in the following sections.

3.3 'The West'

O'Loughlin et al. (2004a: 5) claim that the signifier of the West is 'an organic part of national identity, of individual and group perceptions, values and political ideologies' in Russia. Following Diligenski (2000), O'Loughlin et al. (2004a) distinguish two main geopolitical images of the West in the Russian perception. The first is the West as a community of states in international affairs. In a liberal-Westernist discourse Russia is viewed as an organic part of the Western, Judeo-Christian civilisation and this view holds that only this civilisation is viable in the long term (O'Loughlin et al. 2005: 329). The West is regarded as a role model in terms of social and economic development and adapting Russia's institutions to Western standards is the key challenge of post-Soviet transition. At the geopolitical level, a Westernist discourse would involve putting an end to tinkering with alliances with the countries of the Near Abroad since this poses a threat to good relations with Western countries. Since the interests of Russia and other Western countries hardly deviate from each other, it would be a logical step for Russia to aspire to join NATO, the EU or other regional or security organisations (O'Loughlin et al. 2004a).

At the other end of the articulatory range we find notions of Russia and Russian culture as unique and separate from the West and calls are for a reduction of Western influence in Russia. The vision of a bi-polar world in which Russia still constitutes the nucleus of a coalition contra the West plays a very prominent role in this articulation of 'the West' (Kolossov and Turovsky 2001). In this case, identity construction happens through scripting the West as other and at the same time appealing to wider notions of Eurasian and great power identity implied in other floating signifiers. In many cases, however, a logic of difference seems to prevail according to which the West is seen as different but not necessarily antagonistic and hostile to Russia (O'Loughlin et al. 2004a; Gvosdev 2007).

The second major image according to O'Loughlin et al. (2004a) is one of the West as a socio-economic model. The technological, economic and social achievements of this version of 'the West' are frequently admired in Russia and striving to catch-up with this level of development is seen as highly desirable. In most cases, this image of the West is regarded with considerably more sympathy than the first one, since it is not conceived in terms of rivalry.[5] At the same time, O'Loughlin et al. (2004a) argue that there is significant disappointment among Russians with the still sizeable gap in living standards separating Russia and Western countries. This disjuncture makes for the impression that Russia is frequently considered as inferior by Western countries.

The division into a socio-economic and a foreign policy imagination of the West is analytically helpful for understanding contrasting articulations of the West in different situations. It should not be overlooked, however, that those two images are frequently jumbled up and cannot be neatly separated. Both play a relevant role in the everyday lives of ordinary Russians and therefore merit equal consideration in the empirical analysis.

United States

In Russia, the United States is readily identified as the iconic core of the West. American culture often stands in for Western culture more generally and US political, military and economic strength make it the most salient representative of the West. The geopolitical scripting of Russia's relationship to the US, however, has undergone several twists and turns in the post-Soviet period.

5 It is frequently stressed in anthropological studies, however, that the influx of Western consumer goods has not led to Russians' untrammelled embrace or imitation of a Western lifestyle (e.g. Shevchenko 2002; Patico 2003). Instead, in many cases a hybrid adaptation of these socio-economic elements by which they are merged into Russian culture and rescripted in their meaning takes place.

Immediately after the collapse of the Soviet Union, the United States was Russia's main partner and point of orientation in international relations. The engineer of the Russian transition to capitalism and democracy, the United States was considered the main assistant in helping Russia rejoin the community of civilised states (Lo 2002: 42ff.). With the end of the ideological opposition, Russia and the United States would enter into an equal partnership. Such claims, Lo (2002) argues, were premature and overly optimistic and were soon superseded by a more critical assessment of Russia's relationship to the US.

The quick economic turn-around in a capitalist Russia, engineered with American help, failed to materialise even more than five years into 'transition'. Herspring and Rutland (2005: 262) assert that large parts of the Russian population believed that the US was only taking advantage of a prostrate country. The United States was criticised for its imperialism and unilateralism which did not accord Russia the prominent role it aspired to in international and bilateral relations. Especially in the wake of the Kosovo conflict, in which Russia and the US had serious disagreements, elite and public opinion towards the US cooled down. Under Primakov's incumbency as foreign minister and prime minister from 1996 to 1999 Russia's goal of establishing a multipolar world order was explicitly directed at countering American hegemony (Zevelev 2002). At the turn of the millennium, Zevelev (2002) thus concludes that Russia and the US have strikingly different geopolitical identities and visions of world politics.

A rapprochement was occasioned by the events of 9/11, which are extensively dealt with in a series of articles by O'Loughlin et al. (2004a, b, 2005). Putin was one of the first state leaders to express his support for the United States in its anti-terror actions and adopted a 'common enemy' storyline that placed Russia decisively on the side of the West (O'Loughlin et al. 2004b). In the wake of the terrorist act, large parts of the Russian elites re-affirmed that the place of Russia is in the West – not only from a civilisational but also from a pragmatic perspective of national interests (O'Loughlin et al. 2004b). Consequently, Putin made significant concessions to the US: amongst others he opened Russian air bases in Central Asia to use by the US Air Force and offered to share Russian intelligence data (Herspring and Rutland 2005).

O'Loughlin et al. (2004a) detect in this a turning away from classic sphere-of-influence thinking but also conclude that there are large reservoirs of scepticism towards the US within a geopolitical culture that has generally tended to be distrustful of close international relations with the United States.

Kolossov (2003), however, underscores that while the United States mostly does not enjoy particular popularity as a political actor in world politics, Russia sees the necessity of collaborating with it. The dominant attitude is described as one of pragmatic coexistence, rather than of confrontation. With plans like the American missile shield and the colour revolutions in the post-Soviet states, more recently, Trenin (2006) has detected 'cool estrangement' verging at alienation between the two states, while some commentators and government officials even speak of a 'new Cold War' (see Fischer 2007). Collection of my empirical material took place in 2005 and 2006 and thus happened at a time when US-Russia relations were deteriorating, although not yet having reached the 'all-time low' declared for the year 2008 after the war in South Ossetia.

The East

In Russian history the East has regularly been constituted through exclusion of the West, so that identification with the East has been dependent on opposition to the West. Any eastern orientation of Russian identity is thus more a turn away from the West than a deliberate turn towards Asia (Hauner 1990; Morris-Suzuki 1999; Rangsimaporn 2006: 374). Graham Smith (1999b: 491) argues that while the East has never really had a large identificatory potential for Russia, it still lies at the heart of Russia's geopolitical project to grant it great power status. Kerr underscores that

> Some Russians perceive that the need to colonise and defend the *prostranstvo* [Asiatic Russia] has shaped the history of the country and the balance of forces within it, including politically and militarily (Kerr 1995: 985).

In the post-Soviet period, Kerr (1995) diagnoses an internal push of these regions away from the European centre which is reinforced by an external pull exerted by the economies that surround them. This situation has occasionally given rise to speculations about future pressures to cede parts of Russia's Asian territory to China, a scenario also known as the 'yellow threat' (*žëltaja ugroza*). Generally, fear of 'creeping Chinese colonization' (Pavliatenko 1999: 31) in the Russian Far East is nurtured by growing numbers of Chinese immigrants, cross-border traders and interethnic marriages. Though border disputes between Russia and China have been settled, the border issue has not lost its symbolism for Russians and is frequently evoked to stoke fears of an expanding China (Buszynski 2000; Kimura et al. 1999: 154ff.).

Russia's unresolved territorial dispute with Japan over the Kuril Islands also features in articulations of the East within Russian geopolitical identity. In a three-week war with Japan at the end of the Second World War the Soviet Union occupied this chain of islands and despite repeated attempts at negotiating a compromise to return all or part of the islands to Japan progress in this issue has been negligible (Morris-Suzuki 1999). Rozman (2000, 2002) contends that for both Russia and Japan it seems to have become a matter of national pride not to back down in this dispute. Because of their contestation, the islands have become powerful symbols of Russian identity and Russia's presence in the East, where giving them back to Japan could signify Russian weakness and is feared to buttress further territorial claims by other states.

Pavliatenko (1999) claims that in the early 1990s Russian foreign policy inertia in Asia at that time contributed to a devaluation of the East in Russian geopolitical discourses. This changed with the appreciation of the Asian vector under Primakov which involved an eastward shift of Russian foreign policy. While some observers locate the rationale for this opening up towards the East in pragmatic economic reasons (e.g. Buszynski 2004), others (Kerr 1995; Rangsimaporn 2006) assert that Russia's commitment to the East is a necessary element in keeping up Russia's great power ambitions and insofar is intimately connected to Russian geopolitical identity. The discursive position of the East in Russian geopolitical discourses is thus mostly ambiguous: while it may be perceived as threatening in some cases, the East is also embraced to counterbalance an excessively Western geopolitical orientation and Russian dependence on Western powers.

NATO

Since the breakup of the Soviet Union, NATO has become something like the *idée fixe* of relations between the West and Russia, frequently but not always encapsulating the exponent of an expansive, aggressive Western alliance. NATO enlargement to the east, some authors surmise, is 'considered by practically all social strata [in Russia] as an attempt to erect a new iron curtain, to isolate Russia from the outside world and to transform it into "a problem country"' (Kolossov and Turovsky 2001: 141). Herspring and Rutland (2005: 281) aver that '[t]he very existence of NATO is a problem for Russia, given that the alliance was set up to deter the Soviet military threat to central Europe'. Protection from the 'Russian threat' was in fact a dominant justification in the decisions of Estonia, Latvia and Lithuania to join NATO (Kuus 2007a).

Since the Baltic states joined the military alliance in 2004, and with Georgia and Ukraine actively pushing for membership, NATO has began to establish itself on the territory of the post-Soviet space (Molchanov 2002: 269ff.). In view of these new developments, fears of deliberate isolation in geopolitical and security issues which is designed to keep Russia from gaining power and excluding it in the revamping of the European and global security architecture have been voiced (Kolossov and Turovsky 2001). This is underscored by the Russian perception of the rationale governing Georgia's move to apply for membership in NATO: Georgia is seen to seek a military guarantee for reasserting control of its territory by force and, cognisant of Western support, challenges Russia's hegemony in the Caucasus. Thus, from the Russian perspective, NATO expansion draws new geopolitical lines of inclusion and exclusion in larger Europe (Forsberg 2005; Kuus 2007a; Smith and Timmins 2001: 73-81). In discourses of Russian geopolitical identity, NATO therefore represents a crucial element which is often articulated as a geopolitical opponent and discursive antagonist.

3.4 'Europe'

Over the past centuries, perhaps no single signifier has been more pivotal in the formation of Russian geopolitical identity than 'Europe'. 'Indeed, the idea of Europe is the main "Other" in relation to which the idea of Russia is defined' (Neumann 1996: 1). Defining Russia through establishing differences and equivalences vis-à-vis Europe is a recurrent trope in articulations of Russian geopolitical identity, or, as Neumann (1996: 2) put it, 'Russian identity is caught up in the relationship with Europe'. Quite separate from 'the West', in Russia Europe has always occupied a special place. If Russia is seen to be entailed in a geopolitical confrontation, it will usually be with the West, not with Europe. Europe therefore is not simply a geopolitical subset of the West (Morozov 2003: 1503).

What is more, the meaning of Europe in Russia has been highly contested and ambivalent – not only since the demise of the Soviet Union (Neumann 1997: 149) but for several centuries:

> For Russia, Europe was always both charming and frightening, appealing and repulsive, radiating light and darkness. Russia was anxious to absorb Europe's vitality – and to ward off its contaminating effects; to become a fully fledged member of the European family of nations – and to remain removed from it; to become an object of its courtesies and even its devotion – but at the same time to inspire fear and trepidation. Indeed, the whole history of Russia is cast in this contradictory feeling (Baranovsky 2000: 445).

In his seminal monograph Neumann (1996) traces the idea of Europe and examines the multifarious ways Russia and Russians have constructed their identity in relation to Europe, starting with the import of European culture in Petrine times and reaching up to the ambiguous relationship of the present. The idea of Europe and the conscious Othering of it played a central role in the emergence of a pan-Slavic movement in the 19th century and contributed to the emergence of a Eurasian philosophy in the 1920s (Bassin 1991; Heffernan 1998: 23-32, 79-81). The geopolitical aspect to Russian identity that the European signifier represents has historically been fused with political currents: Russian liberalism is often underwritten by Westernist imaginations which position Russia in close association with Europe, whereas conservative nationalism draws close to the imaginations propagated in pan-Slavism and Eurasianism, which tend to view Russia as separate from Europe (Neumann 2002b; Prozorov 2007).

With Europe being the main referent in the formation of Russian geopolitical identity, authors have come up with a multiplicity of imaginations to characterise Russia's identification with Europe (e.g. Baranovsky 2000; Bassin 1991; Mäkinen 2003; Morozov 2003; Neumann 1996; Prozorov 2006; Smith and Timmins 2001; White et al. 2002). If one condenses these accounts, however, it seems that four generic imaginations emerge which are able to adequately describe the main features of the wealth of competing articulations.

Russia returning to the 'common European home'

Initiated in the period of *perestrojka* under Gorbachev, the rhetoric of a 'common European home' to which Russia should return carried over into the post-Soviet period and marked the order of the day in Russian foreign policy in its early years under foreign minister Kozyrev. The equivalence between Russia and Europe, Russia's European identity, is established mainly through culture and history, stressing humanist ideas about the superiority of the individual vis-à-vis the state, the common history of Europe and Russia and the shared cultural legacy (Neumann 1997). To some degree in this particular imagination the return to Europe is also addressed as a return to the community of civilised countries and which would therefore ensure the approving recognition of Russia by other states. As a 'Europe in the making' Russia becomes an apprentice of Europe for a limited time with the prospect of becoming the full member of the European civilisation it should always have been.

While this imagination quickly lost currency in Russian society and politics in the 1990s, it continued to be popular in (Western) European constructions of Russia as 'a learner who lacks insight into his own need to learn, but who will eventually, after a series of self-inflicted knocks, see the value of going to school with Europe' (Neumann 1997: 158). If not as a learner or apprentice, Prozorov (2007: 324) argues that nevertheless the 'overall telos of integration into Europe has been virtually uncontestable for most of the postcommunist period'. Accordingly, several authors regard Russia's positive identification with Europe as the hegemonic imagination, both among the ordinary population and in Russian political practice. Hopf (2005: 240) maintains that '[t]he average Russian understands herself as European, as part of European culture and civilisation, and as engaging in European daily practices' and Splidsboel-Hansen (2002: 406) similarly writes that 'the *dominant* narrative in Russia is still one where state and nation are placed firmly within the framework of European identity'.

Russia as the true Europe

Representations of Russia as embodying and conserving the true European values which the rest of Europe has abandoned reach back to the 19th century, when Russia persevered in upholding the *ancien régime* as a form of European aristocratic reign at a time when the Western European states had already overcome its mainstays. In the communist period, Soviet Russia was addressed as the caretaker of a true socialist model Europe the adoption of which the rest of Europe had spurned, thus failing the best in its own tradition (Neumann 1996: 194; 2002b: 202-203). In post-Soviet Russia, the imagination of Russia as the true Europe shifted to signify a dichotomous logic whereby Russia is taken to conserve the humanist values which the 'false' Europe had foregone in an all too indiscriminate pluralism which has led to its moral decay (Prozorov 2007).

Morozov (2003: 1507) argues that imagining Russia as the true Europe is motivated by the peculiar relationship of Russia to Europe which is characterised by the constant fear of exclusion from Europe. This exclusion is furthered and subverted by delimiting Russia as the true Europe against a false Europe which has strayed from its moral path, thus elevating true European values in Russia over false European values in the rest of Europe. As a marker of difference this distinction between true and false fractures Europe into an excluded 'us' and the excluding 'them' and serves as a means of representing Russia as European without having to adopt a submissive posture and passively wait for this consecration to be bestowed on Russia by European states (Morozov 2003; Prozorov 2007).

Russia as another Europe

Perhaps the most wide-spread imagination regards Russia as a specific eastern branch of the European civilisation with which it shares common cultural and historical roots. At its core, Russia is seen as being part and parcel of European civilisation, whereas its political and economic institutions have taken a different development path (Gvosdev 2007). Russia and the Western European states descend from the same 'family' and therefore share common ground in fundamental questions, while possibly having diverging opinions on more fleeting political issues. This imagination 'sees Russia as both European and an exception; rightfully part of the European world ... but distinctive within that world' (Gvosdev 2007: 139f). This points to a rather ambiguous identification with Europe which extends to some areas but not to others. Authors underline that the stress on specific Russian conditions is linked to the idea of Russia's great power status which, it is held, cannot be squared with a wholly European Russia (Gvosdev 2007; Neumann 1997). Imagining Russia as another Europe envisions a Russia which actively chooses to maintain close links to European states but at the same time is independent enough to pursue a course of development which does not conform to EU-European expectations.

With the accession of ten new members and states like Ukraine and Croatia about to take up negotiations for accession, sentiments of Russian marginalisation in Europe have recently gained in currency (Smith and Timmins 2001). '[R]emaining outside the EU as it expands its territorial space and functional scope may exacerbate Russia's concerns about its own role in Europe'

(Baranovsky 2000: 453). Concern about Russia's position given EU enlargement has buttressed the imagination of Russia as another Europe which, through a combination of exclusion and purposive self-exclusion, does not take part in the institutional development of the European Union but nevertheless shows high affinity to the cultural and spiritual idea of Europe (see, for example, Prozorov 2007).

Russia as not Europe

In another interpretation, narratives of exclusion from Europe by Europe merge with narratives of conscious self-exclusion from Europe on the part of Russia to create an imagination of Russia as *not* Europe. This self-exclusion may be based on cultural or historical grounds, as advocated by the adherents of pan-Slavism. Aleksandr Solženicyn, for example, has elaborately argued to the effect that Russians are morally superior to people in the West because of the spiritual growth engendered by the hardships the Russian people had to suffer in their history (Neumann 1996: 199f.). Russia represents a civilisation on its own, almost completely dissimilar to European civilisation, and it is therefore not in need of looking to Europe for identification. Other articulations draw primarily on political signifiers and propose to act on the insufficiently reciprocal state of and Russia's subordinate status in Russia-EU relations which do not adequately reflect its great power aspirations (Fischer 2006). They stress the growing political, military and economic strength of Russia vis-à-vis Europe to speak out in favour of its dissociation from Europe and reorientation towards the post-Soviet space (O'Loughlin et al. 2005; Trenin 2007).

Instead of building relations of equivalence to 'Europe', imagining Russia as not Europe constructs antagonistic relations to Europe and the signifiers associated with it. In this kind of imagination narratives of exclusion and self-exclusion from Europe have rallied around 'Eurasia' as a complementary signifier for Russian geopolitical identification. However, even when imagining Russia as *not* Europe, possibly as Eurasia, Europe still remains at the heart of Russian geopolitical identity through serving as the constitutive Other against which this non-European identity is defined.

3.5 'Great power'

'Great power' is perhaps the most frequent signifier in Russian geopolitical discourses today and can rightfully be considered as a hegemonic nodal point in large parts of Russian society. The hegemonic interpretation holds that it is part of Russian geopolitical identity that the country commands a place among the world's most powerful states and that after the demise of the USSR a new strategy was needed to regain or sustain this status as a great power or *velikaja deržava* (e.g. Bassin and Aksenov 2006; G. Smith 1999). The term *deržava*[6] denotes the state as a power, foregrounding the aspects of strength, assertiveness and cultural uniqueness. *Deržava* is an approving qualifier and is frequently applied to Russia as an ideal of Russian statehood (*deržavnost'*). It reflects a primacy given to state interests in civil society and thus the preference of a strong, paternalistic state (Allensworth 1998; Graham 2000). As a title of honour it is associated not only with Russian military strength but also with cultural, musical or literary achievements. The idea of *deržavnost'* in Russia, i.e. the idea of 'great-powerness' and the view that Russia ought to play an important role in world affairs (Kolstø 2004), can be traced back to myths of Russia as the Third Rome which identify the Russian empire as cultural and political successor to Rome in the world (Sidorov 2006).

Talk about Russia as a *velikaja deržava* did not cease with the collapse of the Soviet Union. Already back in 1992 Andrej Kozyrev considered Russia to be 'doomed to be a great power' (Kozyrev, quoted in Baev 1997: 186), even at a time when the role of Russia in world politics was discounted. His successor Primakov immediately set about putting this Russian manifest destiny into a practical agenda in the firm belief that 'Russia was and remains a great power and its policy in the outer world must correspond to this status' (Primakov, quoted in Baev 1997: 186). The Putin administration has pursued an active foreign policy which is commonly regarded as geared towards restoring Russia's status as a *velikaja deržava* (Tsygankov 2005). It is not surprising then if much recent literature sets out to examine Russia's great power identity (e.g. Hopf 2005; Sakwa 2008; Trenin 2006; Tsygankov 2005, 2008). An edited volume entitled 'Russia: re-emerging great power' (Kanet 2007) is devoted to tracing Russia's rise to great power status under Putin. Marshall Goldman (2008) and Alexander Rahr (2008) analyse how Russian petro dollars buttress

---

6 *Velikaja* is an attributive adjective and means 'great'.

the reassertion of traditional great power thinking, just to name a few examples.

The geopolitical identity formulated around the hegemonic nodal point of Russia as a great power connects up with a number of signifiers from notions of spheres of influence and national interests to different articulations of Eurasia and the Near Abroad (Baev 1997). The West, for example, is imagined as separate but not hostile to Russia as a great power.

> Too close an identification with the West became seen as tantamount to a subjugation of national identity and interests. Russia, it was argued, could never hope to be an equal of the West on the latter's terms ...; it could only remain a major global actor or great power as long as it preserved a distinct ... identity (Lo 2002: 59).

This common mode of great power thinking does not advocate integration with the West but rather espouses a kind of foreign policy which seeks to establish Russia's position as an actor who is able to negotiate with the West on equal terms in the international arena.

Eurasia

A number of authors note that the concept of Russia as a *velikaja deržava* is closely linked to the signifier of 'Eurasia' (Humphrey 2002: 382; Lo 2002: 59; Rangsimaporn 2006: 377; G. Smith 1999b: 488). Eurasia and Eurasianism assume many different forms in Russia (see Rangsimaporn 2006; Tsygankov 2003a) but most of them coalesce around the key idea that Russia represents an independent civilisation, both separate from Europe and from Asia. While the idea of Eurasia evolved historically for the main purpose of differentiating Russia from Europe, in post-Soviet Russia it has come to denote the re-emergence of Russia as a great power, assuming a hegemonic role in the post-Soviet states and negotiating with European states on equal terms, as well as the importance of the Asian vector in Russian foreign policy (Humphrey 2002; Kerr 1995; G. Smith 1999b). Amongst other things, Eurasianism holds that *qua* its unique geographical location Russia has been entrusted with playing the leading role in establishing a Eurasian civilisation. Addressing Eurasia as a civilisation in this way contributes directly to identity formation:

> To evoke a "civilization" is to call up a foundational identity, a mystical and mythical transcendental presence that is vague yet absolutely fundamental. ... It is to impose a closure upon events, situations, and peoples (Ó Tuathail 1996: 244).

As a floating signifier, Eurasia usually stands in for the uniqueness of Russia's geopolitical identity and often serves as a unifying term for a diverse conglomerate of Russian special characteristics (*specifiki*). Today, as Smith writes,

> [w]ithin Moscow foreign-policy circles, the place ascribed to Russia within global affairs has become increasingly scripted as part of an explicitly geopolitical discourse based on competing representations of Russia as inextricably bound up, both geopolitically and culturally, with the idea of Eurasia (G. Smith 1999b: 482).

This notion assigns to Russia a leading role in Eurasia and calls on it to pursue its own distinctive societal and geopolitical path. However, articulations of Eurasia differ in the extent to which they view this special role of Russia as providing a potential bridge between Europe and Asia, i.e. Russia as both European and Asian, or as an alternative. Eurasianism as a geopolitical school of thinking is sometimes used to justify territorial or great power ambitions of post-Soviet Russia, while on the other hand it may serve as a legitimation of giving equal weight to Asia and Europe in foreign policy. Rangsimaporn (2006: 385), for example, argues that interpretations of Eurasianism by the Russian elite have primarily been instrumental and directed at how to reap the maximum of benefits from utilising Russia's uniqueness. Humphrey (2002: 380) on the other hand holds that Eurasianism has always been directed against the influence of the West in Russia. For her, it constitutes a national idea of sublime character under whose umbrella Russians have united in pursuit of a unique identity.

The imaginary division of Russia into a European and an Asian part began in the Petrine era, when the Russian Empire was being modelled after a European image. The Ural mountains were then fixated as the boundary between the Russian colony in the east and the Russian core in the west. This division was increasingly questioned in the 19th century, when physical-geographical features were adduced to confute the claim of Russia being part of both Europe and Asia. Instead, the Russian Empire was regarded to form a cohesive, unipartite region of its own; a region which was called 'Eurasia'. On the basis of this geographical imagination Russia was identified with Eurasia in an all-encompassing form – economically, culturally, socially and historically. In contrast to pan-Slavic notions of Russia, Eurasia was perceived as a far greater civilisational entity including Turkic and Asiatic ethnicities (Bassin 1991). The precursor to present day Eurasianism as a (geo-)political movement developed originally in the early years of the Soviet Union and lent ideational support to the unity of Slavic and non-Slavic people in the USSR. It also favoured an authoritarian regime as the kind of government most appropriate for a Eurasian civilisation (Shlapentokh 1997).

The Near Abroad

For many people in Russia, Eurasianism today fulfils the role of a filling function after the identificatory dislocation of the early 1990s (see also the contributions in Kolossov 2000). In many senses, the re-articulation of the Eurasian signifier thus can be seen as marking the continuation of Russian geopolitical identity during Soviet times. More than the citizens in any other of the republics of the USSR, Russians identified with the Soviet Union as a whole and less with their ethnic backgrounds (G. Smith 1999a). According to O'Loughlin and Talbot (2005), this affinity to the states which made up the Soviet Union has carried over into the post-Cold War time and manifests itself for example in the desire of ordinary Russians to seek closer cooperation with states like Ukraine and Belarus (O'Loughlin and Talbot 2005). The emergence of a Eurasian discourse can thus be interpreted as catering to the need for identification with a subject position that represents the geographical imagination of Soviet unity (Lynn and Bogorov 1999).

After 1991 the 14 republics of the Former Soviet Union were dubbed the 'Near Abroad' (*Bližnee Zarubež'e*) to denote the special status and relationship they enjoyed with Russia. A significant proportion of Russian citizens had themselves either lived in those republics, still had relatives or friends there or were even born there. What is more, in the Soviet Union cultural and economic exchange between the member states was actively fostered and Russians were frequently sent on missions to other republics. It is not surprising, therefore, that emotional ties to the post-Soviet states of the Near Abroad are still strong and that there is a sense of geopolitical identity which extends beyond the present territory of Russia (O'Loughlin and Talbot 2005). 'Russian identity cannot confine itself only to the boundaries of the Russian Federation because of the legacy of the Soviet Union, in which Russian and Soviet were the same' (Kuzio 2003: 437).

The identity tie to the Near Abroad is thought to underpin Russia's claim to special rights and responsibilities for maintaining security in this region and to a role as *primus inter pares*. Graham Smith (1999b: 488ff.) places the Near Abroad as the nucleus around which notions like Russia's claim to great power status, geopolitical security, the Russian diasporic space and economic space congeal. While in the first half of the 1990s the Near Abroad was, by and large, neglected by Russian foreign policy, by the mid-1990s almost all states of the Near Abroad had Russian forces on their territory, either in a peacekeeping mission or to guard the external borders of these states (Baev 1997; Smith and Timmins 2001). Moscow's foreign policy then cited the defence of the interests of Russian minorities and the necessary establishment of a zone of security as rationales for asserting its hegemonic role in the Near Abroad (Menon 1999; Zagorski 1999).

Except for the three Baltic states, all ex-Soviet republics became members of the Commonwealth of Independent States (CIS), the principal international successor organisation to the Soviet Union which is mainly concerned with coordinating the relationships between its members.[7] The official rationale for founding the CIS was seen in the need to find a substitution for the coordinative function of the Soviet Union in the areas of economy and security and to organise, as Putin put it in 2005 and as is frequently repeated at MGIMO, a mechanism for 'civilised divorce'. As a political body the CIS has remained largely dominated by Russian interests which has led to it being regarded as 'a geopolitical smokescreen aimed at preserving Russian security interests' (G. Smith 1999a: 158). In recent years, the CIS has been challenged by centrifugal tendencies among its member states. Turkmenistan discontinued its full membership in 2005 and Georgia and Ukraine started to review their membership following the colour revolutions in 2003 and 2004. On the whole, authors judge that the CIS has increasingly become dysfunctional and is gradually replaced by more focused organisations with a smaller number of members, like CSTO or EurAsEC or the common economic space between Russia, Belarus and Kazakhstan (e.g. Buszynski 2004; Lo 2002; Molchanov 2002).

---

7 A subset of CIS members later founded regional organisations with more focused missions (see also Figure 1). In 2002, the charter establishing the Collective Security Treaty Organization (CSTO) was signed and by the end of 2008 Armenia, Belarus, Kazakhstan, Kyrgyzstan, Russia, Tajikistan and Uzbekistan had joined. In 2000, the Eurasian Economic Community (EurAsEC) was established with the goal to work towards a full-scale customs union and common market. By the end of 2008, signatory states were Belarus, Kazakhstan, Kyrgyzstan, Russia, Tajikistan and Uzbekistan.

Ukraine

Ukraine has always occupied a central position in Russian geopolitical identity. According to Kuzio (2003), it was and is still regarded as *the* quintessential Slavic brother state, cradle of the whole Slavic empire and reliable junior partner for Russia in the Soviet Union. Myths of a common origin of the three east Slavic people, myths of separation and reunion frequently establish a close connection between Ukraine and Russia and the idea of a pan-Slavic identity is deeply rooted in the two countries (Smith et al. 1998: 23ff.). As Molchanov (2002) and Kuzio (2003) contend, Russia frequently tends to look upon Ukraine not as an entirely sovereign state and in the past Russia has reacted highly sensitively to Ukrainian political decisions concerning the relationship with its larger neighbour.

In the 1990s, and even more so in the new millennium, the relationship between Russia and Ukraine has become increasingly ambivalent. On the one hand, people in the two countries still often regard each other as Slavic brothers which share similar identities. This view is enforced by the presence and strong influence of a Russian minority in Ukraine and the economically and societally strong ties between the two countries (D'Anieri 1999). On the other hand, there has been a strong dissociation of Ukraine from Russia which was accompanied by a re-orientation of the hegemonic geopolitical discourse. Already before the Orange Revolution in 2004, Ukraine embarked on a course which saw it steering towards closer integration with the West and the European Union in particular. This was marked by an outspokenly pro European and pro-NATO rhetoric which, to a growing extent, drove a wedge between Russia and Ukraine (Molchanov 2002).

More recently, the dispute with Russia over a steep increase in gas tariffs at the beginning of 2006 has fuelled mutual resentment. Ukraine on its part voiced its discontent with the presence of the Russian Black Sea Fleet on Crimea and declared its intention to revoke treaties that allowed the deployment of Russian military forces on Ukrainian territory. What we have witnessed recently therefore is a revived struggle for the articulation of 'Ukraine' as a moment in discourses which construct subject positions of Russian geopolitical identity. Frictions between Russia and Ukraine have grown to a point where, increasingly, Ukraine was being recast as a defector from the pan-Slavic project; a defector, however, who needed to be proselytised and brought back on track.

Nationalism and patriotism

In many cases, a patriotic loyalty to the Russian state underpins the Russian strive for great power status in world politics. Frequently seen as a predominantly domestic phenomenon, Russian nationalism is, as Simonsen (2001) explains, intimately linked to imaginations of territory. He distinguishes between a 'core-oriented nationalism' and an 'empire-oriented nationalism', corresponding roughly to different interpretations of Eurasia as depicted in Table 2. The school of Eurasianism, in its various variants, is as much nationalist as it is geopolitical, since it formulates a Russian national idea in geopolitical terms (Laruelle 2004). More broadly, for Tuminez (2000), the rise and fall of Russian nationalism has always been linked to foreign policy. She argues that whenever the international environment was hostile for Russia, a rise in nationalist sentiments could be observed. She applies this to the Kosovo crisis in which Russia experienced international humiliation which in turn sparked intensified calls for re-establishing Russia as a strong state. Lo concludes that

> we should not underestimate the strength or sincerity of much of the nationalist impulse. If nothing else, Russia's imperial past established an image of itself as a great nation and global power – crucial elements in any powerfully felt nationalism (Lo 2002: 57).

Drawing this connection between nationalism and great power ideology is important for addressing the linkages between domestic, national and foreign, geopolitical identity formation.

Nationalism experienced an upsurge in Russia after the collapse of the Soviet Union and received much scholarly attention in the 1990s (e.g. Brudny 2000; Allensworth 1998; Tuminez 2000). Brudny (2000: 23) claims that the strong appeal of nationalist ideologies in Russia can be attributed to the ideological void left behind with the demise of communism, which liberal-democratic notions of Russia were unable to fill. Russian nationalism, as Tuminez (2000: 266f.) observes, has frequently been equal to patriotism, serving to strengthen the state and to uphold its power vis-à-vis the people. I shall regard patriotism here as a special form of nationalism, a statist nationalism primarily denoting loyalty to one's country, without the ethnic or cultural moments that are often associated with nationalism. *Patriotizm* is also the approving term used in Russia, whereas *nacionalizm* is a derogatory expression reserved for hard-line extremists like Vladimir Žirinovskij who hold violent xenophobic views.

Patriotism is largely naturalised as a hegemonic discourse in Russia and enacted as part of many 'banal nationalisms' (Billig 1995). Banal nationalism refers to the everyday representations and enactments of nation that are often considered as insignificant for formal political analysis: expressions of nationalism appear in sport events, the TV news, the national press, advertisements, consumption and so on. Talking about *the* weather, *our* team, readily waving national flags at all kinds of events or dividing news into a 'domestic' and a 'foreign' section all contribute to instilling a sense of togetherness and common belonging in people. Of course, Russia has its fair share of official patriotism, ranging from Victory Day parades to propaganda campaigns with appeals to a 'strong Russia'. But more important for my research setting are the everyday articulations of national identity which do not carry overtly ideological character. Billig (1995: 86) calls such details 'universal signs of particularity', universalising the nation while at the same time underscoring its particularity vis-à-vis other nations. Billig's key argument, which also applies to the situation in Russia, is that the mundane nature of banal nationalism makes it a very powerful ideology which is often not identified as such.

Herspring and Rutland (2005) contend that under Putin, patriotism became the national idea to unify the Russian people. At the beginning of his incumbency Putin declared that the country needed a new national ideology based on patriotism. He defined a 'minimum package' for this new patriotism with the primary goals of

> strengthening the state and the economy, introducing order, securing Russia's territorial integrity, raising its status internationally, and strengthening the military to resist possible attacks by other powers (Simonsen 2001: 282).

The overlaps of this version of patriotism with a Russian great power identity in world politics are obvious: both foster notions of Russian uniqueness and distinctiveness and advocate strengthening Russia. It has been suggested that much of Putin's success as a president lay in the unifying force that his interconnected visions of Russian patriotism and Russia as a great power exerted (Herspring and Rutland 2005; Verkhovsky 2007). Since I conducted my own research during Putin's second term in office, the co-articulation of patriotism, especially in its banal, mundane form, and great power visions deserves special attention in the analysis.

3.6 Conceptual reflection: the lens of Laclau and Mouffe

In the conceptual vocabulary of Laclau and Mouffe the collapse of the Soviet Union constitutes a dislocation: it was an event that could not be represented in the hegemonic discursive order and therefore led to its breakdown. The dislocation prompted struggles over the articulation of signifiers which had previously been fixed but were now returned into the field of discursivity. The dominance of a logic of equivalence during the Soviet Union was replaced by a dominance of the logic of difference in the immediate post-Soviet years: multiple geopolitical positions were able to co-exist with none gaining hegemony. As Laclau and Mouffe have observed, however, 'it is impossible to suppress antagonisms indefinitely in order to maintain a construction of a social field as a peaceful system of differences' (A. M. Smith 1998: 90).

New struggles for hegemony emerge, striving to invest key signifiers with new meanings and thus also to articulate new subject positions with which subjects can identify (Torfing 1999). Hegemonic projects emerge to form 'a new objectivity by means of the re-articulation of the dislocated elements' (Laclau 1990: 61). It is in times of major dislocations which engender deep identificatory voids that, as Torfing argues, the filling function of articulation is more important than the content of the filling:

> It seems to be of little importance to the voters whether the politicians they support are fascists, reformed communists or neo-liberals, so long as they promise to restore order and put an end to chaos, misery and despair (Torfing 1999: 152).

As the right-wing populist Vladimir Žirinovskij touted in October 1991: 'In a rich nation my program would not go over very well. But in a poor, embittered country like Russia, this is my golden hour' (from a Boston Globe article, quoted in Dunlop 1997: 51).

This dislocation perhaps also explains the surging interest in geopolitics in post-Soviet Russia – the interest in a geopolitics that seeks to objectively interpret Russia's position, taking into account geographical and political factors, and draw conclusions about where Russia belongs and how it should act in world politics. It is this apparent objectivity of geopolitical spatialisations, discussed earlier, that makes it so amenable to serving as a bedrock of the re-articulation of identities. From the perspective of Laclau and Mouffe's discourse theory, of course, the supposed pragmatism of geopolitics is but another ideology – a naturalised, hegemonic discourse which emerges to stabilise dislocated structures. In this section, a review of the most important debates and positions surrounding Russian geopolitical identities has delineated the field of discursivity, the range of possible articulations of signifiers. At the same time, however, it has already highlighted several hegemonic projects that are characterised by a closure of subject positions. As many authors observe, the project of Russia as a strong great power – linked to signifiers like Eurasia, the Near Abroad or patriotism – is gaining currency and starting to build chains of equivalence.

Articulatory struggles manifest themselves in myriad ways in post-Soviet Russia, in texts and practices: in newspapers and magazines, in politicians' speeches, in violence against migrants, in border controls, in the flaunting of haute couture. They are carried out on multiple scale levels, from the international to the local. This social multiplicity of the articulation of geopolitical identities in Russia has not found adequate reflection in the relevant literature. Dominated by the discipline of international relations, studies have adopted a position of analytical distance. Bigo and Walker (2007: 5) describe this perspective as an 'almost superhuman view of scholarship that seems to emerge when we engage with systems, states, sovereignties, and so on as more or less disembodied structures, even abstractions'.

Constructivist studies on Russian geopolitical identity have largely passed over an analysis of social practices which involves fieldwork and thus the participation of the researchers in the situations they are analysing. Instead such analyses have focused on geopolitical textbooks and pamphlets (e.g. Bassin and Aksenov 2006; Höllwerth 2007; Ingram 2001; Tsygankov 2003a), the use and interpretation of geopolitical ideas by political elites and organisations (e.g. Humphrey 2002; Mäkinen 2003; Rangsimaporn 2006; Tsygankov 2005; Zimmerman 2002), geopolitical narratives (e.g. Neumann 1996; O'Loughlin et al. 2004a, b, 2005; Prozorov 2006, 2007; G. Smith 1999a, b; Tsygankov 1997), foreign policy strategy and relations (e.g. Hopf 2005; Kolossov and Turovsky 2001; Splidsboel-Hansen 2002; Tsygankov 2007), opinion polls (e.g. O'Loughlin and Talbot 2005; O'Loughlin et al. 2004a, b, 2005; Rose and Munro 2008) or historical enquiries into the genealogy of geopolitical ideas (e.g. Bassin 1991; Shlapentokh 1997). Sources from which authors have gleaned their material are newspapers, books, political speeches, telephone surveys or government documents which usually lay claim to cover large parts of the Russian society and thus, at least to some extent, to be representative of the Russian state and the geopolitical orientations present within it. This focus on representations, mostly at the level of the state, makes for a somewhat one-sided empirical perspective in which the constitution of geopolitical identities and its particular mechanisms in specific locales are largely written out of scholarly accounts (see Megoran 2006; Sharp 2000b). The discourse theory of Laclau and Mouffe, however, advocates a kind of social analysis that goes beyond mere textual analysis to engage with all meaningful signifying practices that constitute the social – signifying practices that are best captured by employing ethnography as a methodology.

4

Of ethnographic methodology

This book has started from a critique of critical geopolitics: earlier studies, I have argued, lack a broad understanding of identity as constituted in language and practice and neglect the institutional context of micro settings. As we have seen in the previous chapters, a re-conceptualisation along the lines of poststructuralist discourse theory is able to theoretically address such shortcomings. But how are they addressed methodologically? In many ways, ethnographic research is an appropriate methodology for filling this conceptual model with life. It is able to provide a detailed picture of social life within a given setting and devotes considerable attention to everyday meaning construction. What is more, through the active involvement of the researcher in the research process ethnography also fosters the kind of reflexivity about scientific knowledge production that is still mostly absent in critical geopolitics research.

Discussions of methodology are inseparable from the field setting in which research takes place. In my study, geopolitical identities are situated in the institutional context of Moscow State Institute of International Relations (MGIMO). An appropriate methodology needs to be able to address the contextual factors of identity production in the specific setting of MGIMO. It needs to pay increased attention to practices as the small details through which identities are articulated (Thrift 2000). This chapter offers a methodological discussion of my ethnographic research at MGIMO so as to provide the backdrop of the messiness and complexity of the real world from which I have gathered my data. Inevitably, substantial parts of this messiness get 'written away' in the academic homogenisation of establishing a 'reconstructed logic' (Silverman 1985: 4) in the process of data analysis in the following chapters. It is all the more important to reflect on the unevenness and limitations of fieldwork data in order to develop a critical awareness of the inseparability of questions of methodology from the knowledge we produce. The discussion of research ethics will be woven into the description of the research process as a means to present the research process and the results at which I have arrived through my interpretation as transparently as possible. The chapter concludes with a section on the methods of data analysis which is designed to make the process of analysing data and drawing conclusions explicit.

4.1 Data collection: participant observation and interviews

My research at MGIMO took place from late August 2005, when I arrived in Moscow at MGIMO as an exchange student, until May 2006, when I had finished my interviews and left for Germany. One substantial part of my field research consisted of *ethnographic participant observation.* This involved living the lives of students to the degree this was possible for me as an exchange student from abroad. This research created two main data sources. First, my field diary and materials like photos, leaflets or magazines I collected *in situ* and, second, recordings of lectures and seminars at MGIMO, totalling 25 hours. The second substantial part of my research consisted of *interviewing students* about their assessment of Russia's role in world politics. This created the third data source of 35 interviews with third and fourth year students. The following sub-sections describe in greater detail how and why these data were collected and processed. I will try to link a theoretical treatment of research methodology to practical issues that came up during my time at MGIMO.

Ethnographic research

> It may appear to some that ethnographies are impossible to 'get right'. This may be true, and neither of us feels that we have ever fully succeeded in doing our own 'properly'. However, it is far more satisfying to feel that you have addressed these issues rather than tried to avoid them under some quantitative epistemology (Cook and Crang 1995: 91).

Ethnography prioritises the specificity and context-dependent nature of knowledge. If viewed in conjunction with theory-building, ethnography is a methodology rather than simply a method. Hypotheses, insights and generalisations emerge from the ethnographer's progressive socialisation into the life of the group studied instead of being derived from overwrought concepts (Cook and Crang 1995). Ethnography's key advantage over other qualitative research methods is its ability to listen closely to the routine ways in which people make sense of the world in everyday life (Hammersley and Atkinson 1995: 2). In so doing,

> [e]thnography creates a fuller and more differentiated picture of postsocialist transformation from a spatially and historically distinct position. Rather than seeking to eradicate the difference that place makes, it strategically employs positionality to provide a grounded perspective that explains how large-scale processes are interpreted, responded to and (re)produced by social actors in specific locations (Hörschelmann and Stenning 2008: 348).

It is particularly well-poised for comprehensive investigations of social interaction within settings that are often off-limits to other research methods, either because entry is difficult or because the everyday nature of the social phenomena makes it difficult to capture them through interviews or other texts. In the analysis of discursive identity production ethnography animates the practice-component of discourse by paying close attention to the everyday activities and symbolic constructions of the social group that is researched.

In my research, the ethnographic approach thus fulfilled a twofold purpose: it granted me access to a setting which would have been difficult, if not impossible, to study with other research methods and it resulted as the logical continuation and empirical substantiation of the concept of discourse and identity as I have developed it in the earlier chapters. As a method it seemed particularly suited to my research focus on a specific social group of Russian society and not the high-profile elites of public life who have hitherto attracted most attention in studies of post-Soviet critical geopolitics. At MGIMO the ethnographic approach provided me with the opportunity to join the regular, day-to-day process of sitting in lectures, chatting, preparing for exams, listening to talks etc.

> When I entered MGIMO through an exchange programme in August 2005, coming to grips with the educational process at MGIMO was a tedious task and took me a long time of asking around, both among my fellow exchange students and at various offices at MGIMO. To be fashioned with the necessary documents was an extremely time-consuming exercise but at the same time provided me with a useful *tour d'horizon* and *Who is Who* of MGIMO and gave me an impression of the administrative procedures and red tape that accompanied the study process. Since it was not my first time to Russia and I had already gone through the ordeal of Russian bureaucracy several times I tried to make a virtue out of these trials and jotted all of them down into my field diary while I was sitting and waited to be called.
>
> Timetables of lectures and seminars were posted as the beginning of the academic year drew closer and I immediately began to seek out the ones that sounded most in-

> teresting in terms of geopolitical content. I started off with a heavily loaded schedule of about twelve courses which I visited in the first few weeks and which I reduced to five after I had got an idea of how relevant they were going to be for my research. I tried to take part in courses across all years but it was mostly in the advanced courses that I found the kinds of individual assessment and discussion of political issues I was looking for, while the basic courses still concentrated very much on facts and figures. All the while, in my observations I strove to note everything that seemed somehow relevant to my research. This ranged from taking notes of casual conversations or comments that I had overlistened in the corridors to photographing leaflets or posters and collecting all kinds of printed material. As my ideas gelled, my observations grew ever more focused on specific aspects and specially sought out certain encounters or events that I hoped would add a piece to the evolving mosaic.

As noted by Herbert (2000) and Megoran (2002, 2006), ethnography leads a marginalised life in most of contemporary human and political geography. Unjustly so, argues Herbert (2000: 551), 'because its intensive analysis and fine-grained detail provide the optimal way to illustrate and explicate the oft-stated connection between the lifeworld of a social group and the geographic world they construct.' He commends ethnography for its aptness to gauge the specificities of place and how sociality and spatiality are intertwined in the reconstruction and deconstruction of social life. One might add here explicitly that although ethnography unfolds on an extremely limited fraction of physical space, its reach can and should be far greater than this fraction. It is the link between macro level social phenomena and micro level dynamics that shines up in ethnographies – just like in Nick Megoran's (2002) exploration of borderland perceptions in the Ferghana Valley. In it he connects political events at the national levels with the local responses of the Ferghana Valley population and vice versa and maps the oscillating attitudes towards the border during a period of intense political stirs. In this vein, he is able to establish an interrelationship between his local observations and the international dynamics at work in the border conflicts.

Much ethnographic research still fails to connect the situated insights of ethnographies to the wider social picture. All too often, Hörschelmann and Stenning (2008) argue, ethnographies remain stuck within their apparent discreteness in space and time. The specificity of their case frequently keeps ethnographic researchers from locating their findings in historical contexts or linking them to other scale levels. Locating the Other in the ethnographically far-away, disconnected from larger social processes, becomes problematic, however, with the effects of globalisation and transnationalism that fold different scales into each other. There is reason to believe that much can be gained from discussing the insights based on the unconventional empirical perspective of many ethnographies in the context of larger social phenomena, even if traditional criteria of quantitative research like representativeness do not hold. This challenge also entails shifting political responsibilities for the fieldworker in opening up the 'possibility for dialogue rather than observation and for cultural critique rather than description' (Hörschelmann and Stenning 2008: 343).

Perhaps more than any other method, ethnography heavily draws on the idiosyncratic experiences and perceptions of the researching individual (Atkinson 1990; Stewart 1998). Definitions of what kind of research counts as ethnography are exceedingly broad. Most authors concur, however, that the central methodical technique of ethnographic research is participant observation, the immersion of the researcher into the everyday life of a social group with the aim to render an authentic account and interpretation of different facets of social interaction. The degree to which this immersion takes place is one of the defining elements of every ethnography. It involves walking the fine line, or shuttling between, participation and observation, between gaining inside knowledge and keeping a critical distance to the phenomena under question (Stoddart 1986). Both are critical to establishing credibility: too little participation may compromise the validity of a researcher's account; too little distance, on the other hand, may jeopardise the critical analytical purchase.

> My age and similar status as a student were certainly two crucial factors that allowed me to carry out the research as a participant observer, which would have been impossible for other researchers older than me. At 23, I was young enough not to stick out in courses of the third or fourth year in which students were about two to three years younger than me. Although I had just completed a Master's degree a few months before, I did not feel that my advanced education gave me an advantage over other students. On the contrary, the kind of knowledge and knowledge (re-)production demanded at MGIMO was so foreign to me that as far as participation in classes or writing essays was concerned I always felt somewhat uneasy and, accordingly, scored badly.

The ethnographer must thus both empathetically live her or his life as a member of the community and engage this emotion-laden data with comparatively neutral theory. This trade-off, or alternation, between going-native and hands-off is one of the recurrent themes in discussions of ethnographic research methodology (e.g. Fuller 1999; Harrington 2002).

The choice of favouring one or the other side depends both on the research aims and on the conditions of the research setting. It must be cautioned against the assumption, however, that defining the degree of immersion always happens at the researcher's discretion. In many cases the researcher cannot help but adopt a certain role which has been ascribed to her or him by the social context she or he studies. Moreover, the personality of the researcher equally plays into decisions and possibilities to participate in the lives of one's research subjects and shapes the perspective of every ethnography (Moser 2008).

The question of immersion is almost inseparable from the question of obtrusiveness. The classic position advocates the minimisation of obtrusiveness by blending in and therefore getting a supposedly authentic picture of social processes which can then be presented to the reader (e.g. Glesne and Peshkin 1999; Lofland and Lofland 1995). Much of the credibility of ethnography rests on the claim that it avoids methodogenesis, i.e. the problem that the research itself creates the data, and the problem of presence, i.e. a bias on the research data caused by the presence of the researcher (Stoddart 1986). This pretence at authenticity assumes that the ethnographer merely records an objective reality that is 'out there', waiting to be retrieved, but does not partake in its construction. From a constructivist perspective, however, the subjectivity of the researcher is inevitably implicated in every ethnographic account and therefore has to be addressed.

> My old-style leather-bound field diary accompanied me every day, even when I was taking days off at the weekends. The content of notes varies: some of them were taken in lectures, verbatim recording salient quotes or summarising the general line of arguments; others sprang into life when I was sitting on one of the many benches in the corridors and watched and listened to people passing by. In the first weeks, I realised that I had to sharpen my observational skills and attention to details, all the more since the university, even if it was located in Russia, was a familiar environment and at first I did not notice many details that I later thought worth recording. In most cases, note-taking could be done unobtrusively, since all students were scribbling into their notebooks during classes or doing their homework while sitting around and waiting for the next pair of classes to begin. While the setting ensured that I would not draw unnecessary attention when taking notes, sometimes I was so consumed by trying to follow and understand what was being said that I forgot to take notes immediately and had to write them from memory afterwards.
>
> The procedure of note-taking slightly differed for conducting ethnographic interviews, i.e. when recording relevant data that resulted more or less naturally from casual conversation. In this case I tried to memorise the key points and wrote them down immediately after the conversation. As I developed my own style of writing field notes, guided by Emerson et al. (1995), I grew more and more fond of my little notebook and kept it like a treasure. In general, I adopted a rather terse style of writ-

> ing, at least when I listened to lectures which I was recording anyway. When observing events or occurrences without much talk I see my field notes primarily as stimuli to conjure up memories of certain situations. Wolcott (1995, 1999) describes a variety of possibilities, largely dependent on individual preferences, to organise and process one's field notes. Unlike many other ethnographers that report sitting at their desks all night typing their field notes, I did not process my notes in any significant way but completing them from memory on the same day. This is mostly because the hand-written notes, full of arrows, abbreviations, highlights, underlines and little symbols, seemed to me to serve a better purpose than the rather sterile, type-written pages of word-processed field notes.

Conducting unobtrusive research places a high ethical responsibility on the researcher. For the most part, the semi-overt or covert nature of unobtrusive ethnographic research makes it impossible that it follows the principle of informed consent. That is, subjects are often not aware that they take part in a research project and that what they say and do is recorded as data. One of the primary justifications for covert research is often adduced for settings where subjects may react sensitively to the presence of a researcher and, as a consequence, alter the behaviour one expects to study. This was the main motivation for Humphreys (1970) in his study of homosexual encounters in public toilets. For others who study street gangs or criminal groups (e.g. Thompson 1967) the cloak of anonymity guarantees personal protection and bodily integrity and is the very condition for gaining entry to a certain setting.

None of these two major reasons played a significant role in my own research. My bodily integrity, of course, was not an issue and the problem of reactivity could largely be avoided, because groups were sufficiently large to cushion the effects of my presence and because the information that I retrieved was not considered sensitive or intimate. From my own experience it seems that researchers usually grow into a role on the continuum between concealment and disclosure. Their functioning as (new) members of a community who are met with certain expectations already maps out the conceivable positions. If socialisation with the same, narrow circle of people takes place over an extended period of time achieving relative overtness is more likely than this could occur on the basis of passing encounters. In this sense, the degree of covertness in my ethnographic research evolved gradually and adjusted to the specificities of the research setting, just as in many other studies (e.g. Bain and Nash 2006; Schwalbe 1996).

> During my time at MGIMO, it was impractical to inform everyone I spoke to or observed about the aims and methods of my research. Like Bain and Nash (2006), who

> attended a queer women's bathhouse event, the circumstances and type of interaction made research transparency difficult: interactions tended to be fleeting and cursory and the nature of them sometimes allowed and sometimes did not allow to broach the kind of project I was involved in. However, whenever I was collecting verbatim material, most notably in lectures, I always sought permission to do so by stating my status as a research student and the goal of my research project.
>
> I established contact and presented my research proposal to a member of the professorial staff at MGIMO who agreed to sponsor my project and gave me feedback on what to expect and where to look. He subsequently invited me to social gatherings with students of his and tried to point me to literature and studies I might find relevant. This approval at the faculty level was important for me as a reassurance that I could go ahead with what I intended to do and would not violate any unwritten rules or codes of conduct. What resulted was a kind of semi-overt research in which I was candid about my aims whenever the natural flow of conversation led that way or whenever I was recording with my dictaphone but could not help gathering data from people who were not informed of my intent.

Some authors assert that covert research cannot be justified by any ethical guideline, since for one thing it fundamentally undercuts the guiding principle of informed consent and thus violates the right to informational protection of the research subjects (Herrera 1999, 2003; see also Fine 1994). Other authors like Hilbert (1980) or Parr (1998, 2000) argue the case that there are no strict ethical or moral dividing lines between overt and covert research since both forms of research are fraught with complex power relationships and personal positionings. In fact, overt and covert research are usually intertwined, since 'participant observation is irremediably covert to some degree, because of the essential glossing practices any member engages in to produce typicality' (Hilbert 1980: 74). Full disclosure thus is as much a meaningless ideal as full concealment is. Rather than by the degree of secrecy, the ethical quality of qualitative research must be judged against the criteria mentioned above: emancipation and self-determination of the research subjects, and transparency and reflexivity of the research(er). As Bronfenbrenner (1952: 453) remarks, '[t]he only safe way to avoid violating principles of professional ethics is to refrain from doing social research altogether'.

Interviewing

While it constitutes an important data source in its own right, the ethnographic material gathered also serves to lend background to the interviews which followed in the later stages of the research process. Dexter (1970: 15) confirms that ethnographic interviewing, i.e. interviews that are backed by ethnographic observations, allows a much richer interpretation, especially if the interviews have been conducted in a setting the researcher would usually be unfamiliar with. A preceding phase of participant observation enabled me to tailor my interviews more closely to students' realities and to become clearer about what it is I wanted to know from them. Participant observation and interviews thus complement each other as data sources.

Interviews, for example, suffer from a series of shortcomings which may be effectively counteracted by ethnographic data: Silverman (1989, 1993) stresses that the ability of interview statements to reflect the experiential reality of the interviewee is limited by the artificial situation of the interview which prompts answers that are considered appropriate for this particular interaction context. In their responses, interviewees have already processed their answers through various interpretive lenses and present them in their own terms, a problem exacerbated when interviewing highly-trained, well-educated respondents (Hammersley and Atkinson 1995: 189).

> I experienced this first hand when I conducted an interview with a student who made clear at the beginning of the interview that he viewed Russia's 'Sovietness' as the leitmotif in all issues regarding Russian politics and society at large and who subsequently offered me an analysis of the topics at hand along these general lines.

This kind of double hermeneutics is inevitably involved when conducting social research using interviews. Hammersley and Atkinson (1995: 119) on the other hand maintain that the artificiality of the interview situation can serve as a special stimulus and thus can provoke the production of data which would otherwise have been difficult to come by.

Semi-structured interviews as I have employed them in my research at MGIMO have long been the staple research method in the social sciences as well as in human geography. Their main purpose is to get access to information that would not be available otherwise and do so in a relatively systematic fashion using an interview guide. Semi-structured interviewing occupies a middle ground between the in-depth, open-ended interview, which is more akin to a casual conversation and is frequently used in ethnographic research, and the standardised interview typical of opinion polls and surveys. Semi-structured interviews avoid the kind of undirected meandering which characterises narrative interviews but at the same time they are flexible enough to respond to unexpected twists and turns of the conversation and pick up new threads that appear during an interview.

The genesis and compilation of *interview guides* often appears as shrouded in mystery in much social science research involving semi-structured interviews. Somehow they are just 'there'.

> My interview guide for this research has a distinct history and its evolution reflects the changing conceptions of my research. I entered the setting at MGIMO having read little about post-Soviet (critical) geopolitics, apart from several articles by O'Loughlin et al. (2004a, b, 2005) which had appeared shortly before I left for Russia. As it turned out, this was not to my detriment, since I was able to listen first-hand to lectures and talks on geopolitical themes at MGIMO and read up on the literature in this field in parallel.
>
> In general I tried to connect questions in the interview guide to recent events so as to draw them from the abstract into the concrete. This was the case with the questions on the use of Russia's oil and gas as a political instrument, with Russia's relation to Georgia and with Russia's attitude towards NATO. Since my ambition was to tie in the interview guide with the relevant literature but at the same time make it address the issues that were considered relevant at MGIMO, it turned out to be a compromise between the two. On the one hand it works with concepts and regions that regularly appear in lectures at MGIMO. The CIS and the countries of the Near Abroad, for example, play a much more salient role at MGIMO than it could be guessed from the literature. Similarly, the concepts of a unipolar versus a multipolar world are ubiquitous at MGIMO but less so in the academic literature. On the other hand I was intent on bringing in issues from the literature on post-Soviet geopolitics such as Russia's imputed role as a renascent great power.
>
> Starting to interview I soon realised that I had tacitly expected to be talking with experts in the field – just as I had become one by reading up on the literature. But, at best, I was interviewing future experts and possibly only students who were interested in everything else but politics. All in all, I had significantly overestimated the familiarity of students with foreign policy issues and their ability to deliver individual assessments of pressing and current questions. (see O'Loughlin et al. 2004a: 34 for remarks on the generally low level of knowledge about foreign affairs among ordinary Russians). This made it necessary to adapt some items to the knowledge of students. In particular, I tended to replace open-ended questions like 'What are the most pressing questions in Russian foreign policy at the moment?' with more concrete, case-based questions such as students' take on the American war on terrorism. Similarly, I extended the interview guide on a rolling basis by adding new issues that were raised in interviews and which I had not thought of before. Russia's relationship with Iran at the height of the nuclear crisis in early 2006 was one of those themes that I had not included from the outset but which yielded highly revealing responses. The evolution of the interview guide thus accompanied my process of learning more generally.

Developing a *sampling strategy* was one of the tasks that I had set myself for the period of predominantly ethnographic research. During the time I spent as a participant observer I had found that the lectures most relevant for my research questions concentrated in the School of International Relations (IR), the School of Political Science (PS) and School of International Journalism (IJ). It also seemed sensible to focus on more advanced students, since it is predominantly in the later stages of the education at MGIMO that students are confronted with issues like foreign policy analysis and asked to develop their own stand regarding important questions of Russian international relations. Taking these issues into account, my sampling strategy aimed to primarily recruit students from the third and fourth years and from IR and PS into the sample. As becomes evident from Table 4, I also tried to maintain a gender balance in the sample. Apart from these three criteria I did not perform any additional preselection.[8]

Table 4: Social and academic characteristics of students interviewed

Sex	Female	18
	Male	17
Year	Third	9
	Fourth	26
Department	International Relations (IR)	18
	Political Science (PS)	8
	International Journalism (IJ)	5
	Others	4
Place of Origin	Moscow	19
	Russia outside Moscow	11
	Abroad	5
Funding	Stipend (*bjudžetnyj*)	26

8 This sampling strategy resulted in an overrepresentation of students funded by scholarships vis-à-vis self-funded students, who make up about half of the MGIMO student body. This imbalance can probably be attributed to a self-selection bias: self-funded students probably felt less knowledgeable about the issues in the interview and therefore were more likely not to turn up for the agreed interviews.

Self-funded (*kontraktnyj*)	9

My aim was to carry out enough interviews to allow variations in the answers to show up but to stop when further significant variations did not seem to occur any more. The recursive collection and coding of data in grounded theory works according to this principle, for example (Titscher et al. 2000). It also proved to be a workable premise for my situation and since I was not pressed for time, keeping the number of interviews open would ensure that I would not have to rush to get a certain number of predefined number of interviews but could adapt my interview schedule to the research requirements.

> Typically, I contacted potential interviewees before the start of lectures when people began to gather in the lecture halls. As class timetables are posted publicly on the notice boards of the respective departments, it was relatively easy to seek out lectures which were only frequented by students from my target group. I picked people at random, introduced myself and my project to them and asked them whether they would be available for an interview. If they consented, we agreed on a time and date when we could meet for the interview. Since timetables at MGIMO are tight and rather rigid, the time windows available for interviews were rather few. On an average day I could not secure more than one or two appointments, although there were few outright rejections to my request. This was exacerbated by the fact that interviewees regularly 'forgot' about the interviews. I tried to avoid this problem by writing the date, place and time of the interview on a sticky note which I gave to the potential interviewee. This effort of mine notwithstanding, the turn-out rate was at only 65 %, i.e. in order to get 39 interviews I had to make 60 contacts.
>
> Interviews were usually scheduled during the lunch break, which made it easier to find a free lecture hall for conducting the interview, but limited the total length of the interview to about 45 minutes, or in a so-called *okno*, a 'hole' in the tight timetable. These 'holes' permitted the interview to last longer than one hour but complicated the question where to conduct the interview since almost all lectures halls were usually occupied during the day. In this case I resorted to conducting the interview in the university cafeteria which used to be quiet when classes were on. Both interview sites, lecture halls and the cafeteria, offered the advantage of being reasonably familiar for respondents and providing some quasi-neutral territory as opposed to if I had conducted the interviews in my dorm room which was conveniently located right next to the university building and would have offered more privacy. By locating the interviews within the university I was trying to keep the playing field of power as level as possible (cf. Elwood and Martin 2000).

On average, one interview lasted 37 minutes with some lasting longer than one hour and some lasting only about 25 minutes. Questions seemed to be generally well understood by interviewees and where this was not the case, I tried to circumscribe the idea of the question and rephrase it in the interview guide for the following interview. Occasionally, an informal chat developed after the interview, often with students who had been to Germany or who studied German as a foreign language. In one or two cases this evolved into a casual friendship for the time I was at MGIMO. However, my nationality also made some interviewees reluctant to comment unfavourably on Germany, the European Union or even Europe in general; a reluctance sometimes expressed openly in the interviews and sometimes tacitly present.

A central element which determines success and failure of semi-structured interviews is the establishment of rapport in the interview situation. 'Without rapport, even the best-phrased questions can fall flat and elicit brief, uninformative answers' (Leech 2002: 665). Rapport consists of different elements: it is not only making feel people at ease but also convincing them that you are listening and interested in what they are saying. This is all the more difficult to achieve if your interviewees know that you have asked the same or similar questions a number of other people before. At MGIMO several of my interviewees voiced their concern that they might not be able to tell me something new if I had already talked to 25 or so of their fellow students and I sometimes had a hard time persuading them that I was not looking for standard answers but for individual opinions. Recommendations for putting respondents at ease vary: they range from trying to 'appear slightly dim and agreeable' (McCracken 1988: 38) to ensure that interviewees do not lose their face or feel dumb vis-à-vis the researcher to giving the appearance of being knowledgeable without intimidating the respondent unduly so that she or he skips things assuming that the interviewer already knows about them (Leech 2002). In my own research I tried to adopt the position of the student who had come to Russia to learn about relevant issues in Russian foreign policy and the opinion of MGIMO students on certain foreign policy issues. Introducing myself as a student put me on one level with my interviewees who seemed to be more comfortable with talking to a fellow student than they might have been talking to a researcher.

Of the 39 interviews I conducted, I finally selected 35 for *transcription*. I excluded four because in one case my recording device ran out of battery power and in the three other cases interviewees had to leave for lectures or were growing increasingly uncomfortable with the questions asked, giving only monosyllabic answers. Of the more than 150 hours of recordings of lectures and seminars I selected 25 hours by listening to the recordings again and keeping only the most relevant passages. Taking into account the large amount of material and the way I wanted to analyse the data, it seemed most suitable to choose a simple, less time-consuming transcription mode which focuses on the content and ignores the extra-verbal characteristics of speech. Especially since the kind of discourse analysis built on the ideas of Laclau and Mouffe relies on meaning construction and change, and not on language use in concrete situations, it did not appear necessary to devote significant effort to the kind of detailed transcripts that conversation analysis works with.

> Considering the amount of work involved in transcribing recordings in a foreign language and on a keyboard I was not reasonably familiar with, I resolved to outsource the transcription to a Russian friend of mine who is lecturer at a Russian university. I prepared a detailed guideline with transcription rules, which she followed meticulously. Consequently, the quality of the transcribed pieces was very high and when listening to the recordings again in parallel with the transcripts it was only in rare cases that I had to make amendments, mostly when technical terms or abbreviations occurred. Unfortunately, however, the outsourcing of the transcripts turned out to become the major bottleneck in the organisation of the workflow of writing up my dissertation. I had sent the audio documents to my friend in May 2006 and we then agreed on a deadline for the delivery of the completed transcripts in August 2006 at the latest. When she demanded a postponement, we settled for November 2006. It was not until February 2007, however, that I finally received the complete set of transcripts.

All interviews and recordings were transcribed exclusively in Russian, whereas my field diary is trilingual reflecting the situational need to quickly write down whatever thoughts and observations occurred. For a number of reasons I decided not to translate the original material, save for the passages quoted verbatim in this book. First, translation easily erases meaning differences, particularly in cases where the Russian expression is imbued with a culturally specific meaning that can only be circumscribed but never adequately expressed in a corresponding word in English. Second, translation is also a political act imposing a meaning hegemony on the translated material which is seldom problematised (Müller 2007a). Third and finally, working with the untranslated documents significantly reduces the effort needed to process the recordings into manageable transcripts.

> A major part of the preparation for my research at MGIMO, and indeed during my time at MGIMO, consisted of building up my proficiency in Russian to a level where I could engage in everyday interactions as well as in academic discussions. My personal background and the time I had spent working in foreign language settings prior to my doctoral research have engendered a heightened sensitivity to language. Following this sensitivity I kept trimming my interview guide for linguistic precision and correctness and was also highly intent on conducting smooth and flawless interviews

which sometimes got in the way of spontaneity. I remember one moment in one of the early interviews, when I handed the interviewee a piece of paper with a list of recent geopolitical developments and asked him to comment on the significance of each of those for Russia. While talking, he picked up a pen and corrected two typos which I had not seen. This prompted me to put extra care into the phrasing and idiomatic expression in my interview guide.

4.2 Researcher subjectivity and the research process

Its manifold assets as a research methodology aside, ethnography has been challenged on political grounds. Its origin in the study of so-called primitive peoples made for its close connection and sometimes complicity with colonialism in producing colonial subjects. As a Western science studying the noble savage, it tended to script research subjects as the exotic Other and inserted knowledge about them into the colonial administrative apparatus (Asad 1973; Pels and Salemnik 1994). This problematic power relationship between researchers and their research subjects is immanent in any ethnographic research: with a claim to privileged knowledge about a community or social setting derived from intensive participant observation, researchers' representations of their research subjects are fashioned with an authoritative, objective voice. This authority often elides that any knowledge is highly context-specific and situated. Ethnographers' claims to speak for their subjects, to represent their lifeworlds, the meanings they construct, are therefore fraught with what is called the 'representational crisis' – the growing challenge to 'an essentially realistic epistemology, which conceives of representation as the production, for subjectivity, of an objectivity that lies outside it' (Jameson 1984: viii).

The representational crisis calls for acknowledging the role of positionality in the research process or, as Mayne (1990: 8) puts it, ethnographers must learn to look at themselves from both sides of the keyhole. Donna Haraway (1991) introduced the notion that field research is influenced by our 'maps of consciousness' which are drawn up by our own gender, class, nationality, education and so on. Whether we want it or not, we are always already positioned towards our research and our research subjects. The idea of positionality acknowledges that a researcher's take is always partial and subjective, shaped by those maps of consciousness as well as by her or his location in time and space. This is why it has been argued that methodologies need to recognise the existence of multiple viewpoints and incorporate them into their studies.

A number of, largely feminist, geographers have explored ways to make research more transparent and situate knowledge through reflexive re-consideration of the research process and the landscape of opaque power relations it was enveloped in (e.g. Gilbert 1994; Katz 1994; Rose 1997).

Rose (1997) contends that feminist geographers mainly rely upon two kinds of reflexive practices: inward reflexivity and outward reflexivity. In the first variant, researchers are called on to make clear their own position towards the research and explore how their sympathies and antipathies and their relation vis-à-vis the research subjects work in the creation and interpretation of the data (e.g. Routledge 2001, 2002, 2003). In ethnographic research, this tactics has been termed autoethnography (Ellis and Bochner 2000). In the most extreme forms, it turns ethnographies from stories of the Other into stories of the Self. More commonly, it is a means to address researcher subjectivity and thus counteract ethnographies that appear as if they are 'written from nowhere by nobody' (Ellis and Bochner 2000: 734). Outward reflexivity, on the other hand, rests on rendering visible the circumstances and process of data collection and thus to invoke the context of research as a means of situating the research. Rose (1997) argues that this kind of reflexivity is bound to fail, for it assumes the omniscient oversight over a landscape of power in which the researcher herself is implicated. Even so, outward reflexivity still constitutes one of the most promising attempts at addressing positionality, even if it cannot claim to eliminate the influence of positionality. In this subsection I employ these two forms of reflexivity to unroll the research process and context and explore my own role within it.

My first contact with MGIMO was through written reports from foreign exchange students who had studied there and written vividly about their experiences:

> "What do you do here?" "I study at MGIMO." "Ohhhh....". In a way I almost always felt uncomfortable, when an average Russian asked me this question. Either people, especially the elderly in the Russian province, were completely rapt in admiration ("What a smart girl you are, yes, what an industrious girl you are."). Or, and that was the reaction by young Muscovites, I was asked in a provocative and dismissive way what my father did. Thus I always had to explain that I was neither the daughter of a millionaire nor a genius. A taxi driver once said to me, looking at the BMWs parked in front of the university: "Those are the people that are supposed to govern our country in the future.... They don't have a clue of the problems in Russia".
>
> Unfortunately, this frequently seems to be the case. Many are not enrolled because they are interested in the subject but in order to get rich or important, or in order to

> find a rich or important husband. ... You either get into MGIMO if you have got plenty of money or if you pass an extremely difficult admission exam. Those who have been admitted through the latter process are some sort of an eye-catcher among all the others who are clothed in designer rags. ... An excessive amount of boasting takes place at the university. (Catherine Zanev 2003; author's translation from German).

Such was my initiation into the world of MGIMO and it positioned me with unrelenting force: it was the exotic and somehow mysterious air of MGIMO which drew my attention. This Othering of MGIMO as a peculiar concoction of *nouveaux riches* and Soviet nostalgia also characterises reports in Western media, such as the recent article in the online version of the German weekly *Der Spiegel* entitled 'Russia's noble cadre academies: luxury with a touch of Soviet fug' (Schlindwein 2008). Western imaginations of Russia as a Soviet, backward, somewhat uncivilised country striving for new greatness are read into life at MGIMO. It was portraits of this kind that shaped and reflected my own subject position towards education at MGIMO (e.g. Ivanova-Galitsina 2000) and proved Nancy Ries' observation that '[e]thnographers go to postsocialist societies armed with all kinds of nearly unexaminable perceptions, mythic categories, and competitive stances' (Ries 2000: x) to be all too true.

In short, it initially was the interest in the mysterious Russian Other that prompted me to think about a research project related to MGIMO and was my initial driving force.

> Looking back now, it is remarkable how my own position has changed since then. This is particularly well documented in the early proposals for my project. They carried bold titles like 'The pivot of Russian geopolitics' or 'On the anvil of cadres' and stated as research aims to uncover the inner workings of the reproduction of Russian foreign policy elites. Mine was a project with grand ambitions – mapping the functioning of the Russian power apparatus at and through MGIMO – that fit the inclination towards conspiracy theory evident in some critical geopolitics writing. Looking at those proposals and sketches now they betray the masculinist, Western desire of fixing the and unravelling Other, of rendering it visible somewhere out there.

Such positioning is inevitable and contrasts sharply with the ideal of the open-minded, naïve researcher that is postulated so frequently for ethnography (e.g. Fox 2004).

> In the course of my research it would prove hard to step out of this colonial gaze. The other exchange students with whom I mainly socialised would but reinforce those boundaries by bonding together and identifying MGIMO students as arrogant, snobbish and ostentatious. It was not only because I lived with the other exchange

> students in the dormitory but also because I had similar feelings and intuitively agreed to label MGIMO students in this way that I initially was not aware of the discursive moorings of my perspective – and I probably did not become fully aware of them until analysing the empirical material and thinking about its written representation. Too powerful was the everyday experience and situated interaction at MGIMO that I could have chosen to simply 'leave' my subject position behind and, with Judith Butler, 'don' another one which would have enabled me to come closer to the ideal ethnographer and try to blend in.

What initially intrigued me about MGIMO – the flaunting of wealth and the degree of conspicuous consumption – became a defining element in positioning myself vis-à-vis my research subjects: *social status*. Even though I considered and treated it more like an object of study and a factor influencing social interaction and behaviour between students at MGIMO, at closer examination, I found myself not to be as indifferent towards social status as I had thought. In fact, I built up certain mechanisms to protect my difference, perhaps even researcher superiority, vis-à-vis MGIMO students.

> One of those was my refusal to dress so as to blend in with other students. During the time I was in the field, I had never reflected on my reasons for not dressing as formally as others did. While I have never felt uncomfortable wearing smart casual or formal dress, in retrospect, my act of subtle resistance at MGIMO consisted in wearing sports or leisure clothes. Of course, this ran completely against the grain of the typical advice given to ethnographers. Impression management through wearing the right clothes is a central part of empathy and creating rapport (e.g. Bain and Nash 2006: 101). In this case, however, maintaining my own identity fundamentally collided with what are generally considered the requirements of a 'good' ethnography.

From my own experience, researcher identity and researcher roles are thus far from being as freely negotiable in the field as some methodological literature in ethnography assumes. Like their research subjects, researchers cannot escape the performative recitation of discourse and identity in social fields.

In the conduct of research, I gradually grew into the classic position of the unobtrusive researcher. This way the influence of my presence on the interaction was comparatively small and I was able make my observations in a largely undisturbed setting. This is not to imply, however, that I am presenting an objective account of geopolitical identity production at MGIMO. Quite to the contrary, my own subject position within geopolitical discourses marks my interpretation of the empirical material.

> As someone positioned within the hegemonic Western discourses of geopolitical identity, I initially found myself to have a stance of reservation or even repudiation

towards Russia's aspirations to great power status and, as a consequence, reacted more sympathetically when talking to respondents with similar views. Although I tried not to let my own geopolitical identity manifest itself in the interview guide, it is inevitable that the researcher's subjectivity becomes a central feature of ethnographies (Fine 1994).

Over time, however, as I grew into the institutional setting of MGIMO, I felt increasingly comfortable with many geopolitical positions expressed in lectures and interviews. Russian distrust and concern about NATO enlargement in Eastern Europe, for example, became quite natural for me, just as the exclusion of Russia from many important questions of world politics by the West. This, then, also was the position I adopted in exams where I had to analyse foreign policy. In this sense, I experienced the naturalising power of MGIMO as an educational institution first-hand, as contingent knowledge gradually turned objective in the course of the educational process.

4.3 Methods of data analysis

Data analysis is often somewhat of a black box in qualitative research: it somehow in some way works by 'mixing analytical approach (e.g. grounded theory) with data (e.g. field notes, transcripts) and technology (e.g. ATLAS/ti)' (Schiellerup 2008: 164). Coffey and Atkinson (1996) write that 'data analysis' for some authors only comprises data handling, i.e. coding, sorting, retrieving and so on, whereas for others it includes the more creative process of the interpretation of the data. While the former can be formalised, the latter usually resists formalisation. After all, interpretation is a very individual enterprise that is different for different contexts and, as Schiellerup (2008) points out, not only goes on in dedicated moments of focused data interpretation. As was the case in my own research, some of the most revealing moments come in conversations with friends or when working on unrelated projects – or when simply leaving the manuscript alone for several months and working on a different project.

Rather than in a smooth, orderly progression, this book developed in leaps and jolts which are not reflected in the current structure. This retrospective logical framing all but elides, for example, that the decision to employ post-structuralist discourse theory for analysing my empirical material was not an a-priori decision but emerged after collection of the data. The same applies to the present methods and structure of data analysis, which were developed inductively after I had first read through the material and tried to make sense of it with a different analytical scheme. In my case, therefore, theory and methods of data analysis largely followed the empirical part of my research. This conceptual order has enabled me to better live up to the call for a methodological bricolage in assembling a discourse analysis.

As mentioned before, I do not regard discourse analysis as implying a certain choice of methods. In my own attempt at a methodological bricolage, the data analysis proceeds in three steps which reflect the key elements of my conceptual framework for discourse analysis. It starts to describe the institutional context as the primary condition enabling the powerful working of discourses in positioning subjects in step one. In step two, it maps the meaning structure of geopolitical discourses at MGIMO. Step three finally interprets and discusses the data explicitly against the theoretical framework and the existing literature in a bid to draw out implications of wider significance.

Step 1: Institutional practices

Discourses as systems of meaning production are always situated and draw their power from institutional contexts. This institutional context is constituted through particular institutional practices which are explored in the next chapter. My aim in this step is twofold: I want to characterise MGIMO as a university and its status and position within the reproduction of elites in Russia on the one hand. On the other hand, I identify practices which make up MGIMO as an educational institution and contribute to the fashioning of identities. In this step, I primarily relate to notes in my field diary as well as to documents about the educational philosophy and educational process at MGIMO. I initially coded the material in my field diary into general categories like 'everyday interactions', 'chats', 'lectures' or 'facts and figures'. During the data collection I had already added marginal notes which I checked for their validity and expanded along the process of coding. These memos served as the basis for a second coding cycle in which I colour-coded the material into more specific categories like 'admission procedures', 'student-teacher interactions', 'fashion', 'consumption' or 'future career'. These categories were then compared for similarities and differences and possible cross-connections. Finally, I grouped together the different categories into four different forms of practices, each of which reflects a particular way of meaning making and subjectivation at MGIMO:

- practices of consecration;

- practices of discipline;
- practices of knowledge;
- practices of consumption and banal patriotic politics.

Step 2: Meaning of signifiers

Chapters six to eight attempt to recover the structures of meaning ascriptions to signifiers and thus the discursive constitution of geopolitical identities according to the theoretical concepts of Laclau and Mouffe's discourse theory. In those chapters, I have given preference to a mode of presentation which tries to let the material speak in its own right, although I have organised the presentation and, inevitably, added my authorial interpretation. Transcripts from interviews and lectures were coded using the software programme MaxQDA 2 for qualitative data analysis which considerably sped up the potentially arduous process of reorganising and retrieving coded segments. Codes were developed inductively from the material (cf. Hammersley and Atkinson 1995: 168ff.). I initially used a mixture of geographical codes (e.g. 'Europe', 'Eurasia', 'post-Soviet states' etc.) and in-vivo codes (e.g. 'geopolitical crisis', 'multipolarity' etc.) that appeared suitable from the material. Reflecting this exploratory phase, I wrote memos along the way to capture ideas, establish interconnections between different themes and already note possible interpretations.

Having coded about one-third of the material in this way, things suddenly and unexpectedly fell into place. I began to see how the ideas of Laclau and Mouffe should link up with the empirical material in a totally different way than I had previously expected. The code structure I had used to that point was unable to capture this new orientation adequately. I thus reorganised the code structure and reassigned the new codes to the passages already coded. The final hierarchical structure that emerged is shown in Table 5 and reflects the organisation of chapters six to eight.

Table 5: Structure of first- and second-level codes

Loss and crisis
Geopolitics
Dissociation of brother states
Internal crisis
Soviet references
Strength and independence
Reasserting Russian influence
Eurasia/Near Abroad
The West: dependence and cooperation
Economic strength
Russia's special position
Danger and exclusion
Alienating the post-Soviet states
Threatening Russia
Exclusion and marginalisation
Aspiration and reality

Step 3: The production of geopolitical identities

While the previous two steps stay very close to the material, this last step finally seeks to abstract from it and interpret the empirical findings against the conceptual foundations of poststructuralist discourse theory. This is achieved in two ways. First, each of the subsequent empirical chapters is followed by a brief conceptual reflection, situating the empirical findings in the conceptual framework of my work. In this way, the conceptual embeddedness is not lost out of sight while reading the substantial empirical part. Second, chapter nine weaves the different threads into an overarching discussion of how the discourse analytical toolbox constructed in this book can help us understand the production of geopolitical identities. In particular, this chapter asks how the findings that emerge relate to the existing literature on geopolitical identities in post-Soviet Russia and how they perhaps challenge us to rethink some parts of it.

5

Producing subjects: practices of everyday life

> The social world presents itself to us, primarily, as a sedimented ensemble of social practices accepted at face value, without questioning the founding acts of their institution (Laclau 1994: 3).

5.1 Practices of consecration: producing elites

MGIMO (*Московский Государственный Институт Международных Отношений*, Moscow State Institute of International Relations) has about 5,500 students of which about 1,000 are enrolled in so-called *vtoroe vysše obrazovanie* (a kind of secondary higher education or mid-career professional degree). The university comprises ten departments, shown in Table 6. Students in Russia enter higher education at the average age of 17 and study for four years to receive a bachelor's degree (*diplom bakalavra*). A large proportion continues another year to be awarded a specialist's degree (*diplom specialista*) or another two years, after which they can pass the examinations for a master's degree (*diplom magistra*). In its founding charter MGIMO has been placed under the authority of the Russian Ministry of Foreign Affairs. The legal basis of education at MGIMO is provided by a number of federal laws and decrees and by normative documents issued by the Ministry of Foreign Affairs.

Table 6: Departments at MGIMO

School of International Relations	School of International Law
School of International Economic Relations	School of Political Science
Institute of Foreign Economic Relations	School of International Journalism
Institute of European Law	International Institute of Administration
School of International Business and Business Administration	International Institute of Energy Policy and Diplomacy

MGIMO was founded by the USSR People's Commissariat for Foreign Affairs in 1944 as a response to the perceived need for a department of international relations at Moscow State University to train cadres for the Soviet diplomatic service. It is speculated that the reasons why it was finally conceived as a separate institution and not as a part of a larger university are probably related to its mission, which required both confidentiality and a focus on professional training rather than on research. A large proportion of the initial staff of MGIMO was drawn from Moscow State University and the size of the class of 1948, the year of the first graduation, was still quite small at 118.

Traditionally, MGIMO's student intake has been focused on the member states of the former Eastern bloc. Quite early in the 1950s, MGIMO began a tradition that it still continues today: it started to invite students from other, then socialist and communist countries in large numbers to study at MGIMO. Among the first to receive this kind of professional and ideological training were students from Albania, Bulgaria, Hungary, Vietnam, GDR, North Korea, Mongolia, Poland, Czechoslovakia and China. In the late 1980s more than 1,000 students from other socialist countries were enrolled at MGIMO, underscoring its importance as an international training hub for communist international relations. Since 1951, more than 4,600 foreign students, or about 15 % of all graduates, have graduated from MGIMO with the former GDR (750 graduates) and Bulgaria (600) occupying the top of this list.

During much of the Soviet period MGIMO remained a secluded institution in two respects: admission was highly selective and the institute itself was shrouded in mystery. It was a government institution belonging to the Ministry of Foreign Affairs, training students to occupy leading positions in the Soviet state apparatus. As such it was off-limits to the majority of the Soviet population and subject to stringent ideological regulations governing its work. Every applicant had to present recommendations from the local party organs, foreign language publications were stored in separate archives and the admission of women to MGIMO was kept low by imposing limitations. The official ideology also dominated the approach to teaching international relations, which was framed in Marxist-Leninist ideology as a class struggle between capitalist and socialist societies (Torkunov 2004).

It was only during the years of perestroika that the thrust of de-ideologisation prevalent at that time paved the way both for a more open engagement with international relations beyond the tenets of Marxism-Leninism and for a disciplinary broadening of the education offered at MGIMO. The already existing departments of International Relations and International Economic Relations were complemented by new ones such as the School of Political Science, the International Institute of Energy Policy and Diplomacy or the School of International Business and Business Administration. In 1994 MGIMO was conferred the title of a university, a fact that is repeated in almost every official publication by MGIMO and that is emphasised by the change of the official name to *Moscow State Institute of International Relations (University)* or MGIMO (U). Torkunov (2004) opines that this act was merely a formal acknowledgement of what had already become the de facto status of MGIMO. By stressing its university status, MGIMO strives to get rid of the image of a closed, elitist institution, dating back to Soviet times, and arrive at the reputation of a 'dynamic, open and future-oriented' university (MGIMO 2005: 23).

MGIMO's university status is usually cited in conjunction with other attributes that award MGIMO the stamp of international scientific excellence and are meant to demonstrate its inclusion in the ranks of world-renowned universities (MGIMO 2005). With MGIMO's participation in the Bologna process, which is more a fact on paper and had not yet trickled down to the educational process by 2005, MGIMO prided itself with being a truly European university (Torkunov 2004). It is especially the processes of achieving international openness and of complying with international standards which are frequently highlighted. But getting diplomas recognised can still present a significant obstacle, as one American graduate of MGIMO explains:

> I don't know if my Master of Arts degree from MGIMO will be recognized in the States ... When I was choosing a graduate school, I read on the MGIMO website that

> this school was participating in the Bologna process, a 1999 agreement on common standards for higher-education systems throughout Europe. I believed that it would help me make my future diploma convertible. Nevertheless, despite the school administration's promises, I still have no Bologna certification! (Yulikova 2008)

Greater internationalisation is a declared aim, included in MGIMO's strategic development programme (MGIMO 2005: 11, 21), and addressed as the primary external deficiency in MGIMO's development. The importance of exporting Russian international relations education to neighbouring countries is stressed both in official publications and in lectures as a crucial contribution to building closer relationships between Russia and its partner states. Now, about 800 MGIMO students come from abroad, but the majority of those are from the former Soviet republics which did not count as 'abroad' until 1992. In response to the challenge of internationalisation MGIMO has undertaken some institutional reforms one of which I myself experienced first hand as an incoming exchange student.

> Until recently MGIMO had one administrative department dealing with all incoming international students, regardless of their nationality (*Dekanat po rabote s inostrannymi učaščimisja*). This department is now in charge of students from the CIS and other formerly communist or socialist countries. Its staff is composed mainly of women aged 50 and above. Upon arrival I mistakenly reasoned, judging from the department name, that this department was also in charge of helping me along during my stay. It was courteously explained to me by one of the elderly ladies that I was at the wrong department and she referred me to the new department of international relations (*Otdel meždunarodnyx svjazej*), located at the other end of the building. It had been newly created to deal with all incoming Western students and academics and was, by and large, staffed with employees about my age who had just finished university.

> The two departments reflect the two different visions of the old, traditional MGIMO of Soviet times and the new, modern MGIMO of post-Soviet times. Still keeping up the relationships with the formerly socialist brother states, MGIMO has moved to respond to the chances of interaction with Western countries. Styling itself as a leading European university with international reach, it carries on to be primarily a centre of education within the post-Soviet space.

Internationalisation is indeed going slow at MGIMO when compared to other Russian universities. Although there exist dual Master's degree programmes , for example with Sciences Po Paris and the Free University of Berlin, MGIMO is lagging behind such universities as St. Petersburg European University or the Higher School of Economics (HSE), both founded after 1991, in terms of international experience of staff and internationalisation of curricula. There are hardly any lectures or seminars in languages other than Russian and most professors have spent all of their academic careers in Russia or the Soviet Union. As analysed by Lazuech (1998) for the case of the French grandes écoles, internationalisation can serve as major asset in the competition for educational primacy among universities. It is in the acquisition of this new kind of capital that established universities, like MGIMO, can be challenged by new or middle-ranking institutions which more successfully pursue a course of internationalisation.

Unlike the majority of Russian state-owned universities, MGIMO is comparatively well-funded. In the 1990s and at the turn of the millennium, MGIMO was quite successful in introducing new educational programmes and whole new departments as a means of tapping funding through tuition payment. It was especially in the areas of business administration and law that its prestigious status helped it acquire financially potent students who expected a high return on their tuition investment. In 2008/2009 tuition fees ranged from about RUB 140,000 (approx. EUR 5,500) annually for the sociology major to RUB 210,000 (approx. EUR 8,000) annually for the management major, which corresponds roughly to the annual disposable income per capita in Russia. The budget of the university hovers currently at around EUR 30 million, approximately half of which is made up of tuition fee payments.

Every year MGIMO admits about 1,000 applicants. Roughly half of them receive a tuition waiver and a nominal stipend (called *obučenie na bjudžetnoj osnove* or *bjudžetniki* as a shorthand), while the other half has to pay full tuition fees (*obučenie na kontraktnoj osnove* or *dogovorniki*). There is no need-blind admission process so that, naturally, the applications-to-place ratio is higher for the tuition-free places than for the tuition places. In the 2006 admission cycle, there was an average of 4.5 applications for a scholarship place over the whole university, with individual departments ranging from 3 to 12 applicants per place. In the competition for paid education the maximum ratio was 2.5 for the most popular department with average ratios not published but probably somewhere close to 1.5, so that the majority of those students who are able to pay the tuition are also admitted. Application ratios show that departments with an economic orientation are the most popular with applicants, whereas MGIMO's traditional education in the School of International Relations is at the lower end of the ratio range and therefore seems to be less sought after.

Of the approximately 500 tuition-free admissions in 2006 there were about 75 international students, mostly from countries of the Near Abroad and Asia, who were admitted on the basis of mutual agreements between MGIMO and the Foreign Ministries of their home countries. Another 75 Russian applicants did not have to pass the general competition because they qualified for admission through a separate channel. The most common way to access this separate channel is through external competitions like the pan-Russian olympiads for pupils or the famous nation-wide TV show *Umnicy i Umniki*, a kind of talent show in which the seven finalists get to choose the department in which they want to study at MGIMO.

The dichotomy of the selection process and the double standards of academic achievement versus financial potential have a number of curious effects on the education process and on life at MGIMO. First, the dependence on financially strong students puts downward pressure on academic standards at MGIMO, which is seldom spoken about publicly but was a serious concern voiced by some teachers. *Dogovorniki* typically face much greater problems in keeping up with the pace of instruction and the high work load. Second, this diverging performance often makes money act as a substitute for talent not only during admission but also during examination as a means of compensating for academic deficiencies. Third, at the social level this dichotomy tends to translate into a separation along the dividing lines of talent versus money. In a highly stylised fashion, three types of students can be distinguished at MGIMO: sons and daughters of the *nouveaux riches* almost exclusively admitted as *dogovorniki*; students from rather poor families admitted as *bjudžetniki*; a growing number of students from middle-class families, often from the intelligentsia, who are typically *bjudžetniki* but may also be *dogovorniki*. This social composition makes for an extremely heterogeneous student body and is a result of the adaptation to external pressures brought about by the post-Soviet transformation.

Notwithstanding the profound transformations in the post-Soviet period, MGIMO's central mission of preparing cadres, both at the national and the international level, continues to be as central today as it was at its foundation. This image of MGIMO as the 'anvil of cadres' is supported by the large number of MGIMO alumni who occupy positions of power in Russia and the Near Abroad. Today, a large proportion of the staff in Russia's Ministry of Foreign Affairs have graduated from MGIMO, a vast majority of Russian ambassadors are MGIMO alumni just as the Russian foreign minister, Sergej Lavrov. Vladimir Potanin, one of the most powerful Russian oligarchs, is probably the most famous alumnus of MGIMO in Russian business and is still connected to MGIMO through a fund in his name which awards scholarships to future MGIMO students. Beyond the boundaries of Russia, MGIMO alumni have risen through the ranks of foreign ministries in countries of the former Eastern bloc, some making it to foreign minister like Eduard Kukan in Slovakia, Eduard Nalbandian in Armenia, Luvsanginin Erdenechuluun in Mongolia or Kasym-Shumart Tokaev in Kazakhstan or even to head of state, like Ilham Aliyev, President of Azerbaijan.

MGIMO also continues to attract Russian students from Western countries, many of whom, having finished private schools abroad, return to MGIMO in Russia for university education. Consider the case of Jurij:

> I love Russia, I believe in its opportunities and I have Russian blood, and that's why I love the free Russian soul, its depth and incomprehensible vastness. I finished an English school, Clifton College, after which I had the possibility to receive an excellent higher education in universities in Britain and Germany. Initially, I wanted to enrol in the London School of Economics and Political Science, but then I realised that if I want to work in the area of the CIS and do business there, I will not only need knowledge but also an understanding of the Slavic culture and mentality. ... I decided to choose MGIMO. Why? Above all, because you get professional education, prestige, a rich history and international relations. Here you can meet a lot of successful people, established scholars and veteran diplomats (MGIMO 2008).

It is interesting to see how in Jurij's statement pride of being Russian and loyalty to the country are bound up with very personal choices like education and future career trajectories. The fact that this interview with Jurij was published on the MGIMO website is indicative of two things: for one thing, it shows, once again, the concern with emphasising MGIMO's elite status and international competitiveness. For another, it officially sanctions the close liaison of elite education and service to the country. This stance of being educated and working 'for Russia' is very typical of MGIMO and resurfaces frequently in my analysis. Elite education at MGIMO is represented as being not primarily in the students' interest but in the interest of Russia:

> It is our mission to prepare highly capable elites – opinion leaders, business captains, who can serve as a role model and who will be of use for the Russian society and our state (Rožkov 2008).

In the opinion of Aleksandr Losukov, then deputy foreign minister, this approach to elite education 'is correct. Students should be taught to be patriotic, loyal to the country and not to a political system' (Ivanova-Galitsina 2000: 8). In a collection of academic articles on elite education edited by MGIMO, Gennadij Ašin (2002: 13, 43), professor at MGIMO, even specifies the tasks of elite education as a means to achieve the end of Russia's re-emergence as a great power:

> The rise of Russia as a *velikaja deržava* will only be possible if education becomes one of the most important priorities in its social development. Because Russia cannot rise through selling its gas, oil and other raw materials..., but only through developing those traditions of a great culture which have already contributed immeasurably to the development of global civilisation (Ašin 2002: 43).

Nowadays, this loyalty to the country is no longer equivalent to taking up a position in the state service. While in Soviet times a career with the Russian Ministry of Foreign Affairs (MID) was one of the most attractive prospects for MGIMO alumni, today the majority of students prefer positions with private or state-owned companies or international organisations. For one thing, salaries are considerably higher – an aspect that surfaced repeatedly in my interviews with students.

> Our department is oriented towards preparing people for work at MID, but, unfortunately, the pay is nothing special. This aspect plays the main role for my decision against this sphere, because I am not from Moscow and I would have to rent a flat initially to live somewhere and prices here are quite high (Evgenija, 4 IR, 07/87).

For another thing, work conditions at the Russian Ministry of Foreign Affairs generally were met with considerable disapproval by many interviewees. Some complained about the strict hierarchies and rigid structures and the undemanding nature of work. Andrej describes the atmosphere as stifling and uncreative:

> MID has special requirements for the people that are going to work with them. And in the past few years among these haven't been 'showing initiative' or 'creative work'. It's not a question of money. Recently, it has been about the submission to some general directives, to general orders. It has become very difficult to make a career, to show initiative (Andrej, 4 PS, 24/81).

The presence of civil servants that do not have adequate qualification for the job they are doing and that have been occupying the same position since Soviet times, unwilling to leave, was cited as one of the factors that made a career in MID unappealing. Julija even thinks that at MGIMO

> students' attitude towards working at MID is rather negative. I think that it won't be pleasant working there, because chances of moving up the career ladder are low (Julija, 4 PS, 25/66).

Russia does not adequately remunerate its elites and cannot offer attractive work environments in the state service. Patriotism sometimes cannot compensate for this lack:

> Although I love my country, I think that the state does not disburse sufficient funding for its employees. This is not politically correct. By and large, these are people who are very devoted to their work. Unfortunately, a lot of them simply leave because it is impossible to live with such a salary (Julija, 4 PS, 25/64).

It is not uncommon that alumni start off working at the foreign ministry for some years, often as interpreters, and then transfer into business, taking with them a highly useful network of contacts in the Russian administrative apparatus. These relationships ensure that officials at MID may receive lucrative contracts from private companies, thus improving the meagre salaries, while at the same time giving private companies informal access to the state bureaucracy.[9]

In its role for the production and reproduction of elites MGIMO can be best compared to the French *grandes écoles,* as described by Pierre Bourdieu in his monograph on elite education in France (Bourdieu 1996).[10] Of course, MGIMO as a single school is too insignificant to produce the same effects as the system of grandes écoles in France, but its social function and disciplinary techniques are comparable in many ways. The structure and nature of education at MGIMO and at the grandes écoles in France is more geared towards preparation of specialists and professionals for the administrative apparatuses and not towards the education of academics. At MGIMO the use of the expression *podgotovka* (preparation, training) instead of *obrazovanie* (education) in many cases is indicative of the focus on teaching practical, professional knowledge. Similar to the grandes écoles system, promising prospective students at MGIMO who do not yet fulfil the criteria for admission have the possibility to complete a preparatory course over the period of one year (*dovuzovskaja podgotovka* in Russian, *classes préparatoires aux grandes écoles* in French, see Bourdieu 1996: 73ff.), after which they take the entrance examinations. This preparatory course is designed to ensure comparable standards

9 During the Soviet period, this kind of networking and informal exchange was also known as blat and carries on to be important in post-Soviet times (see Ledeneva 1998).

10 Frequently, MGIMO is dubbed the Russian Harvard, but there are little commonalities in the organisation of education beyond the metaphorical level.

of academic knowledge at the beginning of education at MGIMO, particularly regarding language proficiency.

The close contact between students during the five years most of them spend at MGIMO often knits them into communities that last for a lifetime. In the first year every student is pre-assigned to a certain group of about three to seven students which is determined by the foreign languages he or she is going to study. Almost 50 % of total class time is devoted to foreign language instruction, which takes place for each group individually, whereas for lectures several groups are combined. These groups usually stay together over the whole course of study at MGIMO and hence represent the level of closest social integration. This tight social structure creates an extraordinary community spirit and in fact most initiatives originate at the level of the language groups. But at the same time it makes it difficult for outsiders like myself to penetrate the social fabric. My feeling of not being noticed by other students, which I and virtually all other exchange students had at the beginning of the year, for example, later turned out to be mostly a result of closed, rigid social structures not allowing for the easy integration of new members. Similarly, the majority of informal information – changes of the location of a lecture, cancellations of lectures, adjusted deadlines for turning in an essay – is transmitted within these groups, which made it notoriously difficult for me to stay up to date with recent changes.

Bourdieu (1996: 103) describes the social function of elite schools as consisting in

> producing special, separate, sacred beings merely by getting everyone to be aware of and to recognize the boundary separating them from the commonplace, by making the consecrating distinction public, widely known, and guaranteed by the *consensus omnium*, and by creating thereby the conversion of belief that leads the chosen people to (re)cognize themselves as different.

The production of elites thus depends as much on outside recognition as on self-recognition. The formation of community spirit, or *esprit de corps* – 'the prolonged togetherness of like-minded individuals' (Bourdieu 1996: 183) – has become weaker at MGIMO since the composition of the student body has been characterised by the growing rift between the groups mentioned above. Nevertheless, it is still addressed as a salient social element and part of the distinctiveness of MGIMO. Again, the case of Jurij is an illustrative example:

> The longer I study at MGIMO, the more I love it and become a patriot of my alma mater. Of course, after finishing my studies I will always be willing to help the University, its alumni and students and I will give it all that is possible in admiration of what it has taught me (MGIMO 2008).

This idea of belonging together is also expressed by the term '*Mgimovcy*', a nickname for MGIMO alumni which serves as a marker of distinction and mutual recognition. MGIMO students bond together: at MGIMO they find their partners for life, for business and for leisure. Each MGIMO alumnus helps the others, be it in launching a successful career or starting up a business. As the MGIMO alumnus and Russian foreign minister Sergej Lavrov underscores: 'MGIMO is a special way of life, a special style. You can easily tell MGIMO alumni from the crowd, it is easy to find a relation with them' (MajorDom 2005: 2). In this vein, a sense of difference vis-à-vis ordinary people is instilled and a sense of likeness among each other. This idea of superiority and community spirit is encapsulated in iconic, condensed form in the MGIMO anthem, whose lyrics were authored by Lavrov.

We were born under the shelter of the great MGIMO/
As the most excellent of all dynasties on earth/
Here, so many generations are forever intertwined/
God give it immortality and fortune.

It opened us the path to foreign shores/
And it taught us to love the fatherland (*Otčizna*)/
And to equally share pride and shame with it/
To share all with it that happens in life.

Chorus:
This is our institute, this is our common mark (*klejmo*)/
And we will never need another one/
Last forever incomparable MGIMO/
A bastion of student friendship.

For the first time we raised our voices here/
For the first time we started to think about the key things/
May MGIMO have changed its name, may it have changed its address/
But it hasn't changed its glorious traditions:

To study relentlessly, to make friends that last to the very end/
Not to fall and to walk straight towards the goal/
Scattered over the earth are passionate hearts/
Dependable in business matters and in joy.

Chorus

It helped us to experience our steadfastness/
And through glory, misfortune and riches/
It taught us how not to grow tired of the world/
And how to conserve the student fellowship (*bratstvo*).

Wherever we end up in the world – we are always/
In every country and on every path/
Certain that a guiding star shines to us/
Over the arches of our home institute.

Chorus

Far from being an overblown remnant of old times, MGIMO's anthem with its patriotic pathos can be downloaded as a mobile phone ring tone from the MGIMO website and thus clearly appeals to a student audience. As an anthem, this piece bears an official, representational quality and transports an institutionalised image of MGIMO. This image has many facets. One is the community spirit, expressed in formulations such as 'our institute', 'our mark', 'a bastion of friendship' or 'student fellowship'. MGIMO binds people together 'to the very end' of their lives and thus creates a unique community which weathers any storm and shares joy and pain. Another one is the sense of superior distinctiveness that results from this unique community, invoked when speaking of 'the most excellent of all dynasties' and through having the foreign minister write the lyrics. Finally, the patriotic moment is also appealed to through exhortations to love and live for the fatherland. In sum, education at MGIMO is represented as invariably tied to distinctiveness and to categorical loyalty to Russia.

The recruitment via *concours* (*konkurs*) is another characteristic that MGIMO shares with its French counterparts. It is a comprehensive written test of knowledge in various subjects. Russian literature, Russian history, geography and foreign languages are mandatory parts of this test taken by all candidates, whereas creative writing, mathematics and 'knowledge of the society' (*obščestvoznanie*) are only required by some departments. The general examinations at MGIMO are characterised by the same division between 'talent subjects' and 'work subjects' that Bourdieu (1996: 17) identifies. High performance in subjects in the humanities like Russian language, literature or history is generally attributed to a certain talent; a talent which in fact is nothing else but inherited symbolic capital acquired through socialisation and the 'familiar rapport with culture that can only be acquired through the diffuse teachings of familial education' (Bourdieu 1996: 14). Work subjects like geography or the natural sciences, on the other hand, tend to tilt the selection bias towards those who invest industriousness and labour. The concours, not only as a process of selection but also of election, constitutes a rite of institution, of bestowing symbolic capital upon those who successfully pass the trials. Drawing the line between the student with the lowest passing grade and the student with the highest failing grade at the same time means drawing social boundaries, instituting a social order which is societally legitimised.

With Bourdieu, symbolic capital necessary for good performance in the talent subjects is significantly more abundant in the intelligentsia families in the capital regions of Moscow and, perhaps, St. Petersburg than in the Russian provinces. This uneven distribution causes an uneven selection of applicants at MGIMO: applicants from 'the regions' (in Russian jargon this includes everyone not from Moscow) currently make up only about 40 % of the newly admitted students. Although this number has grown over the past few years from a nadir at less than 20 % in the mid 1990s, it is still low when compared to the fact that about 90 % of the Russian population live in 'the regions'. In 1960, under the Soviet regime, the proportion of students from the regions was as high as 60 % but declined steadily in the decades after. One of the major concerns at MGIMO is the poor level of high school education in the regions which does not manage to prepare students well enough to pass the entrance exams at MGIMO, especially in the field of foreign languages.

In a similar vein, the social composition of the student body has shifted significantly since the 1960s. The proportion of students from working class or farming households dropped from 23 % in 1960 to 5 % in 1999 and in the same period the proportion of those from upper middle-class and upper-class households rose from 15 % to 48 % (Temnickij 2002). These figures somewhat contradict the message of openness that MGIMO management is trying to disseminate but rather points towards Bourdieu's conclusion that elite schools and their concours represent a means for elites to reproduce themselves and institutionalise consecration. The increased presence of students from well-off families has given rise to the image of MGIMO being a university for the 'golden youth' (*zolotaja molodëž*) which is especially nurtured by the media. Students from other universities in Moscow often display a reserved attitude towards MGIMO students. Rumours and jokes about MGIMO circulate that say, for instance, that female students are admitted to MGIMO in a beauty contest, that male students are obliged to wear suits, white shirts and ties or that there is no public transport link to MGIMO because all students have their own cars.

Elite schools bestow consecration on some selected few and withhold consecration from the rest and hence contribute to the reproduction of elites at the societal level. MGIMO can thus be conceptualised, in the Bourdieuan sense, as an institution through which the reproduction of societal elites with symbolic capital is realised and sanctioned. Students lacking symbolic capital can still gain elite consecration by presenting significant material capital to pay for the preparation courses, the tuition fees and so on. In this way, elite schools convert material into symbolic capital, money into distinction (Bourdieu 1996). This conjunction of material and symbolic capital clearly shines up at MGIMO. Unlike at the French grandes écoles, at MGIMO consecration can be gained either by successfully mastering the concours or, alternatively, by investing sufficient material capital. This material capital can also take the form of various degrees of veiled corruption, a starker form of transforming material into symbolic capital, as a means to guarantee admission or successfully passing examinations.[11] Another form of this capital transformation can be found in the various agencies offering ghost writer services on leaflets handed out right in front of the main entrance to MGIMO.

5.2 Practices of discipline: producing docile bodies

Discipline is one of the constitutive elements of education at MGIMO and its extensive presence distinguishes MGIMO from other Russian universities that I have experienced. Students are required to adhere to a plethora of rules, regulations and expectations. In many ways, this highly regulated environment recreates a school-like atmosphere.

> When I walked into a lecture hall for the first time, I felt slightly uneasy. I had arrived well ahead of time since I had not been sure whether I would be able to immediately find the right room in the convoluted building. The whole set-up reminded me not of a university but of a classroom. There were benches for two, arranged in three rows. I was not sure where to sit down but chose a bench in the front for better quality of the records. Gradually the room started to fill with chattering students who com-

---

11 MGIMO recently has taken measures against corruption, such as the institution of independent, external observers, which indicates that it apparently constitutes a problem that needs to be addressed.

> pletely ignored my presence. When the lecturer finally came in, all got up from their benches and stopped talking immediately. It suddenly became clear that the class had begun.

Not dissimilar to school instruction, students have to follow a rigid timetable of classes which leaves little room for personal preferences. Students are usually assigned two foreign languages at the beginning of their studies and may choose a third one freely if they wish. Attendance at all classes is mandatory. These usually take place in four doubles of 80 minutes each from 9 to 15.50 every day, excluding Sunday. The basic unit of organisation is the language group. An example of a timetable for a second year student in the department of international relations is reproduced in Table 7. Language classes are generally taken more seriously by students than seminars or lectures, since they require considerably more and constant preparation and since groups are very small, which makes it difficult to 'hide' behind other students. A peculiarity of the second year is the so-called General Military Training (*obščevoennaja podgotovka*) which acts as a substitute for military service and teaches the theoretical and practical basics of the military.

Timetables not only structure students' daily and weekly routines, but are the kernel of the whole educational process at MGIMO. Timetables list classes, times, instructors and rooms for each of the language groups and are displayed at central locations all over the MGIMO building. This allows comprehensive observation, since the timetables chart where a particular student or lecturer should be and what they should be doing at any moment in time. It instructs students and lecturers when and where to go and organises their daily lives: lunch breaks, times to relax, times to study. Timetables break up the day into ever smaller units to be filled and used ever more efficiently. They represent a central disciplinary instrument without which the educational process could not function properly. Therefore one of the first things memorised or copied in the academic year is the timetable.

Table 7: Timetable of a male second-year student in international relations

Time	Monday	Tuesday	Wednes day	Thurs-day	Friday	Saturday
9.00 - 10.20	General Military Training (*Obščevoennaja Podgotovka)*	English	Turkish	Turkish	*Free*	English
10.35 - 11.55		Lecture 1: Institutions of Modern Diplomacy	Physical Education	English	Lecture 3: Ethnopolitical history of Russia	Lecture 4: General and social psychology
12.10 - 13.30		Seminar on Lecture 1	Seminar on Lecture 2	Lecture 2: History of the East	English	Seminar on Lecture 3
13.30 - 14.30		*Lunch Break*	*Lunch Break*	*Lunch Break*	*Lunch Break*	*Lunch Break*
14.30 - 15.30		*Free*	English	*Free*	English	Turkish

Most disciplining of students takes place in the classroom. In one first year lecture I attended the professor was particularly clear about his requirements in terms of discipline:

> "There are a couple of principles that govern my classes and I want everyone to adhere to them. Your failure to do so will get you expelled from this class and you won't be able to write the exams at the end of the year. So listen closely: First, no-one is allowed to enter the room after the first bell signal or to leave it before the second bell signal. Second, there is no eating or drinking in my lectures. You are not in the cafeteria. Third, I will not admit anyone wearing outer clothing (*verxnjaja odežda*). We are not in a train station here. Fourth, I ask you now and for the future to fill up the rows from the front and to leave the last two rows empty. Whoever sits in the last two rows will be asked to leave the class immediately."

Especially in the early years presence in lectures and seminars is monitored on a regular basis and teachers tend to enforce their rules strictly. This creates a school-like atmosphere with clear divisions between teachers and students.

The strict order enforced in classes makes it easy to spot deviant behaviour. I also experienced a fair share of being reprimanded for a lack of discipline, which was rather a lack of being able to blend in with the rest.

> Not writing at times when all others in the class are writing can also provoke irritation. This happened to me once, when the professor was dictating references and I did not quite understand the names of some Russian authors. As she was dictating at a rapid speed anyway, I decided to copy the references from another student afterwards. My not writing was much to the discontent of the professor who reprehended me for not writing down what she read out: 'Do you think that you don't need this, young man? Write!'.

As both Bourdieu (1996) and Foucault (1979) observe, writing exercises are a frequent means of establishing discipline. In the French concours for admission to the grandes écoles and in the grandes écoles themselves very strict rules of composition apply for the format of work to be handed in. Poorly formed letters, for example, will get students a deduction. Errors in spelling and punctuation lead to the severe downgrading of an essay. Foucault (1979: 154), in particular, emphasises how the 'gymnastics' required to produce acceptable handwriting is linked to control over bodies. At MGIMO, excessive writing and dictation exercises are not uncommon.

> I once sat in a classroom, waiting for a particular lecture. However, apparently the lecture had been moved or postponed and instead another seminar took place in the room. It was not until the seminar had started, that I realised my mistake, but I was too afraid to stand up and leave. So I sat through the whole class which consisted of writing down tax brackets for different countries. The lecturer dictated the tax brackets and tax rates and students copied them into their notebook.
>
> *1 – 7,825 USD = 10 %*
> *7,826 – 31,850 USD = 15 %*
> *13,851 – 77,100 USD = 25 %*
> *77,101 – 160,850 USD = 28 %*
> *160,851 – 349,700 USD = 33 %*
> *Above 349,700 USD = 35 %*
>
> This act was repeated for several countries and for several different taxes until the end of this class. The whole time, the classroom was completely silent. Students had to concentrate so hard on listening and writing down the correct figures that they did not have the chance to chat. In this vein, the classroom was disciplined into obedient silence through the use of scholarly exercise.

Supervision and monitoring of disciplined behaviour are not confined to the classroom, though. Students must be prepared to be admonished even if the timetable does not allocate them to a particular lecture hall and a particular lecture at this moment. It is not untypical for lecturers to reprimand students for just standing around in the corridors. Even outside classes, simply chatting away the time is not approved of and the principle of non-idleness is enforced (cf. Foucault 1979: 154). Spare time should be used to prepare for language classes or get homework done. Several times I heard curt admonitions like the following in MGIMO corridors:

> *Lecturer (to students standing in the corridor):* "What are you loitering here? Don't you have classes?"
>
> *Another lecturer:* "Don't chat! Learn!"

Even outside classes, simply chatting away the time is not approved of. Rather, it should be used to prepare for language classes or get homework done. This ideal of the hard-working student – always busy to form themselves according to the image projected on them – cannot be fulfilled by all students. The high workload creates stress and pressure both for *dogovorniki*, who have invested significant sums for tuition fees, and *bjudžetniki*, who are afraid of losing their stipends if they underperform. One teacher, with whom I had struck a loose friendship, reported that nervous break-downs were not uncommon and that there were occasional incidences of suicide among students.

> While in the first years, students are made to adhere to very stringent rules, disciplining of students slackens over the years as students grow older. It becomes more acceptable to talk during lectures, to come late or to be absent altogether or to pass on notes. The use of mobile phones, very much a persistent element in both students' and teachers' everyday lives, is increasingly tolerated. Also, there are certain bewildering moments when the strict enforcement of discipline suddenly breaks down. One of those moments was when the same lecturer who told me to write down the references accepted a phone call in front of the student group during class. Apparently, her young daughter had just come home from school and rang her up to tell her that she had safely arrived. At this moment the lecturer stepped out of the educational context and the requirements of discipline to act in a completely private context. After finishing the conversation she carried on with her lecture as if nothing had happened.

The enforcement of discipline vis-à-vis students is also achieved by the institution of the pro-rector for teaching (*prorektor po učebnoj rabote*) and his deputy pro-rectors to whom students get called if they fail to live up to the disciplinary standards. This might be in cases when they arrive late, when they fail to deliver their homework, when their performance deteriorates or when they are altogether absent from classes. The pro-rectors for teaching monitor that students conform with the rules of MGIMO and coordinate measures of reprimand and punishment of students within departments. Students say that the pro-rectors know every individual student and her or his personal file of disciplinary measures very well. Pro-rectors for teaching thus function as centralised observers with a surveying over-view who are able to police students' mischiefs. They represent an authority of control that enforces discipline.

> This disciplinary technique is not without its loopholes, however. Students say that sometimes the pro-rectors can be talked into waiving an entry into the student file and are generally more lenient than might be expected from their tough outward appearance. Having or devising a good and credible excuse for coming late ("Gennadij Ivanovič wanted to talk to me about next week's English competition") or for not having done the homework ("I did an elective on the art of diplomacy yesterday and did not come home until nine in the evening") can spare students reprehension.

In addition to the outside disciplining by lecturers and pro-rectors, there is also a significant degree of self-disciplining among students.

> Most prominently, this happens through the *starosta*. The *starosta* is a student who is in charge of monitoring the attendance and academic performance of his group. She or he usually registers present and absent students for every class and is responsible for maintaining high general attendance rates. Moreover, she or he is also supposed to motivate the group to study hard and do the homework. At MGIMO, some faculties hold a competition in which they select the group with the best academic performance. The *starosta* often plays the role of mediating between lecturers and students and wielding disciplinary power on part of the lecturer. It is not uncommon, for example, that a lecturer will ask the *starosta* to silence the class or to collect assignments.

Choosing students in this way to monitor correct behaviour and ensure the smooth operation of the educational apparatus internalises disciplinary techniques and exhorts students to become self-governing subjects

Perhaps the most efficient technique of producing docile bodies texams are closely linked to practices of knowledge. '[T]he material taught is less important in and of itself than what is taught above and beyond this material through the ordeal required for its acquisition' (Bourdieu 1996: 111).

> Language classes probably come closest to Foucault's dictum of the school as an 'apparatus of uninterrupted examination' (Foucault 1979: 186) in which drill guides students to the mastery of knowledge. Language classes ask the biggest effort of students and the majority of studying time is invested into the constant and regular preparation for them. Students progress in learning the vocabulary is regularly

> checked through small tests or grilling in front of the group. Homework such as translations or compositions is regularly given and marked. If in the lectures it is possible not to come prepared, this applies considerably less so for the language classes. Failures to complete the exercises can usually not be covered up and hidden from the instructor.

It is the regular repetition of this ritual examination four or five times a week which turns them into a powerful instrument of subjecting students to the disciplinary mechanisms of the school.

The most successful students in examinations at MGIMO are called *otličniki*. *Otličniki* must constantly score very high in oral and written exams (usually over 90 %) to maintain their status and receive a bonus on their stipends. They are also awarded the most prestigious stipends such as the stipend of the President of Russia, the MID stipend and so on and are given preference in the assignment of prestigious internships in the MID. On the other hand, students may lose their stipends if they do not satisfy the minimum requirements for academic performance. Almost every department has a public notice board on which it posts the faces and names of its *otličniki*. This public posting of excellence has a normalising effect: it institutes academic performance as a central criterion of judgement and elevates the best of the best as a model for all to see and imitate. The model student is thus scripted as a student who subjects her- or himself to the logic and primacy of academic performance by striving to become an *otličnik*.

5.3 Practices of knowledge: producing objective truths

With Foucault, disciplinary practices and the production of docile bodies at an educational institution are always bound up with the constitution of knowledge. At MGIMO, knowledge sublimates into objective truths through a variety of practices such as through exams. The first exam students have to pass at MGIMO is the entrance exam. While a significant part of the entrance exam covers foreign language proficiency, subjects like geography or history are geared towards the reproduction of facts and figures. In geography, typical questions are of the following kind:

1) Belarussia[12]

12 The document uses the Soviet, russified name for Belarus.

1. Peculiarities of the national structure. Economic geographical location.
2. Assessment of the natural resource potential of Belarussia.

2) Political and economic geography of Russia
   1. Change of political and economic geography in comparison to the Soviet Union. Territory, land and marine boundaries, Russia in the CIS.
   2. State structure of Russia.

3) Political map
   Indicate on a blank map the member states of OPEC, specify their form of government and territorial structure.

A description of the relevant knowledge in the field of Russian history contains the following elements:

> Great Patriotic War 1941-1945: Reasons for the entry of the USSR into the Second World War. Beginning of the Great Patriotic War. Reasons for the failures of the Red Army in the initial period of the war. Course, main stages and major battles of the Great Patriotic War. Military leaders and heroes of the war. ...
>
> The Soviet interior during the years of the war. War economy. Labour heroism of the people.

By and large, successful performance in the entry exam is dependent on the meticulous accumulation and reproduction of facts and figures. This is not dissimilar to the structure of exams during the course of studies. As Table 7 illustrates, each lecture is usually accompanied by several seminars which are designed to practically apply the content of lectures in smaller groups and provide exercises to train students for the final oral (*začët*) or written exams (*ėkzamen*) that constitute a requirement for classes. In the majority of cases, there is a complete list of possible questions for the exams available beforehand from the lecturer and preparation for the exams is geared towards the knowledge canon demarcated by this list.

The conduct of seminars and lectures reflects the nature of knowledge to be imparted: methods of preparation for exams favour memorising and learning by heart as the premier approaches to acquiring knowledge. Classes mostly resemble a monologue without much interaction with the audience and, in most cases, with complete absence of visual aids. Some seminars are a mere 80-minute dictation in which the teacher reads out sentences and students pen them down in their notebooks. This method is applied when dealing with highly structured subject matter such as statistical data. Other seminars consist of teacher monologues or the teacher catechising students on literature they are supposed to have read at home to prepare answers for the questions. In the early years students are supposed to memorise information from a standard set of textbooks which can be borrowed from the MGIMO library. Asking students mainly to reproduce this knowledge turns exams into arbiters of objectivity, especially since academic performance is tied to the correct reproduction of knowledge.

In the classes students are required to be able to immediately retrieve the information they have acquired. It is not uncommon for them to be called up by the lecturer and to be confronted with questions of the following kind:

> *Lecturer (addressing himself to a student)*: "What is the definition of GDP?" Student stands up and answers rapidly. "And what is the total amount of Russia's GDP?" Student gives correct answer. "How many hectares of arable land per capita in Russia?", "How many litres is a barrel?" and so on.

> In another seminar, the lecturer wants to know the definition of politics. When the student stands up and is unable to give an answer, the lecturer scolds him and asks how he could possibly dare to come to his lecture if he did not master even the basics of world politics.

The necessity to give immediate and unambiguous answers in such situations fosters the uncritical reliance on facts and figures. Even in the case of more openly phrased questions that demand an assessment by the students, the immanent logic of urgency favours the recycling of the same topoi of argumentation. Resorting to similar answer schemata allows satisfying the demands of examination – to give an immediate answer to any possible question – at the lowest cost. With Bourdieu (1996: 87f.) such practices of rapid knowledge (re-)production at almost any cost make elite schools 'genuine executive training grounds' that prepare students for working life rather than for doing in-depth research.

There is a clear distinction, communicated to the students, between right and wrong, good and bad answers. This kind of rigid knowledge structure promotes the uncritical consumption of pre-fabricated viewpoints. While it is especially dominant in subjects that primarily deal with the comprehensive acquisition of so-called 'objective' knowledge, it also marks knowledge culture at MGIMO in general. The nature of exams espouses the accumulation of masses of facts, dates and figures; as a mainstay of academic performance this kind of knowledge acquisition is held in high regard by teachers and students alike and rewarded, through disciplining practices, with good grades. Knowledge is something to be mastered through drill and accumulated – the more the better.

It is not only exams, however, that fashion knowledge with objectivity. The structure of arguments in lectures also relies heavily on seemingly objective facts and figures to support conclusions. This way of reasoning shares many similarities with the natural sciences. One lecturer even argues that the application of natural laws to social and political processes is a highly useful way of doing analysis, because of the similar structure of nature and society (61/14). The stability of social systems, the balance of powers, the theory of Pareto distribution can all be explained with the help of laws from the natural sciences. Lecturers sometimes contrast this objective, scientific assessment in political *science* with the subjective views expressed in politics and society. Russia's role in world politics is one of those topics where a lecturer proposes a 'scientific' treatment of the question:

> Thinking about Russia's place in the world, we will orient ourselves towards simple, scientific things like the share of GDP, the share in world trade, territory, armed forces, the number of warheads and so on. This is not as poetic as Tjutčev or Bunin but it allows, at least, to draw unambiguous conclusions (Lecture 11/7).

Such unambiguous conclusions, it is argued, can also be derived from analysing the 'objective core' (Lecture 13/7) of Russian national interests. Arguments and conclusions presented in classes are therefore always based on a meticulous recounting of facts and figures. Collection, analysis and synthesis of the facts at hand are the main instruments of judging international relations. This approach is regarded as 'professional' and MGIMO students are to be taught to follow this example:

> I may be wrong, ... I don't know the absolute truth. I am a student just as you are. I see, analyse and try to draw some conclusions. This is why they might be right or they might be wrong. Look to me as an example and learn how to do analysis of international relations. That's what you will have to do all of your remaining life, if you work professionally: analyse events that are happening and make conclusions and predictions (Lecture 31/1).

While this lecturer openly acknowledges the possibility of wrong judgements, the objectivity of the process of arriving at such a judgement is not questioned. What is more, the relatively hegemonic organisation of classes favours a climate in which interpretations of international affairs, for example, are taken for granted and not questioned. The attitude towards knowledge as something to be acquired is irrevocably applied to those more openly 'subjective' forms of knowledge such as interpretations of international affairs current and past. Every teacher does make certain political assumptions that are transported in the classes. These assumptions, however, are rarely problematised as subjective fixations, all the more because of the high premium placed on absorbing as much knowledge as possible which discourages dealing with multiple, possibly contradictory interpretations and positions. It is therefore not the case that there is no general openness towards different viewpoints, but rather do the disciplinary mechanisms of knowledge production enforce premature closure.

Knowing all the details about an event or a situation is a requirement for making an informed judgement. As one lecturer cautions:

> I don't know the details of the talks and that's why I hesitate to comment on this question. You have to know all the details. I don't want to say anything about this topic, because you have to be a professional (Lecture 31/18).

A similar reservation to making judgements was evident in my interviews with students. Many students were concerned to lay out how their views are backed by objective reasoning. Whenever possible, they quoted events, statistical data or expert analyses to support their positions and were afraid to make assessments without having detailed knowledge about an issue. When they did so nevertheless, they qualified their assessments as 'subjective' or 'without proper foundation' and expressed their concern about 'getting it wrong'. Conversely, however, this assumes that once all the details are acquired there is nothing that would stand in the way of an objective conclusion.

5.4 Practices of consumption and banal patriotic politics[13]

Up to this point, I have mainly focused on the classroom and the formal practices of education that make up MGIMO as an educational institution. A substantial part of the practices that underpin identity production, however, takes place outside of the classroom. The cafeterias and cafés of MGIMO are virtually the only meeting places with an opportunity to sit down and have a chat or do one's homework. They represent the nodes of social life at

---

13 For a more detailed rendition of these practices refer to Müller 2008b.

MGIMO and in an almost ideal typical way they also mirror the social fault lines between MGIMO students.

> MGIMO has three cafeterias. The staff cafeteria is located on the top floor and has nicely decorated tables with a cotton table cloth and curtains draped around the lunch counters to separate them visually from the dining room. Even during the lunch break the atmosphere is usually quite serene and calm. The food served is the same as one floor below where the MGIMO student cafeteria is located. In contrast to the staff cafeteria, there are bigger tables, often several in a row, with plastic table cloths and little space between them. Food is handed out by kitchen staff wearing white and often relatively dirty aprons and the checkouts are staffed with people in funny uniforms wearing funny hats. Beverages offered are of the classic Russian sort, e.g. *mors* and *kompot,* and the same is true for the food. Both of these cafeterias are MGIMO-run and staffed with middle-aged and older employees in traditional work clothes. The average bill is about EUR 4.
>
> On the bottom floor we find a fast food restaurant which opened in 2004 and is operated by Rostik Restaurants Ltd. The fast food chain invested EUR 1 million into a food court of 4,000 square metres which seats 230 students and offers various kinds of fast food, ranging from sushi to pizza, and the usual Western brands of beverages. The food area has a stylish design with brightly coloured tables and chairs, and rap and hip hop music is played at high volume. Besides ordinary tables and chairs there also bar stools and bar tables and sofas. Employees are about the same age as the students and wear modern uniforms. The average bill runs to EUR 10 or more for a full lunch.

This dichotomy between private and university-run catering also applies to the two cafés at MGIMO. MokaLoka, a chain of cafés run by Rostik, represents the type of expensive swanky café with cosy sofas and wooden tables. It is primarily frequented by wealthy, expensively-dressed students able to pay the RUB 100 or more for a cup of cappuccino. The other café, strangely named Boeing-737, with its ascetic decoration, sulky service staff, sterile atmosphere and standard selection of ordinary food and drink corresponds to the MGIMO student cafeteria. It has simple plastic tables and chairs which do not encourage to stay for much longer than the very business of eating and drinking. The contrasting possibilities of having lunch or a coffee create completely different atmospheres and a separation between two different groups of students. This social rift and its manifold articulations constitute an omnipresent hallmark of MGIMO life. Notwithstanding their differences, students of both groups are usually dressed up neatly and elegantly – only the budget they spend on clothes seems to vary. This professional dress code is a characteristic of MGIMO and develops as students are socialised into MGIMO (for a similar observation at a Canadian university see Turner and Coen 2008).

While first year students are dressed in a motley mixture of clothes, the way of dressing becomes considerably more stylish and oriented towards the latest fashion over the years.

Besides clothes, the possession and use of cars is another social marker that plays a central role in MGIMO life.

> In one of my first conversations with a MGIMO student I was asked: "Do you drive?" Due to the unspecific character of the question I misinterpreted it as meaning: "Do you have a driving licence? Do you know how to drive?" Having answered affirmatively, I thought I could usefully clarify the real intention of the question but she pre-empted me and started complaining about the traffic jams in Moscow and that it often takes her half an hour to get from Jugo-Zapadnaja metro station to MGIMO (which, incidentally, is a 20-minute walk). Quite obviously she thought that I had really bought a car in Moscow, although in most cases using public transport is often much faster than driving by car.

The inconvenience of using a car is offset by the prestige gained. There is a clear unwritten pecking order that big cars with chauffeurs wait in front of MGIMO, crowding the clearway, whereas smaller cars and cars without chauffeurs are left at one of the parking lots.

In the course of their education at MGIMO the majority of students at least once have the chance to travel to Europe. Other than ordinary Russians, the majority of whom spend their holidays in Egypt, Turkey or the Near Abroad, MGIMO students are more centred on Europe. Many of them can afford to be frequent visitors to European countries or have even grown up in internationally mobile families. Language courses or internships concentrate in European countries and most educational exchange programmes have been concluded with European universities. European universities are the ones most actively pursuing academic cooperation and European companies and cultural institutions have gained high visibility at MGIMO. Startravel, the local travel agency, maintains an office in the dormitory right next to MGIMO and regularly advertises flights to Russian and European destinations.

> While going abroad is a necessity in the professional development of MGIMO students, the choice holiday destinations often is a question of prestige. During the time I was at MGIMO there was a highly advertised contest, centred around the leitmotif of Phileas Fogg's journey around the world, in which students were called on to participate and compete with Fogg (and other students) in how many countries they have visited. The greater the number and the more exotic the culture, the better the chances of winning the trophy. In the same vein, clothes that carry the names of places abroad are the only exception to the professional or exclusive fashion style

> described above. Venezia, Goethe-Institut, Key West and Oxford University t-shirts compete with more elegant brands as insignia of urbane internationality.

Not only culturally but also in terms of future career prospects Europe provides a frame of reference for MGIMO students. Western companies woo MGIMO students, for example through the English-language newspaper *The Moscow Times* which is freely available at MGIMO. *The Moscow Times* is the most frequently read international newspaper at MGIMO. Since it is distributed free and provides an opportunity of English language exercise, it has a competitive edge over Russian newspapers. With the Moscow labour market a strong buyers' market for most of the new millennium, especially for highly qualified personnel, job opportunities for MGIMO graduates abound. It is especially companies in the oil and gas sector, in auditing, consulting, real estate and law which attract the interest of MGIMO students through special career fairs or internships. Indeed, careers with international organisations or international companies enjoy a high reputation with MGIMO students, even with those who do not specialise in an economic subject.

The kind of consumption prevalent at MGIMO is almost epitomised by the magazine *MajorDom* which appears quarterly in an edition of 5,000 and is especially produced for MGIMO students and alumni. Despite being a magazine primarily aimed at students, *MajorDom* is more akin to a lifestyle and executive magazine. This is also reflected in its self-description:

> A publication for a selected audience, the journal is read by the future elite of the country and people who have already been successful in their lives. The in-house audience at MGIMO reads quality publications and prefers expensive brands.

The contents of the magazine present a curious amalgamation of business and politics on the one hand and lifestyle and consumption on the other hand. It features sections named 'Institute of Style' or 'Institute of Money' (where 'Institute' refers to MGIMO) which give fashion and styling tips and advertise the latest collection of dakine or Estée Lauder. Another section entitled 'Institute of Automobile' runs regular photo reports in which female students are photographed in various positions while exploring a luxury car. These reports are accompanied by adverts for executive cars by major Western manufacturers such as Mercedes, BMW or Jaguar. 'Institute of the World' publishes the latest travel report from a holiday trip to Goa or to Columbia University in New York. According to surveys carried out by *MajorDom* among its student readership, 65 % own a car, 85 % regularly travel abroad and 67 % regularly renew their outfit (MajorDom 2005).[14]

The image of the successful young MGIMO graduate working in a responsible and advanced position with a well-known company is further nurtured by *MajorDom* in its career section. This section features brief portraits of those who 'have made it', mostly in international business, and shows how MGIMO lays the foundation for future success. It reiterates all the important attributes mentioned in the previous paragraphs: the importance of fashion and style, the centrality of cars and other luxury items and international versatility as mainstays of professional success. Established politicians or high government officials, usually of advanced age, represent the other type of person that is frequently portrayed in *MajorDom*. People like Evgenij Primakov or Sergej Lavrov are less presented as immediate role models but rather addressed as mentors who, over the course of decades, have acquired the necessary oversight and knowledge to give useful advice to aspiring students. They have climbed the apex of power but still belong somehow to the MGIMO community – a community that not only educates people academically but also socially.

In many respects, much of the consumption at MGIMO described up to now appears to be geared towards adopting what is often seen as the model of a Western, or, more precisely, European, lifestyle.[15] This holds true both for students from a wealthy background and for students with comparatively little financial means. With Oushakine (2000) or Rausing (2002) one might therefore argue that the consumption of products of Western origin is linked to the expression of a similarly Western or European identity. At first glance, this seems to be all too true. In fact, looking at MGIMO one could be forgiven for thinking that this little part of Russia has already arrived where many in Europe and the West would like to see Russia as a whole: in Europe.

It would be premature, however, to equate the enactment of conspicuous consumption of Western products, which immediately catches one's eye, and the imitation of a Western or European lifestyle in many respects with the adoption of a Western or European identity. 'When interpreted in the context of post-socialist culture and society, these seemingly Western practices reveal

---

14 Although many MGIMO students read MajorDom, this survey should not be taken as representative of the whole student body.

15 See Müller (2008b) for the argument of Western vs. European lifestyle.

their fundamentally local, yet contemporary, logic' (Shevchenko 2002: 148f.). Many superficially Western or European attributes appear in natural juxtaposition with elements that obfuscate and dissolve the clear enactment of a Western or European identity that I have proposed up to now. Western and European products and practices become interwoven with local practices which disrupt the initial impression of European- or Westernness.

One of the striking juxtapositions is the encounter of this imputed European identity with elements of war and the military. This happens most visibly during the annual celebration of Victory Day on May 9 for which veteran alumni of MGIMO are invited to a programme at MGIMO honouring their braveness and heroic deeds during the Great Patriotic War. The pompous celebration of Victory Day is a custom throughout Russia and it is unsurprising that this also applies to MGIMO. What is quite striking, however, is the uncritical and unconditional glorification of war actions and the Soviet participation in it which seems oddly out of place if viewed in conjunction with the ubiquitous presence of European attributes. The following poem, written by a fifth year student of international journalism and published in *Meždunarodnik*, the regular bulletin of MGIMO, is instructive in this respect:

> Five
>
> 1941: Withdraw. Go back. Surrender. Leave the city to the fascists. And the buttonholes (*petlicy*)[16] ripped off in captivity. Forgetting that I was a communist.
>
> 1942: Not surrender. Stand firm. Wait, dying in the cauldron of Stalingrad, and take into weak hands the subdued shield of Leningrad.
>
> 1943: Attack. Assail. Lie down my life at the altar of victory. Face falling into a puddle of blood and die like our grandfathers have died.
>
> 1944: Cut. Finish off. Blow up, and with casualties advance towards Berlin. All who stood on the way – kill. May splinters pierce my spine.
>
> 1945: Crawl. Run. Walk over the torn stairs of the Reichstag. Victory! The end of the road. The wind strikes the cloth of the flag.

While the celebrations of Victory Day may be viewed as an isolated event imposed and propagated from above, the military also plays a role in everyday life at MGIMO. For one thing, there is the requirement to complete General

16 Signs of military honour sewn to buttonholes.

Military Training which is integrated into male students' curricula in the second year. While it is impossible to receive a full military training within the period of time spent in General Military Training the programme appears rather to be designed to familiarise students with the Russian armed forces as a central part of the Russian state and instil a sense of patriotism in them, as one student intimated to me. *MajorDom* and *Meždunarodnik* regularly carry articles on military-related issues. In the career section of its third issue in 2005 *MajorDom* ran a story on how to become an arms exporter for the Russian Ministry of Defence in which it laid out the advantages and prospects of a career in the Russian arms trade. Another series of photos in *Meždunarodnik* shows a female MGIMO student model playing around with weapons (Figure 2). The articulation of military elements at MGIMO thus occurs alongside and is jumbled up with markers of a seemingly Western identity.

Figure 2: Girl and gun from Meždunarodnik

It is my contention here that the presence of the military should be read not so much as an intentional and overtly political or militant statement than as a naturalised articulation of patriotism. The armed forces acts as a symbol of Russia's strength and national pride and honouring war veterans is a reminder of Russia's great past. Such naturalised articulations of patriotism are scattered throughout MGIMO in more or less obvious forms. In the best sense of Michael Billig's (1995) 'banal nationalism', they are enmeshed with everyday life: omnipresent portraits of the Russian president, the three colours of the Russian flag as recurring motifs in festive decoration like the balloons in Figure 3, ties that depict the Russian flag and the double-headed eagle, badges worn on suits that show Russian symbols.

Figure 3: MGIMO with white-blue-red balloon decoration (Photo: Martin Müller)

As Sergej Lavrov emphasises in an interview with *MajorDom*, the best graduate of MGIMO not only has professional skills and creative talents, but also 'truly goes for (*bolet'*) his or her country'. This interpretation of patriotism as a necessary personal quality can also be found in the recruitment adverts of companies in *The Moscow Times.* A significant number of companies pad their adverts with reverence to Russia and try to tailor them explicitly to the patriotic or at least to the proud Russian. The most striking example is an advert by flexsearch, a Russian headhunting firm, which has adopted the slogan: 'Rebuilding Russia's self-image as a great power: rebuilding Russia together' (Figure 4).

All the while highlighting the desirability of international competence, the career section of *MajorDom* similarly makes a point in emphasising that the people portrayed have been successful in Russia and sometimes have even opted *against* taking on a job opportunity abroad. Others, like Jurij quoted earlier, even return from the West to study in Russia. This sentiment of staying true to one's country, of devoting one's career not only to one's own profit but also to the advancement of Russia also resurfaced in the interviews:

certainly, gaining international experience and making international contacts is important, but when it comes to more fundamental choices, many expressed their desire to perhaps work for an international company but nevertheless to stay in Russia.

Figure 4: Job ad 'Rebuilding Russia as a great power'

What is most striking, however, is the fusion of everyday student life at MGIMO, and its importance of consumption and living 'a good life', with high politics and big business. This is a recurrent feature and perhaps best exemplified on one of the title pages of *MajorDom* (see Figure 5). It features a girl wearing a dress with plunging neckline, her skirt slightly lifted to show her thighs, next to a smaller picture of the President of the Republic of Kalmykia, a subject of the Russian Federation. The teasers advertise the following contents: 'MGIMO-UN: students solve the problems of the world', 'Missteria 2006: the most beautiful girls at MGIMO!', '12 ways of getting rich without doing damage' and 'Grandson of national[17] significance: Andrej Brežnev on the student years of stagnation'. This pastiche-like juxtaposition of politics and lifestyle is most evident in the contents of the magazine where in another issue Evgenij Primakov is framed by a Dolce & Gabbana model and a student-driving a Mercedes car (Figure 6), while the whole opposite page is covered in a lingerie advertisement.

17 The word used in the original is sojuznij which refers to Soviet times and means 'union-wide'.

Figure 5: Banal politics I: title cover of a MajorDom issue

В нашей жизни много треугольников. Какова их роль?

56

64

46

50

Босые модели в платьях от D&G напоминают принцесс, таких-сяких, сбежавших из дворца, расстроивших отца

78

72

Актер Евгений Миронов не покорял Москву, она сама к нему пришла

Figure 6: Banal politics II: table of contents of a MajorDom issue

The fusion of at first glance disparate worlds, of mundane things and high politics, destabilises the image of a prevalence of Western identification at MGIMO which might arise by looking superficially at consumption practices:

the seemingly Western lifestyle is always wedded to a naturalised, patriotic politics. In lectures, professors chat about how they attended crisis summits or how they took part in negotiations about nuclear disarmament in a very informal tone. Decisions about war and peace thus are fashioned with a certain intimate character as they are recounted to the closed community at MGIMO. World politics is discussed as casually as the Miss MGIMO election or the night out yesterday. Sitting in the café and sipping a cup of frappuccino while 50 Cent raps from the ceiling, we read the interview with our fellow MGIMO alumnus Sergej Lavrov. It is wedged between a model photo shooting in a Maserati car and a photo story of General Military Training. The interviewer asks Lavrov, using the familiar address with first name and father name:

> Sergej Viktorovič, is Russia a *velikaja deržava*?
>
> *Lavrov*: Of course. ...
>
> *Interviewer*: Will we remain a *velikaja deržava* in 15 years' time?
>
> *Lavrov*: I think that we will even strengthen our position.

5.5 Conceptual reflection: practising subjectivities

MGIMO is a sedimented ensemble of different social practices. The formative power of this educational institution for the making of subject identities can only be understood by taking apart those practices: practices of consecration, practices of discipline, practices of knowledge and practices of consumption and banal patriotic politics. Subjects are constrained through the objective, sedimented structures of discourse: it is only within this field that they can position themselves, not realising the limitations they submit to. This objectivity, which is characteristic of elite schools and elite eduction more generally as Bourdieu (1996) remarks, comes into being because those – like teachers and students – who embody MGIMO as an institution submit to this status and show active complicity. 'Symbolic efficacy', as Bourdieu calls it, is conferred on MGIMO only through the embrace and, indeed, the incorporation of these structures.

> The miracle of influence or – the word is not too strong – *possession* succeeds only insofar as the one who submits to it [to the elite school] contributes to its efficacy; and that it does not constrain her unless she is predisposed by prior experience to *recognize* it. This only truly happens when the categories of perception and action that she puts into practice in the individual acts through which the "will" and the power of the institution are accomplished ... are in direct conformity with the objective structures of the organization because they are the product of the embodiment of theses structures (Bourdieu 1996: 3).

This submission to the educational apparatus – the production of docile bodies – can be better understood through Foucault's (1979) concept of discipline. For Foucault, there are three disciplinary techniques, all of which are put to work at MGIMO. *Hierarchical observation* refers to the constant surveillance and monitoring of student conformity with the rules of MGIMO:

> The exercise of discipline presupposes a mechanism that coerces by means of observation; an apparatus in which the techniques that make it possible to see induce effects of power, and in which, conversely, the means of coercion make those on whom they are applied clearly visible (Foucault 1979: 170-171).

Checking regular attendance, reproving loitering students, monitoring academic performance are some of the observational techniques employed for this purpose. Hierarchy in this case should not be understood as uneven power relationships between lecturers and students, though. Hierarchical observation also takes place among students, just take the example of the *starosta*, and among lecturers. Disciplinary power that produces docile bodies is thus not wielded by lecturers but is immanent in the educational institution itself.

Normalising judgement distinguishes between good and bad behaviour, good and poor performance, and treats students as cases which, to different degrees, do or do not live up to the expectations of the institution. *Otličniki*, the best students of each department, are exhibited as show-cases of excellent performance. Success and performance are quantified and measured through fixed instruments and allow to classify every student along a continuum of excellent to poor. This establishing of standards which promote the normalising of judgement puts considerable psychological pressure on students to satisfy the normative expectations. The *examination*, finally,

> combines the techniques of an observing hierarchy and those of a normalizing judgement. It is a normalizing gaze, a surveillance that makes it possible to qualify, to classify and to punish (Foucault 1979: 184).

The examination is not only instituted through oral and written exams, but also through the use of instruments such as the timetable which separate and partition time into 'ever more available moments' (Foucault 1979: 154) and extract time and labour from the disciplined bodies. Similar to the timetable, the function of pro-rectors for teaching is to make students clearly distinguishable, each irregular behaviour assignable to one particular person. It thus becomes impossible to hide anonymously in a big group. The aim of this 'disciplinary space', as Foucault calls it, was to 'know where and how to locate individuals, … to be able at each moment to supervise the conduct of each individual' (Foucault 1979: 143).

Discipline is the key moment in the objectivation of knowledge at MGIMO: the combination of discipline with knowledge makes knowledge objective. The highly structured character of teaching and examination at MGIMO engenders an understanding of knowledge as an object to be accumulated – the more the better. Within education at MGIMO, foreign policy and the political decisions it involves have become professionalised to such a degree that, by and large, they are perceived as objectivities which are not up to debate. Whatever view one adopts is seen as the outcome of an objective process, based on the analysis of facts such as national interests, military power or economic influence – on objective knowledge.

MGIMO 'trains' and 'prepares' students with the knowledge and analytical skills that will be required for occupying important positions in the future Russian elite. The practices of discipline and knowledge involved in education at MGIMO constitute the mechanisms through which the closure and ensuing objectivation of identities become functional. A recognition of the contingency of this fixation and its dissolution into equally legitimate subject positions would undermine the special status of MGIMO in the system of elite reproduction. Insofar as MGIMO serves as an institution reproducing elites, drawing on this distinct 'elite' knowledge constitutes an element of fixating an identity vis-à-vis other societal groups. As an elite school, we can understand MGIMO therefore with Bourdieu as a locus of consecration.

> In selecting the students it designates as the most gifted, that is, the most positively disposed toward it (the most *docile*, in the true sense of the term), and the most generously endowed with the properties it recognizes, the elite school reinforces these predispositions through the consecration that it bestows simply by separating its students from the rest. ... This social function consists in producing special, separate, sacred beings merely by getting everyone to be aware of and to recognize the boundary separating them from the commonplace ... and by creating thereby the conversion of

> belief that leads the chosen people to (re)cognize themselves as different (Bourdieu 1996: 102f.).

MGIMO's privilege of consecration is not uncontested. While in Soviet times it was a unique gateway to positions in the *nomenclatura*, recent years have seen rising challenges to this position. Other universities are successfully offering similar or better academic programmes and academic standards have come under pressure. Nevertheless, MGIMO's social function of producing elites is still recognised and frequently reiterated both by those within and outside MGIMO. But it is not an elite educated for its own interest or for the mere acquisition and creation of new knowledge, but with a clear societal purpose: to serve the country.

Patriotism – devotion and loyalty to one's fatherland – is enveloped in social practices at MGIMO at different levels. It is seen as a central element of education and as a pre-requisite for any good graduate and future diplomat. This categorical loyalty to one's country naturalises, of course, Russia's domestic and foreign policy decisions. If Russia is not to be questioned, this constitutes a hegemonic intervention on an undecidable terrain in Laclau and Mouffe's terms. Patriotism forms the ideological screen that obscures the contested political element of foreign policy knowledge at MGIMO. If in doubt, a good student should always act so as to advance her or his fatherland, subordinating other considerations. This articulation of patriotism in the institutional context of MGIMO already foreshadows patriotism as the basis of establishing Russia as a strong and respected country in world politics.

Such a naturalisation of an 'Advance Russia!' position not only takes place in the classroom, though. In everyday life, the prevalence of Western style consumerism would suggest cultural closeness to the West. Language courses, holidays or internships in Western companies or organisations all figure prominently in the lives of numerous MGIMO students. In the pursuit of a lifestyle that includes a car, travels abroad, stylish clothes, a well-paying job, lots of ambition and a number of other attributes MGIMO students appear to embody the Western model of 'a good life'. One aspect of this consumption certainly is the contrast and escape it offers from the disciplined world of the classroom. Especially for those who cannot or do not want to live up to the disciplinary expectations of the educational process, indulging in stylish clothes or expensive food is a mechanism of compensation for failures in the classroom. But consumption at MGIMO has a far more important political effect. Far from representing a simple imitation of Western lifestyle, superficially Western attributes are conjoined with often patriotic politics. The fusion of career opportunities with Russia's rise as a great power is but the most easily discernible example of such an amalgamation.

Combining the official and the everyday, combining grand gestures and banal elements makes high politics and big business seem banal; bereft of their mystic aura they become a natural part of everyday life. The banalisation effected through this conjunction glosses over the political quality of many aspects of life at MGIMO and the fixations of identities underlying them. When Evgenij Primakov appears side-by-side with beauty and styling tips and career perspectives in the arms trade are treated together with a review of the best party locations, the political is incorporated into the realm of the everyday and fashioned with the same objective qualities, failing to problematise or even recognise its fundamental contingency. In everyday life at MGIMO, the political has become banal as a natural element of the quotidian practices of students.

The production of identity is rendered uncontested and objective by the combined workings of discipline and professional, objective knowledge on the one side and the banality of everyday life on the other. Together they serve as a veil that naturalises the political fixation of elements and thus clouds and depoliticises the construction of identity. In this vein, an educational institution can function as the political apparatus through which discourses become functional, hegemonies can evolve and subjects can be positioned. Now that we have an idea of how discourses at MGIMO work, how they acquire the power to position subjects within this institutional setting, we can turn to examining the meaning and structure of geopolitical discourses at MGIMO.

6

Dislocation: crisis and loss

6.1 Geopolitical loss and instability

The deeply rooted feeling of loss and crisis in the aftermath of the collapse of the Soviet Union is a recurrent topos at MGIMO. One lecturer stresses the unique historical significance and unprecedented scope of the events following December 1991:

> The destabilisation which began right after the break-up of the USSR was linked to the change of all, to the change of socio-economic orientations against the background of the break-up of the USSR. This is very important from the point of view of history. There is not one single example of a great empire collapsing not only from the point of view of its territorial boundaries but also from the point of view of its interior structure. Nobody has ever changed the interior structure from one extreme to the other. A *dual geopolitical collapse* happened here, that is, the borders broke down, a new state was created, and at the same time the interior foundations were destroyed (Lecture 01/2, emphasis added).

Loss and crisis thus have many facets, relating both to the wider geopolitical changes in the post-Soviet time and the social restructuring that has taken place.

The diminished geopolitical role of post-Soviet Russia is something like a constant at MGIMO when talking about world politics. The lecturer above explicitly uses the term 'great empire' (*velikaja imperija*) to refer to the previous status of Russia within the Soviet Union. One lecturer vividly recalls the very document that set the seal on the end of this powerful position, citing from the following passage:

> "We, the Republic of Belarus, the RSFSR, Ukraine, founding states of the Union of Soviet Socialist Republics, ... declare that the Union of Soviet Socialist Republics ceases its existence as a subject of international law and as a geopolitical reality." ... And the most agonizing passage, I think, uncanny, mystic, you know, how little you

> are, I will finish you off – "ceases its existence as a geopolitical reality". That is, political space, territory, geopolitics, anything – you have nothing left (Lecture 62/12).

The deviation from the usually rather objective style of reasoning in lectures which becomes evident here underscores the emotional importance of the collapse event as one which deeply unseated Russia's role in world politics. The element of loss plays an important role, a loss of strength and power which leaves Russia in isolation.

> We became unimportant. Economically unimportant, militarily unimportant. We lost the system of alliances and coalitions of the Soviet Union. We were left more or less alone (Lecture 22/15).

To forcibly demonstrate the incisive drop in geopolitical importance Russia experienced after the break-up, a comparison with the geopolitical influence of the Soviet Union is inevitable.

> We understand that Russia is not a superpower anymore. Russia is not integrated into a sytsem of foreign policy alliances in the world, except for CSTO (Collective Security Treaty Organisation). Russia lost half its territory, population and economic capital compared to Soviet times. And from what was left, it lost still another half (Lecture 22/2).

In expressing Russia's degradation, the country is explicitly equated with the Soviet Union in this extract. This identity has been a common phenomenon since Soviet times, when Russians were encouraged to identify with the Soviet Union as their homeland (*rodina*) (G. Smith 1999a). It is not surprising therefore if many articulate the post-Soviet transformation in relation to what the Soviet Union was in the past. Maksim (17/4-6, 4 IR) thinks that 'in politics, Russia's voice is listened to much less often than was the voice of the Soviet Union'. This view is shared by many others who regret the loss of greatness and the degradation of Russia in world politics that followed the events in 1991. Julija, for example, emphasises that

> Russia cannot claim the role of a hegemon. ... It can no longer dictate the terms. ... It seems to me that many do not acknowledge that the role which Russia had earlier is already gone (Julija, 25/9, 4 PS).

It is especially in the relationship with the United States that Russia's significantly diminished position becomes obvious. One lecturer elaborates that earlier Russia and the US were comparable and had a very close relationship (Lecture 22/14). This, however, has changed radically with the end of the Cold War: While the US is now busy defending and expanding its leading position in the world economy and as a military power, Russia has to find some niche in the globalising world. 'For this reason we can no longer talk about partnership, about equally great greatness' (Lecture 22/14).

One immediate result of this degraded geopolitical position is Russia's weakness, almost helplessness, in the years following the collapse of the USSR. The conflict in Yugoslavia is given as an example where the powerlessness of Russia in the new world order became painfully obvious:

> The ambition (*zamax*) was very serious: not to let NATO beat up Slavic states, to stop the bombardment. But apart from turning a plane around over the Atlantic Ocean, Russia could do little. This were completely new realities (Lecture 01/17).[18]

The Russian army in the 1990s, the world's biggest army during Soviet times and the national pride of the Soviet Union, is regarded as a poor copy of its predecessor, which evoked trepidation in the capitalist world. Being severely underfunded, it accelerated the decline of Russian geopolitical influence.

> In the 1990s the Russian army did not receive one single piece of new weaponry or new military technology. That is, the money was just enough for feeding the soldiers and maintaining the trousers of the generals. Not more. We did not modernise our weaponry. That's only, what is evident, what lies at the surface. I could give many other examples of the degradation of the Russian potential in the 1990s. This is a sad history, but we have to assess it objectively. In fact, in the 1990s Russia's potential as a player [in world politics] was significantly reduced (Lecture 22/3).

Again, the professor urges to separate emotion ('sad history') and scholarly analysis ('assess it objectively'). The geopolitical collapse and decline of Russia are perceived as highly personal, emotional events that nevertheless need to be analysed through an objective lens.

Besides disparaging Russia's geopolitical position, the break-up of the Soviet Union is also held to have contributed to geopolitical instability. Touching on the global consequences of the events of 1991, lecturers at MGIMO like to quote Vladimir Putin. In his annual-state-of -the-nation address to the Russian Duma in April 2005 the president of the Russian Federation called the

18 This refers to the first NATO attack against the Federal Republic of Yugoslavia, when Prime Minister Primakov, then en route to Washington, turned his plane around over the Atlantic in a move that signaled Russian fury at being ignored in this issue.

collapse of the Soviet Union 'the greatest geopolitical catastrophe of the 20th century'. It is the key event which brought the stable world order into disarray and ushered in an era of crisis and uncertainty. In the eyes of many, the bipolar system meant greater predictability, as a stable balance was achieved between the US and the USSR. Boundaries could be clearly drawn between the capitalist and the socialist world, and between the nuclear and the non-nuclear world. These boundaries have now been erased and not been replaced by equal certainties. The conflicts on the Balkans, in Afghanistan, in Iraq and around Iran are at least partly attributed to the collapse of this stabilising system. The stability of the Cold War deterrence strategy is preferred over the upheaval in the 1990s. If only Russia had remained a strong, stabilising power, many of the military clashes could have been avoided.

> Look, during the time of the Soviet Union the US could not enter Iran. We entered Afghanistan and they had Vietnam. And that was it. They could not afford to do more. ... Why? Because they were afraid of a conflict. And now, Iraq, Afghanistan, the threat of Iran, the Near East, Yugoslavia, Sarajevo, Bosnia and so on. Do you really think the world has become more stable after the collapse of the Soviet Union? (Lecture 61/38)

Russia's geopolitical weakness has precipitated crises like those in Yugoslavia but has also led to destabilisation within the country. The conflict around Chechnya is construed as one incident which could have led to the break-up of the whole Russian Federation if Russia had just been a little weaker.

> I am not for the USSR as a communist state, I only talk as a systems analyst. Any system is more stable than a unipolar one. When the Soviet Union collapsed, a huge number of problems immediately appeared. Would the Soviet Union have allowed such a break-up of Yugoslavia? No, of course it would not have allowed it. They would have shouted on the grand-stand, they would have threatened with their ballistic missiles (*pokričali by na tribune, potrjasali by ballističeskimi raketami*), but nothing would have happened. And that's the tragedy. Look at Kosovo. Kosovo – Chechnya. Draw the parallel. Chechnya – Kosovo. If we had been weak enough, we would not have thought of intervening. That's what it is like (Lecture 61/38).

Again, the Soviet Union embodies the good old times of certainty, whereas the new world (dis-)order is seen as confusing and objectionable. Russia was too weak to act as a stabilising element in world politics, all the more so since the country itself was affected by disintegration and internal crises. Whereas the Soviet Union had a strategic, clearly developed foreign policy, Russia in the 1990s had to rebuild its foreign policy strategy but did not successfully manage to do so, according to another lecturer (Lecture 01/27). This failure to re-establish a strong Russia in the image of the Soviet Union also resulted in declining respect which Russia earned in the West and which further contributed to the erosion of its geopolitical position.

> The first five or six years [after 1991] it was just shameful to be Russian. I was in contact with Germans and in fact saw what relations were like. When you came as a Soviet representative, relations were such. But when you came as a Russian representative ... you felt a certain disdain (Lecture 61/46).

6.2 Loss of brother states

The notions of crisis and loss are also very pronounced in assessments of developments in the formerly socialist brother states of the Soviet Union. The image of the divorce of a married couple, used by several interviewees and lecturers, reflects the deep significance of the forced dissociation that followed the collapse of the Soviet Union.

> This is similar to imagining that husband and wife lived together, and lived, and lived, and then got divorced. But the husband still sees himself as the most important, although the wife does not live with him any more, but with someone else. If he continues to behave towards her as if she were still his wife, if he dictates to her, if he imposes his terms on her, this would at least be injudicious (Lecture 61/11).

This metaphor is instructive in that it pinpoints the close relationship between Russia and the Near Abroad and the difficulty, especially for Russia, of accepting such a divorce. In fact, lecturers stress that both ordinary Russians and Russian politicians find it hard to accept that they are dealing with separate states now. For most people, the USSR and their member states have been a homeland, where everybody belonged together in the unity of Soviet peoples (*družba narodov*). Adressing his students, a lecturer tries to make clear, how hard letting go of the newly independent states is for the older generation:

> And for you the CIS, I think, is not the USSR, of course. This is not your homeland (*rodina*). For you Ukraine is a foreign state. But for my generation and for those who are 20 years younger than me, they are soul mates (*brat'ja po razumu*), they are essentially compatriots. Because we were in one state, in the USSR (Lecture 61/5-7).

Lectures emphasise that a significant differentiation has occurred among the post-Soviet states – states that have left the homogenising umbrella of the USSR and now want to be recognised as individual entities. It is believed that this differentiation is not easy to acknowledge from the Russian side, since many Russians have personal ties to the post-Soviet states and do not want to realise how different from Russia they have become.

> It is common to think that in the CIS, just like in football, everyone understands everyone else. ... Because one says, "I spent my childhood in Kazakhstan." Another one, "my wife is Ukrainian, I go there in the summer." And the third says, "and I lived in Kyrgyzstan." And the fourth says, "and my mother-in-law is Belorussian. I know everything about these states." But there are so many nuances. ... [Still everyone thinks] that they understand everything in the CIS. "That's a former part of the Soviet Union, after all." But in fact we have drifted so far apart in terms of our mentality (Lecture 61/7).

Initially, lecturers claim, Russia did not treat CIS diplomacy as a separate field. It did not bother to acknowledge the diverging interests of the new nations. The recognition that the former homeland has been lost and that what was once united has fallen apart began to emerge in a gradual process. It seems even harder to understand that there is not only a differentiation but also a dissociation from Russia, as states seek closer relationships with NATO or the EU and increasingly break with Russia or even rally against it, despite the positive effects of the Soviet Union:

> You know, they are former republics of the Soviet Union. That's what I want to say. In Belarus, for example, illiteracy was around 80 %. After the Soviet Union all were literate. And in all other republics. Too literate even, and now they rail against Russia: "What did you do? You oppressed us!" But I just cannot understand what bad they did to them, except that they developed an industrial base for them, developed culture and significantly increased the level of education (Tatjana, 08/72, 4 IR).

Ukraine is a case in point here. Whenever talking about recent developments in Ukraine, hardly anyone fails to mention that Ukraine and Russia are brother nations. The shared history and the *Kievan Rus'*, the nucleus of the Russian empire, constitute a common reference point that is frequently appealed to. It is all the more difficult to understand why, in the wake of the Orange Revolution, Ukraine is trying to break with Russia. This break is not only considered a political statement, but equally a personal one. How, after all that the two states have been through, can Ukraine possibly walk out on

Russia? Even more so, since Russia has always taken care of Ukraine, has helped with cheap gas and other subsidies.

> For us, Ukraine has always been such a sacred cow, because we are closely related Slavic peoples. Though now we are not so close any longer, we are not at all brothers or sisters (Natalija, 29/33, 3 PS).

Students argue that Russia has always unconditionally supported its brother states, but instead of expressing their loyalty in exchange for this support, states like Ukraine or Georgia behave rather disrespectfully towards their larger neighbour. Some countries try to escape from Russia's sphere of influence or are lured away by the US or Europe. To some students, this behaviour appears to be outright irrational and ridiculous, as in the case of Georgia:

> If you put it bluntly, he [President Saakashvili of Georgia] wants to fall out with Russia. He does anything to achieve this. Although Russia helps Georgia in every way, even if not in such a way as the US could do it, but it supports it in a friendly way (Vasilij, 19/51-53, 4 IR).

> He [President Saakashvili of Georgia] is a man who should act in the theatre and not appear on the international arena, I think. ... We have the same faith, they are also orthodox. In Russia there has always been a positive image of the Georgian people as one of the noble (*blagorodnyj*) peoples of the Caucasus. Our relations were always very decent, very friendly towards the Georgians (Vera, 35/68, 3 IR).

Earlier, Vera described relations between Russia and the Near Abroad as 'one family, Russia and the CIS are one family' (Lecture 35/8), picking up on the familial metaphors. If your own brothers and sisters not only let you down but shun you, this is bound to result in disappointment. The dissociation of some CIS states from Russia is therefore more than a purely political process. More importantly, it deals a blow to a Russian identity that is still closely tied to this space and has a strong emotional component. This emotional component becomes evident in Natalija's utter incomprehension of the events in Ukraine which leaves her speechless:

> About Ukraine I do not know what to say. Anything you say will be used against you, because this country is, it is just, I don't have any words to describe this policy, the relations with our country (Natalija, 29/22, 3 PS).

Others locate the reason for the centrifugal tendencies in the Near Abroad with Russia's failure to support the countries adequately. In face of Russia's waning power, there is an absence of a uniting force around which the states of the Near Abroad could cluster.

> Russia does not have the necessary economic strength (*mošč*), it cannot tie the other, smaller states, states of CIS to itself. ... The USSR earlier was able to do so, to tie them to itself, since it had a huge economic potential. They felt more secure than now. Now Russia has a small GDP, little resources, the economy is in such a state that for the time being we cannot operate with global interests (Aleksandr, 14/4, 3 IR).

Once again, one central reason for the crisis in the Near Abroad is the failure to recreate the 'greatness of the Soviet Union', as Konstantin (16/49, 4 IR) puts it. The colour revolutions in Ukraine, in Georgia and in Kyrgyzstan are often read as repercussions of the collapse of the Soviet Union. The Orange Revolution in Ukraine is framed within an extended crisis that affects all states of the Near Abroad, like in this lecture:

> And all that brought some political scientists to shame, who perceived the Orange Revolution with anger and thought that this is a fact, that it turned out like that. But nothing is firm right now, too many factors are involved, too much was brought to the surface after that titanic explosion that happened with the break-up of the Soviet Union in the space of the CIS (Lecture 03/1).

6.3 Soviet times: when everything was forever

In speaking about the past, notions of loss and crisis implicitly or explicitly gain their weight by virtue of references to Soviet times. For the majority of people living in the Soviet system, it appeared as stable and imperishable. Just as if everything was forever – until it suddenly was no more (Yurchak 2006). Lecturers mourn the loss of those aspects of the Soviet Union which had instilled a common identity in people. One lecturer recounts how in lectures he had always appealed to students' common socialisation within the communist youth organisations: the Komsomol, the Young Pioneers and the Little Octobrists. There had always been a common reference point, a shared experience on which one had been able to draw in the lectures. Now, he complains, most students have not even been members of the Little Octobrists[19]

---

19 Soviet youth organisation for children between seven and nine years of age.

(Lecture 61/5). Most, he speculates, would not even be able to name the 15 member states of the Soviet Union:

> Even 10 years ago there wasn't a problem with this. Students got up and said them. Sometimes even the capital. I am sure that now, even if you can name all states, you won't be able to name the capitals. Now you come to the lectures and talk such things that would have sounded funny 10 years ago. This is what time means (Lecture 61/23).

The Soviet Union constitutes something like a timeless reference point in which things hardly ever changed. This does not mean that it is equated with an undesirable standstill. Quite to the opposite, it is contrasted favourably to the fast-moving times in the post-Soviet period in which things change constantly – a situation in which everyone can do everything and all fixed points of orientation have melted away. The Soviet system, in contrast, followed a more orderly, predictable and slower rhythm, which was upset by the collapse of the Soviet Union. The average Russian is not only portrayed as unable to cope with this situation. He is taken not to have wanted this change anyway.

> A normal man who has something to do (*zanjat svoim delom*). An orderly man who has his favourite job. Perhaps he gets paid little for it, perhaps he gets a sausage after waiting in line for half a day. You are no longer able to imagine this. You cannot imagine how you can walk into a shop and there is nothing. A normal, orderly man. And all of a sudden they tell him: "Go on, everything's possible." He has his favourite job, he has something to do. Well, who went on the streets with banners, who went to all those meetings and so on? Those who did not have to do anything. Those who felt insulted in some way. Those who did not have something proper to do were passionate about it (Lecture 61/41).

The collapse of 1991 is constructed as a revolution by those who did not fit the model of the 'normal, orderly man'. As a result, the collapse brought about an abnormal, disorderly situation which, for the majority of people, meant serious, unwanted disruption. With this disruption, the feeling of solidarity among people and states also disappeared.

> In the Soviet block, everything was done for the good of the people. If the most developed countries were in the Western block, then in the Soviet block there weren't. Everyone received free support. Dozens of African states, Muslim states. And they cancelled foreign debts, constructed industrial plants for free, delivered weaponry. ... That is, they delivered energy resources at discounted rates. This was one country (Tatjana, 08/72, 4 IR).

When earlier nobody was left behind and everyone received selfless support, in the post-Soviet period everyone fights for themselves and the feeling of unity has disappeared. Those who propelled the revolution in the Soviet Union, one lecturer argues, were always looking towards the higher standard of living in the West, ignoring that there were marginalised groups in the West, too. Such marginalisation did not occur to the same degree in the Soviet Union. While no-one was particularly rich, everyone earned enough to lead a decent life (Lecture 62/9). Through the veil of nostalgic idealisation, the Soviet Union here comes to embody the good things swept away by the rapid transformation. Actualising its presence becomes a way of mourning the loss of stabilities in times of perceived crisis.

The USSR frequently appears as a country one could be rightfully proud of. A strong state like the Soviet Union would not have allowed such shameful disintegration to take place as it occurred in the 1990s. One lecturer points out that the strong USSR was able to control the drug trade and business which now is rampant in Russia (Lecture 33/36). Others contrast the humiliating situation in the Russia of the 1990s to the achievements of the Soviet Union and the Russian Empire. The Russian Empire spread civilisation over its territories and saved the cultures of its constituent republics. It would be very difficult, another lecturer argues, to imagine the preservation of the Georgian culture if it had not been protected within the Russian Empire (Lecture 13/35). Although acknowledging the faults of the Soviet Union, a professor at the same time cautions against demonising the Soviet Union, as he thinks it is currently done in the West:

> Because if it had not been for the Soviet Union, we would not know what language they would speak now in London. This is not a subjective judgement. The role of the Soviet Union in the defeat of fascism is absolutely unequivocal and decisive. No matter what our strategic partners in overseas, on the other side of the English Channel or, among others, in Europe say: this is an obvious historic fact, which is not propaganda, but which, in fact, is a historic fact (Lecture 61/34).

In this statement there is, again, an appeal to the indisputable facticity of historic events, the common pattern of establishing objective knowledge claims at MGIMO. Highlighting the central role of the Soviet Union during the Second World War, it expresses disappointment with the lack of recognition of this importance, and by implication of Russia's past, in the West.

In retrospect, the rapid turnaround from a pro-communist to a pronounced anti-communist stance that characterised Russian official ideology in the early

1990s is judged as irritating and overdone. Why did Russia have to break so radically with the Soviet Union, both in its domestic and economic and in its foreign policy? This radical break is often regarded as a principal reason why the crisis in Russia hit so hard. It could have been averted or at least attenuated if politicians had steered a line more oriented towards continuity, many lecturers hold (Lecture 01/7; 02/31; 23/6).

> Was the Soviet Union developed or not? It would have been developed, if we had just continued after the Soviet Union. But just look what happened afterwards (Lecture 62/10).

Some believe to see this continuity in the figure of Putin who serves as a guarantor of stability and builds on what is perceived as the positive legacy of the Soviet Union (Lecture 02/20).

Such statements should not be understood as an uncritical glorification of the Soviet Union. In fact, the same students and lecturers who praise some aspects of Soviet times are also quite critical of others. They condemn the closed Soviet society which isolated people from events in the world (Lecture 03/9-10). They also stress that Russia pursues a considerably more peaceful and less aggressive foreign policy than the Soviet Union and thus has already become more 'civilised' (Andrej, 24/62, 4 PS; Julija, 25/3, 4 PS). What is reflected in all those statements that bemoan the loss of the Soviet Union, however, is a longing for the stability that is no more. A longing for the authority, both internal and external, which guaranteed a certainty and continuity that served as a fixed guiding line. In one lecture this reference to Soviet times is aptly qualified:

> I do not defend the Soviet Union. I only talk about the stability of the situation. What I want to say, what I am telling you about is that you never should take a situation at face value (*ocenivat' v lob*) (Lecture 61/42).

Taking a situation at face value in this context means blindly believing in that the Soviet Union was all bad and the new Russia is only good. In the eyes of many, it is regrettable that the good things about the Soviet times, the predictability, the controllability of life and Russia's respected position within world politics were lost with the bad things. A radical break occurred which, seemingly, forestalled every attempt at continuity.

6.4 Conceptual reflection: crisis of identity

The stories of loss and crisis recounted in this chapter are an omnipresent part of making sense of Russia in the post-Soviet period. Within the conceptual framework of Laclau and Mouffe this chapter describes an extended crisis of identity, caused by the dislocation effect of the Soviet collapse. Dislocations are events that cannot be symbolised by an existent discursive order and therefore disrupt this order (Laclau 1990). 'Dislocation is the traumatic event of "chaos" and "crisis"' (Torfing 1999: 149). Hegemonic nodal points become undone and old certainties wane as established discursive orders break down.

The hegemonic discursive order of the Soviet Union experienced a comprehensive dislocation in every social realm. A crisis of identity results from these seemingly objective fixities being dissolved as nodal points for identification and not being immediately replaced by new fixities. The onslaught of a whole set of new developments could not be adequately integrated in the hegemonic discourse. Russia's geopolitical power was annihilated, the ex-socialist brother states started to break away, new conflicts emerged in the wake of the downfall of the USSR, the economy was paralysed and the standard of living dropped dramatically. Eliminating the ideological master signifier of the capitalist enemy has destabilised identities by removing the antagonistic Other.

The feelings of disorder and chaos that are conveyed in many text extracts are potent evidence of this societal dislocation. They reach across the board and extend to geopolitical as well as to very personal aspects of the collapse. Even seemingly distant events like the colour revolutions in the post-Soviet states acquire a personal, emotional quality, as they serve to further displace Soviet notions of belonging together. References to Soviet times, by contrast, are replete with notions of stability and order which are repeatedly compared against the new, insecure times. This is a topos that can be observed more generally in Russian politics under Putin, Morozov (2008) argues. The Soviet past, particularly the time of stagnation (*vremja zastoja*) under Brežnev, is addressed as the golden age in the history of Russian statehood and contrasted to the times of collapse and destruction in the 1990s.

The effects of dislocation are contradictory, however. It not only threatens and destroys identities but also constitutes the foundation on which new identities are built (Laclau 1990: 39). The dominant themes of crisis and loss represent the failing discursive order which produced unprecedented societal uncertainty but at the same time also an unprecedented discursive openness.

The polysemy that arises in the wake of dislocations asks for a rearticulation of relationships between signifiers. A dislocated structure, however, does not have the means for its own re-articulation. The identificatory void, created through dislocation, will be filled by emerging hegemonic projects: 'the response to the dislocation of the structure will be its recomposition around particular nodal points of articulation' (Laclau 1990: 40).

7

Hegemony: strength and independence

7.1 Reasserting Russia's geopolitical position

Regaining Russian influence

Although they are omnipresent, stories of crisis and loss are mostly descriptions of times past at MGIMO. In most cases, Russia is constructed as having already weathered the worst period of decline and as re-emerging, perhaps somewhat battered, but still as a power to reckon with.

> Since the beginning of the [new] century, despite all losses that we have suffered, Russia has looked upon itself as a country that can stand on its feet and stay on this level even considering the transformation that occurred (Lecture 04/11).

Russia's ability, indeed willingness, to stand on its own feet is contrasted to the dominant position in the 1990s which posited that Russia should integrate more closely with the West. At that time, Russia's main avenue for consolidating its situation and becoming an equal partner of Western states was seen as lying with greater alignment. In retrospect, this belief is now interpreted as mistaken, considering that the West has never been willing to accept Russia as a truly equal partner (Lecture 23/15-16).

Russia is currently gathering new momentum even without rapprochement with the West. Pavel paints a picture of Russian recovery in world politics that is shared by many of his fellow students. Russian influence in the world, he thinks,

> keeps growing and growing. I cannot explain this, but there is no doubt that I personally like what is happening at the moment. From my memories and from the conversations I heard when I was a child, from what my parents say, it seems to me

> that the situation in the country improves in comparison to what it used to be like (Pavel, 06/3, 3 IJ).

Pavel's comments reflect the feeling of a generation at MGIMO who has come of age in the rising Russia of the new millennium. Students and lecturers tend to follow this general line of argument but bolster it up with more specific examples. Mikhail (11/68, 3 IR) observes that Russia has made a recent career from a state that was more or less ignored in world politics and needed help to get its things sorted out to one that already counts as a key player as is evident in the Iran conflict or in its membership in the G8. This is underscored by Ksenija (33/3, 4 Other) who claims that Russia is a powerful country that is respected and even feared by other countries. Anton (10/3, 4 IR) emphasises that Russia is actively developing its relations in all world regions, not only in the West. One lecturer argues that Russia, by virtue of its nuclear arsenal, is the second most important state after the US and that it has managed to successfully keep this position which guarantees significant influence in the international arena. Nevertheless, he thinks that Russia still has much left to achieve:

> I personally think that the major foreign policy task of Russia today is becoming a full-fledged member of the G8, that is, our departure from the semi-peripheral situation in which we are and the inclusion in the centre of world society. ... We are not, as they call themselves, a part of the prospering industrial countries of the world. Not yet (Lecture 22/17).

There is little doubt in this statement that Russia will be able to soon become such a prospering industrial state. Students are even more upbeat about this. Andrej (24/35, 4 PS) is confident that Russia already is or will soon become a world leader in key technologies and that its industrial and technological base will form the basis for this global re-emergence. Irina believes that Vladimir Putin is currently restoring domestic law and order and strengthening the influence of the state in order to increase Russia's political leverage:

> Perhaps earlier, under Yeltsin, I doubted [that Russia's will become influential again]. But now that Putin's has taken office, he definitely tries to take everything in his hands (*vzjat' upravlenie v svoi ruki*) and strengthen control. If we just take the example when they sent Xodorkovskij to prison, those oligarchs who grabbed the reins after the privatisation and had control over significant assets which belonged to the state. So, I think in fact, it is absolutely possible that the political rule (*vlast'*) is becoming stronger (Irina, 21/3, 4 PS).

Others agree that Russia is currently gathering new momentum and regaining influence in international relations. The contribution of Vladimir Putin to this re-emergence is frequently highlighted:

> At the head of our state we have really such an advocate of a strong state (*gosudarstvennik*) – Vladimir Putin – and whatever you may think of him, he tries to increase, to boost Russia's weight in every conceivable way (Katja, 2/3, 4 IJ).

> And it is just Putin's policy, as I think, which aims, if not at restoring past greatness, then at least at introducing new directions in foreign policy which can then be used to exert influence (Natalija, 29/3, 3 PS).

Some hold a favourable view of what they consider the recent Russian attempt of trying to expand its sphere of influence into the Near Abroad again and restoring what it has lost there (Oleg, 26/3,7, 4 IR; Natalija, 29/4, 3 PS). Anastasija (20/11, 4 IR) argues that Russia has diverse interests in many regions. It is gradually building its position as a world power and will not be content with that of a regional power only.

The notion of re-emergence is also discussed prominently in the lectures and seminars. In one seminar, students were asked to write short essays about their opinion on Russia's role in the world. They were free to adopt any position they wanted as long as they were able to defend it with proper arguments. The gist of the majority of presentations in class, however, followed the general line from above and sought to argue why Russia occupied, or ought to occupy, a leading position in world politics. It is worth quoting one oral essay defence in full length in which a student argues forcefully (but with a peculiar interpretation of economic theory) to the effect that Russia's economic power has been grossly underestimated:

> [Looking at the different levels of GDP] the question arises whether Russia is really 25 times less important than the US? Or 9 times less important than Japan and so on? There are two approaches. If one counts the GDP according to the exchange rate, Russia is certainly in a losing position. Why? Because the role of the currency ... is depreciated. If we calculate that one rouble is a tenth of one dollar, then, correspondingly, the Russian GDP will always be a tenth of the American GDP. ... If, however, we take the difference between the nominal GDP and the GDP by Purchasing Power Parity, then the difference [between Russia and the US] is only five times. If in the first case it is 400 billion per year, then in the second case we already have a trillion. And this already puts Russia among the top five states in the world by GDP. The difference is tremendous.

> We say that Russia's GDP is comparable to that of South Korea. But who knows whether South Korea will have such a GDP in ten years' time? Russia's GDP won't decrease, because today's GDP is the minimum of what Russia is capable of, that is, it can only grow from here.
>
> By the way, there is another important characteristic – the structure of GDP. The biggest part of the Dutch GDP, for example, is made up of the non-manufacturing industries. What does this mean? That the Netherlands live on tourism ... It is clear that if the world situation becomes a bit worse, then the GDP ... disappears. But Russian tractors cannot disappear, they will always be sought after. This is why the Russian GDP is more solid (Lecture 14/2-9).

He continues to argue further that Russia's GDP is seriously underestimated, because of the pervasive presence of black market transactions and barter trade. But the main line of attack is evident and very similar to that of other students: Russia has a huge, underestimated and underdeveloped potential and, consequently, its power is only bound to grow in the future.

Russia as a great power

While only few claim that Russia's great power status vanished irrevocably with the collapse of the Soviet Union and can hardly be regained, an overwhelming majority believes that in one way or the other Russia is either becoming a great power at the moment or has already become one. Ideas of what constitutes a great power are diverse. Some consider it a designation of states which have a rich history:

> Martin: Do you think that Russia currently is a great power?
>
> Larissa: Yes. Above all, as a patriot of my country I cannot think otherwise. And then, like every country which has a rich history, rich traditions, a rich culture – this is a great power (Larissa, 15/89, 4 IR).

Others interpret the idea of great powerness in a more political sense, according to which great powers are characterised by political and military leadership in world politics. Ekaterina (04/84, 4 IR) reasons that the status of a great power is one of great permanence which a state acquires over centuries and which it cannot lose so easily. Sergej even claims that being a great power is virtually inescapable for Russia:

> In fact, if Russia is fated to make a choice at some point, if it wants to exist, then it has to be a great power. To some degree, even our leadership understands this. The

> phrase that Russia must either be great or not exist at all is attributed to Vladimir Putin. ... Russia must be, and we believe that it is destined to become, a great power (Sergej, 01/71, 3 Other).

The conception that Russian great powerness is virtually ingrained in the Russian people, that Russia is destined to be a great power, is interpreted to be very prominent in Russian society and also analysed in the lectures:

> Words like "Russia – Messiah", "Russia is destined to greatness", "Russia cannot not be a great power", these mottos, these slogans, are deeply rooted in societal consciousness. And if you take the verbatim records of the Duma debates, the declarations of political writers, especially of the patriotic ones, you will see it all. This destiny of greatness is justified in different ways, starting from the assumption that Russia is the biggest country and therefore it must also be the greatest (Lecture 13/19).

Russia's tradition as an empire, its historical mentality continue to have an impact on Russian foreign policy and cannot be ignored, one lecturer argues (Lecture 02/21). Classic geopolitical reasoning plays an important role here: Russia is taken to have a history both of territorial expansion and of expansion of its sphere of influence. Russia grew significantly in territorial size, beginning from the *Kievan Rus'* up to the Russia of Yeltsin. At the same time, because of this huge territory, Russia has always had to defend itself against aggressions from the outside.

> Why are the Kuril Islands so important for Russia? They are small islands, only rock, nothing else. What is important for the Russian is the very idea of losing territory. He lives, he was born in a huge country. For him, [spatial] dimensions are very important. The loss of a small territory already causes painful reverberations. Completely imperial ambitions (Aleksandr, 14/47, 3 IR).

This geopolitical condition, it is concluded, makes for the special character of Russia as a 'land empire' (Lecture 13/9-10, 18). While it is acknowledged that many in the West disapprove of Russia's imperial ambitions, the signifier 'empire' does not seem to have negative connotations. Just like 'great power', it is a status which a state acquires through its history and which constitutes one of many forms of societal organisation, Zoja elaborates (32/70, 4 IJ). The pervasive notion of historical destiny and inevitability indicates that restoring great power status is considered a very natural thing to do, since it must belong to Russia anyway.

It is common at MGIMO to credit Evgenij Primakov with the first serious attempts at saving Russia's status as a great power after the collapse of the

Soviet Union and ending the fatal realignment with the West. Much in contrast to the Kozyrev period, his policy is positively remembered as aiming at creating a multipolar world system in which Russia should constitute an independent centre of force (Lecture 23/41). Such a line corresponds, of course, to the general notion that Russia has the potential to become a great power very soon, with a status perhaps rivalling that of the US:

> I think that Russia is not only a great power because of its nuclear weapons, not only because it is the biggest country in the world, but because it has resources, it has potential. ... With all this potential, with all these resources, being one of the main centres of scientific development in the world, I think that Russia has kept its leadership in this respect. And if we cannot definitely call it a great power now, if we cannot compare with America now, then we can at least say that in the very near future Russia will recoup this status (Andrej, 24/74-76, 4 PS).

The diversity of imaginations associated with the concept of great powerness shows how this idea is able to unify almost all facets of what Russia should be. As such, it is less a distinct geopolitical concept than an expression of patriotism, espousing a strong Russia and exhorting people to work towards this goal. Several students explicitly state that believing in Russia as a great power means being a patriot. Vitalij (28/75, 4 IR), for example, believes that people in Russia just need to be united to achieve Russia's geopolitical revival. In a similar vein, Natalija is convinced that Russia's ascent to great power status starts from within:

> Right now, everyone here fights for themselves. Man is a wolf to his fellow man and we do not yet have ... a national idea. Perhaps it is worth getting everything into order internally and then already move beyond one's borders, beyond the borders of the CIS and so on (Natalija, 29/55, 3 PS).

This patriotic inclination is also shared by lecturers, many of whom more or less openly call themselves patriots and support the mantra of a national idea. In the words of one professor, every foreign policy line needs a 'solid, big, great idea around which everything will be built' (Lecture 02/33). Another lecturer expands on this:

> In this respect Kazakhstan is a good example (*molodcy*). They do neat ideological work like in the Soviet Union: "Kazakhstan is a great power." "In Kazakhstan there is unique wealth." "The future belongs to Kazakhstan." Is that right? Excellent! This is not ideology. That's a sound, natural ideology. A man must be proud of his country and proud of being Russian. Look at the Americans, those knuckleheads (*tupye-tupye*) – but they have natural, national politics. And so should we. ... The most important

> thing is not to allow a national schism. The state, in my opinion, shows very little effort to build the image of a great Russia in society. A Russia where it does not matter which nationality you have got. Where you are just proud of living here (Lecture 61/45-46).

Here, patriotic nationalism coalesces with great power visions of Russia's role in world politics. Only if Russians stand united internally can Russia become the influential player that it aspires to externally.

It is only in rare instances that imaginations of a strong Russia draw critique. In the vast majority of cases, it is either actively promulgated or at least approved as the best way forward. Only those two students in my sample who showed a consistently pro-European and anti-Soviet attitude are openly critical of the current great power ideology – but they also qualify their critique. Igor (03/9, 4 Other) disapproves of what he found were inappropriate measures to push Russia's strength in the world at the expense of moral standards. As an illustration, he cites the recent invitation of the Hamas leadership to Moscow and compares it to the invitation of Chechen rebels to hearings on human rights violations in the European Parliament – a move which incited Russian anger. He thus does not reproach the great power idea directly but rather directs his critique at the ethics of realising it. Boris (27/13, 49, 4 IJ) voices doubts about the great power project, because he perceives it as overdone and not corresponding to the real, rather dire economic and (geo-)political situation of Russia. Instead, he offers a different idea of what constitutes a great power:

> For me a great power is primarily a state which can serve as an epitome of virtue for other states, an example of highly moral, highly cultured political relations with that country. A highly developed society which has a high self-awareness, which has its role in the world and which, finally, has good economic indicators. That's what for me is a great power (Boris, 27/49, 4 IJ).

Boris does not dismiss the great power concept for Russia. He just ascribes a meaning to it which is partly different but also, as we will see in the case of economic strength later on, not so different from that of others.

7.2 Russia's role in the post-Soviet countries

Depending on Russia

In the interpretation of Russia's position in the world the relationship with the countries of the Near Abroad represents an important part. Does the perception of this relationship somehow reflect the imagination of a rising Russia? I shall argue in the following that it does so in several ways. One central way is through the notion of dependency: the countries of the Near Abroad depend on Russia and they would be imprudent if they did not return to Russia. Among other things, this dependency was seen as finding its expression within the structure of the CIS. When I asked students, why, in their opinion, the CIS was important for Russia, it was not uncommon for them to answer that the CIS was less important for Russia than it was for the countries of the Near Abroad:

> I don't think that the CIS is necessarily important for Russia. Not as important as for the other countries of the post-Soviet camp. Because Russia is some indicator of the CIS, like the head. Without Russia the CIS will completely lose its role. So it is key (Anastasija, 20/45, 4 IR).

Russian leadership vis-à-vis the post-Soviet republics is justified on two grounds. First, the Near Abroad, as the term already indicates, is frequently regarded as still representing part of one big family. Students emphasise that all republics once were one country and that common traditions and a shared history continue to prevail. Those commonalities makes the post-Soviet states dependent on each other:

> History shows that we live badly without each other, that we are used to be together. ... That is, the republics of the CIS cannot do without us and, in fact, nor can we do significantly without them (Ljuba, 09/47, 4 IR).

What sounds here still as a rather even, equal relationship, takes the form of a unilateral dependency in several other statements. This dependency is the second reason for claiming leadership, and it is tightly interwoven with the feeling of belonging together. One lecturer sums up the peculiar relationship between Russia and the Near Abroad in the following parable, in which the post-Soviet republics play the role of the unreliable friend:

> You run a business together with your wife. And you tell your wife that your friend sells doors [in this business]. And she says: "If he sells doors, why didn't he give us our money today or tomorrow? Kick out this friend of yours. Let's hire a normal fellow who sells and brings us the returns." And you say: "No. He is my friend. We went to school together, to university. I like him, he is my brother." What conclusion can we draw? Either you are a fool or ...? (Lecture 61/19)

There are a number of interesting elements in this story. First, the general frame of market capitalism in which the value of a social relationship is judged, in this case by the wife, by the generation of profit. Second, the special relationship between the husband and the friend which transcends the narrow confines of profit orientation. Third and finally, the notion of generosity by the husband who helps a friend who is in dire straits. At the same time, the friend is dependent on the grace of the husband. He would have been kicked out by the wife if it had not been for the intervention of the husband. In this example, Russia plays the role of the generous husband. It continues to be faithful to the post-Soviet republics, it helps them in difficult times, although they are not able to pay back their dues.

The concept of the Near Abroad as a region in which countries are dependent on Russia and need its help as a strong partner is also popular with students. In the opinion of students, the countries of the Near Abroad benefit from close relations with Russia economically and politically. Ksenija (33/14, 4 Other) suspects that the countries of the CIS would not last long without Russia's support. Armenia, for example, is regarded as one of those 'poor countries which Russia always helped' (Katja, 02/11, 4 IJ). Pavel states this quite directly:

> Because it is absolutely clear that countries such as Ukraine and even Belarus would face great difficulties without Russia. They can solve their domestic problems on their own, but in the global context they are very dependent on Russia. And the series of recent events [has shown] that such self confidence is absolutely unfounded (Pavel, 06/46, 3 IJ).

The 'series of recent events' – the colour revolutions in several post-Soviet states – are difficult to understand for students: given such dependency and Russia's selfless support, why would the states of the Near Abroad seek to distance themselves from Russia? Why would Georgia hope for support from the US, when Russia as a strong and faithful partner is right across the border? (Ljuba, 09/52, 4 IR) It is only understandable, then, that the colour revolutions are framed as temporary events after which countries like Ukraine or Georgia will return into the Russian fold.

> If we look at all those colour revolutions, I don't think that this is a defeat [for Russia]. Because those republics have strong relations with Russia. And it would take at least two centuries to destroy them, in my opinion. And sooner or later they will come back under Russian influence (Dmitrij, 12/15, 3 IR).

The Orange and Rose Revolutions are thus interpreted as having the reverse effect of showing the republics how pointless their ambitions are. Nevertheless, students are somewhat indignant at the behaviour of the post-Soviet republics. Olga (30/15, 3 PS) says she would have shown Ukraine its proper place long ago and told Ukrainians how dependent they are on Russia. Ljuba claims that the post-Soviet states initially always disparage Russia but then come running back again and expect Russia to help them out:

> And they do it exactly like Georgia, on the basis of their declarations, their words, "we don't need this [Russia's support]". In the end it turns out that all of them need this, but initially you have to say something against it. And that's why for them the door is, if not open, then at least ajar, i.e. "Come to us! We help you!". And they always lock up their door, they always lock it from the other side. But very soon, I think, they will come back and look at us again (Ljuba, 09/56, 4 IR).

Here and in other statements, the image of the generous Russia again comes to the fore. It is a Russia which also displays a certain condescending attitude towards the Near Abroad, as if the countries were unruly children who needed to be disciplined and had a lot to learn in the process of growing up (Natalija, 29/29, 3 PS). When they run away or defy their parents' orders, their parents will nevertheless forgive them and, in the telling wording of Vasilij (19/55, 4 IR), 'feed them'. On the other hand, if the child is not sensible and does not regret its mischiefs, Russia can and should also withdraw its support:

> Ukraine publicly declared that it does not want to cooperate with Russia. No, not that it does not want to cooperate ... – that Russia is an unreliable country, that we do everything wrong. Why on earth should we sell them gas at a discounted price if they want to join the European Union, if they claim some supremacy? Why, if they are a strong country with a market economy, with a developing civil society? Why? Why should we grant them humanitarian aid? (Irina, 21/73, 4 PS)

Russian support, although construed as a selfless act, is therefore conditioned on the loyalty of the post-Soviet countries and on acknowledging Russia's superior status.

Re-uniting what belongs together

Talk of Russia's interests is a second way in which a rising Russia is reflected in articulations of the post-Soviet space. Russia is regarded as being implicated in manifold ways in the post-Soviet environment. Mikhail (11/61, 3 IR) argues that a significant part of the property of the post-Soviet states was built with funds from the RSFSR and that therefore Russia rightfully continues to have an interest and influence in the Near Abroad. Aleksandr (14/8, 3 IR), like several others, points out that there are still a significant number of ethnic Russians who live in the post-Soviet republics and who need to be supported. To him, it appears important that Russia plays a leading role in unifying what should belong together anyway.

> All should be united in one political space, in Eurasia. We should work together, work together more closely. That's beneficial for all. This is always beneficial for all. ... In what context, in what way this will happen is not clear yet. Maybe it will be Russia again. Russia should have the leading role, because it has the biggest assets (Aleksandr, 14/55, 3 IR).

The idea of cooperation between the states of the CIS is also reflected in the lectures. One lecturer draws on explicitly geopolitical arguments to underscore the importance of good neighbourly relations with the post-Soviet states:

> But if you don't live in peace and harmony with your next-door neighbour, then there won't come anything good of it. It is even psychologically important that those who live next to you ... And the world is built in such a way that Kazakhstan cannot just shift into third gear and drive away from Russia. Territory is territory, and geography is geography (Lecture 61/15).

The unity of the post-Soviet states is almost represented as an objective necessity in these statements. Russia's role in facilitating and guiding this unity appears to be similarly objective. The post-Soviet states are so much smaller in size and in political, military and economic significance that equal relationships seem almost impossible (Lecture 03/34). Anton (10/9, 4 IR) thinks that it is not only in Russia's interest but that it is essentially Russia's moral duty to act as a stabilising force in the post-Soviet space. This echoes the paternalistic inclinations from above which position Russia as a guardian of the Near Abroad.

Another necessity for keeping the post-Soviet states together arises from the perceived need for geopolitical security and stability in Russia's backyard. Because of its huge size, it has always been important for Russia to have loyal neighbours which help it protect its borders (Tatjana, 08/52, 4 IR). The CIS is such an instrument which could guarantee stability and cooperation for the benefit of all members (Natalija, 29/10, 3 PS). Evgenija (07/52, 4 IR) considers this all the more important now that several states have begun to break away from Russia. Given the manifold ties to the post-Soviet states, Russia has high stakes in countries like Georgia or Ukraine and cannot possibly allow them to undermine the post-Soviet unity which is so precious to Russia, Anton holds (10/3, 4 IR). This is why Russia so adamantly sticks up for its presence in this region.

> Russia cannot allow that the Kyrgyz upheavals happen every day. This destabilises. Russia simply cannot afford to have weak, uncontrollable neighbours. This is dangerous. This is the reason why Russia wishes to support political stability, even through encroaching on political freedoms, on democracy. No matter what, this is important for Russia. That's why I think that Russia will continue its attempts to build, to construct this space according to its image (Viktor, 18/11, 4 PS).

Acting as stabilising factor and unifying the post-Soviet space is invariably linked to establishing and expanding Russian influence. Maksim (17/42, 4 IR) is convinced that demonstration of Russia's political strength is directly related to the stability of post-Soviet regimes. Yet, Russian interventions like those in the wake of the riots in the Uzbek city of Andijan where Russia supported the heavy-handed, violent actions by the Uzbek government meet with open criticism by students. Although all students are convinced that Russia does not apply the rough methods of the USSR any more, the CIS is still its primary sphere of influence, 'its territory' (Andrej, 24/62, 4 PS). The Near Abroad then serves as a mirror of Russia's influence: If Russia is weak, it falls into disarray. If Russia is strong, it stands united behind it, allowing it to grow even stronger (Olga, 30/26, 3 PS; Zoja, 32/40, 4 IJ).

The re-emergence of a strong Russia is thus co-articulated with its unifying presence in the Near Abroad. But beyond this political component, representations at MGIMO portray Russian involvement in the Near Abroad also as a felt necessity and moral duty. Expanding Russian influence in the post-Soviet space, uniting the post-Soviet space, is therefore not only placed in the context of increasing Russia's geopolitical weight, but also, as the familial metaphors indicate, in the context of restoring age-old bonds. These deeply ingrained notions of dependency and unity connect to Russia's image about itself: the image of a strong Russia which functions as a guardian of its dependants and is able to re-establish the unity on which it can build its strength and security.

7.3 The West: dependence and cooperation

The idea that a strong Russia will have other states depend on it, that a strong Russia can exert influence on other states is not limited to the Near Abroad. Students also mention several ways in which Western countries have come to depend on Russia. The most frequently cited example is European energy security.

> In fact, that's what pays us. Europe and the US need us, because we supply a big part of Europe with energy resources. And the US is highly dependent on how the energy supply situation develops (Katja, 02/67, 4 IJ).

The European dependence on Russian oil and gas is not only viewed as an abundant source of revenue. More than that, it also a source of Russian influence, because it allows Russia to act independently from Western loans. Vasilij elaborates:

> But now, after a certain time, Russia rebuilds its position in the world which it had lost. In many ways, this is not connected to the economy but to the need of the West, of the Western countries, to secure supplies, to secure resources. Russia alone supplies 50 percent of resources, gas supplies to Western Europe. Above all, energy resources mean influence (Vasilij, 19/3, 4 IR).

According to Vera (35/71, 3 IR), this influence on Europe is so strong that the West did not dare to quarrel with Moscow during the Ukrainian gas dispute. The European countries were afraid that they could be hit by the same suspension of gas deliveries and therefore did not support Ukraine in its disagreement with Russia.

Beyond energy supplies, many students also regard Russia as indispensable for the functioning of world politics. Ljuba (09/66, 4 IR) thinks that although the US lays claim to the role of the global hegemonic power, it will not be able to achieve much without Russia's support. In the same vein, Igor (03/71, 4 Other) reasons that Russian strength is necessary for Europe in its attempt to become a centre of power in the world. This becomes all the more true given China's rapid rise and the overwhelming power of the US which, in Tatjana's opinion (08/63, 4 IR), leave Europe no other choice but to cooperate with Russia. In the same measure as Western countries come to depend on a strong Russia, Russia's independence increases. No longer does it have to look for Western assistance or submissively follow Western advice. Quite to the contrary, there is a growing number of situations in which Western countries ask for Russian help. Strength and independence are therefore two sides of the same coin, one presupposing the other.

Highlighting Russian strength and Western dependence does not imply a hostile or uncooperative stance towards the West, though. In fact, many students view cooperation with Europe and the US as essential. For Mila (13/81 4 IR), cooperation has become a necessity in a globalised world if states do not want to fall behind. The clarion call in the foreign policy of today's Russia is cooperation and not, like in the Soviet Union, aggressive conflict. Andrej (24/64, 4 PS) emphasises that Russia strives to always seek compromises and mediate between different interests, often neglecting its own interests. For him, this is part of what it means to be a democracy:

> I think that the first priority in our foreign policy is to preserve what Russia already has achieved. To strengthen the reputation as a country which lives according to the law, which is democratic, which seeks dialogue with any country. And it will solve all its questions, all its problems only in a peaceful way, only through dialogue, because it is interested in cooperation (Andrej, 24/9, 4 PS).

As a democratic country, Russia cannot and will not have any clashes with other democratic countries in the West (Andrej, 24/67, 4 PS). According to Mila (13/64, 4 IR), Russia has already cooperated successfully with European states in a number of instances such as in the actions against Iran's nuclear programme. International terrorism is quoted as another case in which Western states and Russia have common interests which promote cooperation.

Yet, despite this apparent willingness to cooperate, students at the same time set certain limits and conditions to cooperation. Ivan (05/74, 4 IJ), for example, agrees that cooperating with the EU in issues such as the Schengen regime or the development of a common trade policy is a desirable goal. Institutional integration, however, is assessed cautiously by him and others such as Galja.

> I think that we will never join [the EU]. And we do not need to. We will cooperate with them, get some benefit from this. Just as they will. And that's it (Galja, 23/68, 4 IR).

Cooperation with the US is viewed in a similarly self-conscious fashion by Mikhail (11/81, 3 IR). While he generally supports the idea of cooperation, it is more a cooperation between equals:

> Martin: Should Russia and the US try to cooperate?
>
> Mikhail: I think they should. Simply because the US is one centre of power and Russia is another centre of power. ... There should be permanent cooperation, consultations just like in a normal partnership (Mikhail, 11/81, 3 IR).

This self-consciousness in the relations with the West becomes also evident in actions which initially appear to be affronts vis-à-vis the West. The appreciation of the Eastern vector in Russian foreign policy, evidenced by events like the joint military manoeuvres with China, is carried through despite and sometimes even because of the critical reactions in Western countries (Lecture 05/4). Far from being perceived as an affront, for Konstantin (16/7, 4 IR) it seems only fair that through the cooperation with China Russia is giving equal weight to its partners in the East and in the West. Anton renders a similar interpretation of Russia's natural resource policy vis-à-vis other states. He maintains that what is sometimes perceived as political blackmailing is in fact the attempt at reaping the maximum benefit from the export of resources:

> Russia uses its potential, it tries to trade, it tries to get some profit. But I wouldn't say that this economic factor could be used for blackmail, for provocation. We are interested in developing this factor. And if this factor develops, the political factor will also develop. Our country is in no way interested in blackmailing these countries (Anton, 10/63, 4 IR).

Thus, in instances where Russian actions were interpreted as a confrontation or at least as a significant cooling of relations from a Western perspective, the material from MGIMO suggests that it can equally be interpreted as legitimate, assertive behaviour which aims to position Russia as an important player in world politics while still endorsing the idea of cooperation.

7.4 Economic strength

Economic development and economic interests are one of the most prominent themes at MGIMO, especially among students. This prominence seems all the more plausible when looking at students' socialisation and life trajectories. In a time when the Russian economy is booming and companies are scouring the Russian labour market for new graduates, the attention of highly qualified students at MGIMO is increasingly attracted by private business. A similar thing may be said about lecturers, who also experience first-hand the economic upturn in Russia and the new possibilities it opens up in the international arena.

The overwhelming majority of students preferred realising Russian economic interests over Russian political interests, when I asked them directly. This primacy of the economy is often justified as a new pragmatism which has supposedly replaced the ideological baggage of the Soviet Union.

> I think that Russia's position now is pragmatic and ideologically we do not look to anyone specifically. Even economically. In my opinion, the engine of history now is the economy and not ideology, religion or something else. We are pragmatic and develop the relations with our partners, with those who are ready (Ivan, 05/9, 4 IJ).

Viktor (18/5, 4 PS) similarly judges that political confrontation is 'too expensive: we don't have money for all that nonsense'. Foresighted economic policy guarantees stability and improves the welfare of Russian citizens. Only in the case of societal prosperity can a state conduct a successful domestic and foreign policy.

> I think that right now realising Russian economic interests is more important, because political interests follow them. If economic interests are more or less satisfied, then politics follows them anyway. This is inevitable. They always go together. But primarily it will be economic ones, because if people are hungry in your country, they won't support those politicians that will realise the government of the state (Oleg, 26/9, 4 IR).

> Generally speaking, politics – that's words, and economy – that's business (*delo*). It's more important to see something in practice and that's what the economy is all about (Vitalij, 28/9, 4 IR).

Anton (10/11, 4 IR) reasons that there is a lot of catch-up development ahead of Russia which spells out the need to actively promote and push those economic sectors in which Russia still has some competitive advantage. This also involves economic diversification away from the dependence on oil and gas which is perceived as merely a temporary stimulus of economic growth (Ljuba, 09/15, 4 IR).

In a very similar vein, lecturers put an emphasis on the economy, even when giving lectures about international relations or diplomacy. Putin's contribution to the economic boom in Russia is appreciated in clear distinction to the purported attitude towards Putin in the West:

> And when the West reminds us that he [Putin] was in the KGB for 15 years, then I like to emphasise something else: a deskbound career in the civil service (*činovnič'ja škola*) is never as fruitful as an entrepreneurial career. And he was deputy of Sobčak[20] and directly dealt with private enterprise. This is why the economic component, the economic part gained significantly (Lecture 01/11).

Following the successful example of Putin, students are encouraged to similarly focus on economic diplomacy as one of the most promising directions and as the foundation of political diplomacy.

> And finally to Primakov is attributed the highly important, in my view, remark that Russia's foreign policy above all should reflect its economic interests. ... The nature and tasks of foreign policy are to facilitate Russia's economic reforms, to create a conducive external environment, and to explicitly reflect and advance the interests of Russia's economic actors – of companies, financial groups – and the economic interests of Russia as a state more generally (Lecture 23/23).

This orientation towards the economy, however, does not imply that Russia should abandon its geopolitical aspirations. On the contrary, economic strength is seen as a precondition for geopolitical clout. Tatjana (08/3, 4 IR) points to the example of China in this respect. China's influence, she argues, is based on its economic power. In the same vein, Russia should strive to back up its political ambitions with economic strength. According to Tatjana, the neglect of this interplay was one of the primary reasons for the failure of the USSR to survive:

> What is the reason for the disintegration of the Soviet Union? It is because the leaders of the Soviet Union did not understand that when the economy is starting to stall, when it stops working, then one has to direct all attention not towards extending one's sphere of influence, but towards the economy. Because a strong economy means a strong politics, as Marx already said. Now we no longer believe in Marx, but this postulate remains and it is a correct statement (Tatjana, 08/11, 4 IR).

Post-Soviet Russia is taken to have learned from this experience and follow the correct order: first the economy, then politics. In this way, economic relations between countries are the foundation and can help pave the way for deeper political cooperation (Andrej, 24/4, 4 PS). The relationship between

20 The former mayor of St. Petersburg.

Russia and Europe is a case in point where many students think that common economic interests are the basis for political cooperation. To a large extent, Europe's eagerness to engage in political cooperation with Russia is attributed to its dependence on Russian oil and gas imports.

> Almost all countries benefit from relations with Russia, because we have oil. And they want this oil. And we give them oil, because unfortunately we don't have anything else to give. We have huge reserves. It is for this reason that the States, that the EU cooperate with us (Galja, 23/31, 4 IR).

Rapid economic development serves to buttress Russia's claim to a leading position in world politics. Pavel (06/9, 3 IJ) thinks that such development is long overdue in order to draw level with other countries. This is considered especially relevant within the G8 framework. Marina (34/9, 4 Other) complains that Russia is lagging behind the other G8 states by a number of indicators and concludes that Russia has to push hard to accelerate the process of catching up. Mikhail (11/3, 3 IR), on the other hand, points to Russian achievements in the past: when earlier the group was called G7+1, it is now the G8, indicating that Russia has become a full-fledged member. He mentions that he has recently looked up the GDP figures and was proud to find that the Russian GDP level has already surpassed the Canadian one.

In the competition for influence, garnering the big countries' recognition is an important element:

> Improving our economic situation, we become more important in the world arena and the big countries will turn their attention to us. ... I think that we first have to develop the economy as it is necessary, and then they will already address us in a completely different way (Galja, 23/10, 4 IR).

Economic potency not only draws the respect of the world's leading states, but it also enables Russia to play the desired role in unifying the CIS states. For some time, Tatjana argues, Russia has been unable to replace the Soviet Union as a centre of force in this respect. Russia's ambitions to stop the centrifugal tendencies in the CIS must be backed up by a corresponding economic potential:

> [W]ithout economic relations, without economic growth, it is impossible to return these republics to Russia, to tie them closer to Russia just through some political will (Tatjana, 08/3, 4 IR).

Economic strength is therefore immediately linked to the Russian great power project. Russia can be a great power if it just rebuilds its economy.

> I think that by virtue of our history we can lay claim to imperial ambitions, which for some reason are always judged negatively. I don't know why. We have a big country, but it is weak now. It is a weak empire. But I think that if it does not fall apart, it will bring its economic potential up to the level of its political potential (Zoja, 32/70, 4 IJ).

Recovering its economic potential will allow Russia to turn from an object to a subject of international relations and shape international political processes more actively: 'When we have completely got back on our feet, when we have acquired that economic power, only then can we dictate our terms' (Larissa, 15/11, 4 IR).

One of those incidents where Russia began to dictate its terms through economic measures was the gas dispute with Ukraine in 2005 and 2006, when Russia cut off Ukrainian gas supply over a disagreement about gas tariffs. In the Western press this was widely read as constituting a serious threat to European energy security and as a Russian attempt to pressurise Ukraine and punish it for the increasing dissociation from Russia in the wake of the Orange Revolution. Western coverage of this event was framed within the broader picture of Russian authoritarianism and aggressive great power behaviour. At MGIMO, the events surrounding this dispute were interpreted in a radically different way. For one thing, energy resources are regarded as the basis for Russia's current economic and political upswing and as an insurance against any conflicts over resource access. Russia's main advantage, one lecturer reasons, is its independence from energy resources which frees it from the burden of having to secure supply of such resources like in the case of the US (Lecture 03/18). Energy resources are the main foundation on which Russia's geopolitical influence in the world is built:

> Yes, Russian influence becomes big and the profit is big as long as we have oil and gas. And with its help Russia has a significant weight in decision-making processes, exerts pressure on certain countries. Many respect Russia and its opinion because it has these resources. ... I agree that Russian influence is great particularly because it has certain energy resources (Julija, 25/55, 4 PS).

When I asked students whether they thought that Russia was using its natural resources in order to achieve political aims, as in the case of Ukraine, many did not recognise the critical undertone in this question or were surprised that such a policy could be assessed negatively. For the majority, it appears quite natural to employ natural resources as a lever to achieve certain aims. Oksana (31/75, 3 Other) thinks that every big business is always linked to politics, so there is nothing surprising about this liaison. Anastasija (20/62, 4 IR) is convinced that every country would use the economic leverage it has to advance its influence in the world. Russia does not have anything else at its disposal except for oil and gas, which are currently the most effective way of advancing Russian goals:

> If Russia wants to realise only some of its political aims, then today it can only do it through oil and gas. Because we do not have any other of such global resources (Nikolaj, 22/77, 4 PS).

> Yes, we do that because Russian oil and gas are a very strong instrument in foreign policy today. Why shouldn't we use them? At the moment, we do not have a similarly strong instrument. We won't scare anyone with nuclear missiles, this is not the time now, this is not very welcome now. But oil and gas – that's very strong (Oleg, 26/68, 4 IR).

The link between natural resources as an economic instrument and their purposeful application to leverage political strength shines through very clearly. But because this link appears so natural, for Natalija there is nothing condemnable about Russian support of loyal states through discounted gas tariffs. Russia simply wants to defend its influence:

> If it [Ukraine] wants to walk down that path, please, go ahead! If they choose such a policy – independence, democratic orientation. It is another question, however, that they shouldn't rely on discounted gas prices then. That's obvious. That's what we have got. Those mechanisms of applying pressure (*ryčagi davlenija*) that we have. Yes, we are a country that relies on primary resources and our mechanism of applying pressure are pipelines. There is nothing we can do about it (Natalija, 29/29, 3 PS).

Zoja (32/68, 4 IJ) argues that a policy of backing up Russian influence with oil and gas is absolutely legitimate, since increased influence in the world means better living conditions for Russian citizens and this, after all, must be the principal aim of every state. Relatively few students assess such Russian policy more critically. Boris (27/12, 4 IJ), who generally displays a very critical attitude towards Russia's conduct in international politics, likens such behaviour to economic blackmailing and interprets it as an expression of Russia's weakness, making it desperately jump at any possibility of raising its influence.

Other students regard Russia's behaviour in the Ukrainian gas dispute as characteristic of normal market exchange: other countries need resources, Russia supplies them. Why shouldn't Russia take advantage of the benefits of such a relationship?

> Russia uses its potential, it tries to trade, it tries to get some advantage. But I wouldn't say that this economic factor can be misused in the context of any political intimidation or any provocation (Anton, 10/64, 4 IR).

The increase in gas tariffs is contextualised as a reform which is aimed at introducing a market economy which applies to relations with every state in the CIS. Gas tariff hikes are framed within the natural transition to market prices in which Russia only seeks to maximise the profit from the export of natural resources and treats everyone equally: 'the only goal is to get earnings and not political pressure' (Maksim, 17/71, 4 IR).

> It's not Russia's fault that there is oil and gas on its territory. And it's not Russia's fault that they aren't on the territory of Europe, for example. Europe is dependent as far as oil and gas are concerned. I think that Russia acts from an economic position and does not try to exert any influence. Even our minister of foreign affairs says that since the 1990s a market economy has developed in Russia. And now we try, just as the West has taught us, as America has taught us, we try to act according to market laws. That's normal. We sell, we receive money and we do not try to exert any influence (Larissa, 15/79, 4 IR).

In this interpretation, Russia is following the prescriptions for economic reform, issued by Western countries, and now is reproached by the very countries which asked for this reform. They do not seem to be willing to grant Russia the right to reap the full economic benefit from its resources, which would help it rebuild the country. This is regarded as an unfair treatment, given that some already perceive that Russia is selling off its riches to those states without benefiting adequately from them. Soon, Marina (31/67, 4 Other) fears, Russia will run out of resources. If this happens and Russia has not set up its economy by then, Russia's great power aspirations will simply collapse: 'If we don't do anything for the development of our economy, our greatness will fade away' (Anton, 10/74, 4 IR).

Placing high priority on the economy at MGIMO, economic aspects are co-articulated with geopolitical aspects of Russian identity construction in a way that sees the economy as conducive to (re-)gaining the geopolitical position Russia aspires to. Economic strength is thus not an aim in itself but is rather bound up with geopolitics. In order for Russia to regain its position as a strong state, economic recovery is essential. Successful development is thus not only judged against the realisation of political goals but also against economic prosperity. This is summed up in a statement by Anastasija:

> Russia rather tries to become a political than an economic leader. It is good, of course, that their economy is highly developed. But nevertheless, what is most important for them, in my opinion, is the political interest. In order to lead in the post-Soviet space and gain more advanced positions, in the West, in the East, everywhere (Anastasija, 20/9, 4 IR).

7.5 Russia's special position

A unique country: between East and West

Articulations of Russian strength are complemented by articulations of Russian independence. A strong Russia is also an independent Russia which does not look to others for orientation. It is neither East nor West but something special in between and therefore should not align itself with either of the two sides. One lecturer observes that Russia's distinctiveness is often derived from its intellectual succession to the Byzantine empire as a 'Third Rome'. This hereditary line maps out a special destiny for Russia and also accounts for its sometimes obfuscated, wavering diplomacy. Russia has taken over from Byzantine

> a certain deviousness (*dvoemyslie*), a certain tendency towards opaque moves, towards closed diplomacy and so on. We do one thing, think another, talk about a third (Lecture 13/3).

In support of this special position, Winston Churchill is quoted as saying that he 'cannot forecast the actions of Russia. It is a riddle, wrapped in a mystery, inside an enigma' (Lecture 13/2). This lecturer approvingly refers to the air of mystery in which Russia is shrouded in this statement and links it to the age-old traditions of Russian diplomacy and the specific historical trajectory of the Russian empire. Explaining Russia's distinctiveness in greater detail, he operates with the popular term 'Russian specificity' (*russkaja specifika*). Although cautioning against the assumption that Russia was unique, he nevertheless highlights a number of 'permanent Russian specificities' and talks about their historical continuity. The huge size of the Russian territory is one of the most salient of Russian specificities in his view. To a large degree it determines Russian culture and makes for the pioneer spirit which is still present in Russia:

> A trip from one end of the country to the other, for example from Murmansk to Vladivostok, is still an extreme sport. It belongs to the category of extreme tourism. You need an off-road vehicle. But just crossing like, for example, from New York to San Francisco does not work. ... There is a pioneer spirit, a spirit of claiming territory, and in this sense the age of claiming the Wild West, that's our Far East, continues (Lecture 13/47-48).

The assumed fact that Russia is still struggling with claiming land and establishing control over territory is linked to the second Russian specificity of vertical power (*vertikal'naja vlast'*). Vertical power, the centralisation of political power at the national level, is seen as typical and necessary for Russia, given its peculiar territorial constitution: Russian territorial expansion and cohesion could only be realised through a strong central government. Propagating a Western idea of democracy is therefore not appropriate for Russia, Andrej (24/26, 4 PS) holds. Western-led democratisation may have worked in Yugoslavia or the Baltic states, but it is doomed to fail in Russia because of its 'huge territory, very strong influence of traditions, culture, local specificities' (Andrej, 24/26, PS). Russian culture is portrayed as highly resistant to any outside change or influence:

> There has to pass a lot of time for something to change. Really a lot – more than a hundred years. Because this culture, this mentality is very strong in our consciousness. Russia has been in close contact with Europe for several hundred years and nothing particular has changed from this (Oleg, 26/65, 4 IR).

Russia's specificities not only make it unique among other states, though. They also afford an advantage in negotiating relations with other states:

> Moreover, we are the biggest country ... and we unite what at first glance cannot be united: people of different faith, people of different nationality and territories which are completely different in their stage of development, their economic level, their cultural development. And this makes us strong to a certain degree, because we know how to act in relations with other countries, because we learn this within our country. This really has an influence and gives us a great advantage over other states (Ljuba, 09/9, 4 IR).

Independence from and influence on other states thus come together in the conception of Russian uniqueness. Above all, this uniqueness finds its clearest expression in how Russia's interstitial position on the Eurasian continent is construed.

> We are a Euro-Asian country. Even the eagle on our crest looks into two different directions, to Europe and to Asia, and in our country Europe and Asia are interlaced. This is why we are such a unique country. And that's why it is so difficult for us to choose one path of development. We are torn back and forth. Depending on the changing conditions we should not rely on anyone, because there is no other such country. There are European countries, there are Asian ones and we, we combine them. We are in between (Marina, 34/64, 4 Other).

> [Russia] is neither a European nor an Eastern country. I think that it is a separate civilisation, as Gumilëv said, which combines elements of the East and the West, i.e. Asian and European elements (Vera, 35/73, 3 IR).

One aspect of this Eurasian character, of course, is Russia's geographical location, on the one side sharing common borders with the EU and NATO, on the other side with China, Japan and Alaska. The location and size of the country do not allow, do not even make it desirable to speak of Russia as being a European or an Asian country: 'Russia is supposed to be, where it is', Mila is convinced (13/68, 4 IR).

A second aspect is Russian history, which is perceived to have taken a trajectory very different from that of either Europe or Asia.

> I think that Russia is Russia. There is such an opinion that Russia is neither East nor West, that Russia is Russia. And that's really so. And not only because one part of our country is in Europe and the other one in Asia. That's all not because of this, but because of our historical development. We have always gone our way and will probably continue to do so, sometimes of course leaning more towards Europe in some issues. But generally we have our own development path (Ljuba, 09/61, 4 IR).

While students acknowledge that there were times when Russian and European history were intertwined, most of them employ this statement to support a claim of Russian difference from Europe rather than a claim of similarity. Such difference is further reinforced by the argument that Russia is a multi-confessional and multi-ethnic state and as such differs from European states. Konstantin (16/67, 4 IR) argues that the very fact that Russia is an observer state in the Organisation of the Islamic Conference sets it apart from Europe. Moreover, he emphasises that Russia also has a strong a Buddhist presence, which makes out the case for its affinity with Asia. One lecturer speaks out against Russia's alleged 'European choice' and points out Russia's unique cultural constitution:

> And strolling around in Moscow, look at St. Basil's Cathedral in order to understand that in the best case on the banks of the Kazanka River, that is in Kazan', a city that's older than Moscow .... stroll around in those quarters and you will understand that you are somewhere on the edge of Eastern Europe. Moreover, don't forget that there are more Muslims in Moscow than in Damascus. ... If we say that architecture is culture, ... then anything can happen here, for any flavour. Both the European or almost European Petrograd and the completely Asian suburbs of any big industrial centre which Russians, who have a penchant for self-mockery, call "Shanghai" (Lecture 15/1).

Some students claim that there is also an everyday cultural difference between Russia and Europe. Vitalij (28/73, 4 IR) believes that a Russian would find it rather boring to live in Europe: according to him, there is a certain kind of spontaneity in Russians that they would not find in Europe, where life tends to be very structured and organised. A similar sentiment is shared by Galja:

> Honestly, I have never thought of myself as European. And I do not think of myself as Asian. Always something in between. Well, Europe. I was in the EU, I was in Germany. Absolutely different countries, different people. I never thought of myself as belonging to a European country (Galja, 23, 70-72, 4 IR).

Russia's distinctiveness demands, of course, an equally distinctive kind of foreign policy, as one lecturer claims (Lecture 13/44). The Western-centric policy of the early 1990s is evaluated critically by both students and lecturers. Lecturers regularly highlight the greater gains from improved relations with countries like China or India in comparison to relations with the US and support expanding the Eastern vector in Russian foreign policy (Lecture 31/2). By the same token, joint military manoeuvres with China and the flourishing economic relations between the two countries are judged as one of the major recent achievements of Russian foreign policy strategy (Lecture 31/5). Compared to this new situation, the Western vector in Russian foreign policy had been greatly exaggerated in the past and did not correspond to Russia's 'true' geopolitical identity:

> Earlier, after the fall of the USSR, there were very strong tendencies towards the West, very strong pro-Western sentiments. Gradually they took a lot of dollars, exaggerated ... very much Western values, perceived everything very uncritical. There were a lot of good things, of course, in the West. But we must not forget that the

> Russian state always lived in the East *and* in the West. We necessarily need an Eastern component (Aleksandr, 14/14, 3 IR).

Nowadays, Russia's foreign policy is taken to be more successful in living up to this unique position and trying to balance East and West. In this position Russia can serve as a bridge between East and West by mediating conflicts and in so doing expand its geopolitical role by having partners in both parts of the world. Its special status allows Russia not to decide on one direction but rather to flexibly draw on the best of both worlds. After all, Vera (35/37, 3 IR) argues, Russia would be ill-advised to take over elements from the East which do not fit its European orientation, or elements from the West which do not fit its Eastern orientation.

Occupying a position in-between other blocks is by no means perceived to be an easy task. Other states sometimes fail to recognise Russia's interstitial identity:

> At the same time, some countries do not see us as an Asian country and other countries do not see us as a European country. That is, on the one hand such a situation between two worlds is comfortable for us, on the other hand it is uncomfortable. Because when we ask, for example, if they accept us into APEC, questions come up, why do you want to be there, you are not an Asian state (Ekaterina, 04/13, 4 IR).

In a world where everyone forges alliances Russia feels increasingly urged to decide on one direction: East or West.

> This pressure on us, does Russia have to make a decision? Because the international environment after 1991 opened up great chances for our reconciliation (*uregulirovanie*) in foreign policy. Perhaps it is worth strengthening our status as a not so small state with big potential and good perspectives? Today we have the material chance to play on many tennis courts. To play, not jeopardising relations with anyone, keeping up good relations with all (Lecture 02/25).

Other states do not seem to tolerate such a position, though, and try to sway Russia on their side. Europe, Ljuba (09/11, 4 IR) argues, wants Russia to support the European policy line, but this would entail abandoning Russian interests in the East. In order to withstand such outside pressure and defend its independence, Russia must become stronger: 'the more powerful a state, the more independent it will be' (Lecture 02/23). At this point the mutual interdependence between independence and strength comes clearly to the fore: geopolitical strength is a necessary pre-condition for living up to Russian ideas of geopolitical independence and uniqueness, and vice versa.

A sovereign, independent pole in a multipolar world

Independence is a key idea around which Russian self-conception at MGIMO revolves. The Russian leadership, it is held, wants to make Russia an independent country with interests that it can pursue independently and without having to take into account interests of others. In the words of Vera (35/3, 3 IR), Russia is a self-sufficient (*samodostatočnaja*) country. For this reason, integration of Russia into international organisations or regional associations is assessed very cautiously. In a lecture, one student critiques the idea of Russia's joining the EU:

> I want to say that there is no sense in Russia joining the EU, because Russia itself has to become a centre of force. Because all who accede join the EU as a centre of force. But Russia itself has to form something around itself, they should join Russia, this integration in the context of the CIS. That is, Russia should attract others and not the other way round (Lecture 14/74).

Students and lecturers alike fear that as a member state of the EU Russia would never be accepted as a leading player. If Russia were to participate in international integration, it would only be 'with the rights of the core, of the key integrator, of the centre of integration, but not in any other role' (Lecture 15/3). Russia thus wants to keep its independent role and should therefore act as a second global player beside Europe. Such a position resonates in the statement of another lecturer who explains Russia's reluctance to join international organisations:

> Today we cannot and indeed should not join any long-term coalitions or unions. Because in such coalitions with strong partners we can only play the part of the junior partner. But our political mentality does not allow us to do this (Lecture 05/10).

Galja (23/74, 3 IR) sums this attitude up, when she says that she is for cooperation with other states but against integration. Russia should not try to push its status by joining the ranks of organisations in order to receive some benefit, but it should rather work on its own to achieve something. This way, Russia will not have any obligations vis-à-vis other states that it needs to fulfil. In this light, Aleksandr (14/75, 3 IR) reads the gas dispute with Ukraine as a Russian measure of freeing itself from earlier obligations in order to be able to act more independently in the international arena. According to Anastasija (20/3, 4 IR), Russia now no longer wants to play the role of a subject of the West, the US or Europe, but rather that of an active mediator.

Defending Russian independence is often framed as taking seriously Russian national interests in foreign policy. According to one lecturer, when Russia declared itself a democracy in the early 1990s, this conjured up 'a somewhat idyllic picture of the world' (Lecture 23/30) in which every democratic state lives in harmony with other democratic states. This illusionary vision prompted the incongruous neglect of Russia's national interests and precipitated Russia's decline in the international arena, he argues. Seeking to side with other states comes at the expense of one's own independence and runs the risk of being ignored as a separate actor in international relations (Lecture 05/23). Russia has national interests which are frequently incompatible with those of other states and defending them is crucial if Russia wants to recoup.

The idea of independence voiced in these statements applies in different measure to Russia's relationship with stronger and with weaker states. While Russia seeks to defend its independence vis-à-vis stronger states, it does not grant the same right of self-determination to smaller states. A central idea of Russia's becoming a separate pole in a multipolar world is the attraction of the post-Soviet states to this pole. By setting up this bipolar opposition of integration (for small, weak states) versus independence and sovereignty (for strong, big states), Russia's only choice, of course, remains independence. The need for Russia to keep its sovereignty is beyond question:

> It has to be said immediately that if the problem of sovereignty within this or another integration movement, for example the EU, if the preservation of a scope of sovereignty is a topic for discussion, for referenda and negotiations, then Russia does not have such a problem. If money were printed for us somewhere in London and if it were called not roubles but somehow else – the national consciousness has an unequivocal attitude towards this (Lecture 15/3).

For Russia it is virtually inconceivable, this lecturer holds, to give away its sovereignty to some supranational body for important decisions to be taken somewhere else and by somebody else. Anastasija (20/56, 4 IR) and Andrej (24/10, 4 PS) see Europe as meddling too much with Russian affairs already: Europe criticises Russia for human rights abuse, violations of freedom of press and its domestic policy more generally. In their view, however, Russia is entitled to conduct its domestic affairs in whatever way it wants to. The pressure Europe applies to Russia is therefore not justified and Russia should remain stubborn in fending off all outside attempts to interfere with its domestic policy: 'basically [Russia] will do, what it wants to do' (Anastasija, 20/56, 4 IR).

This image of Russia as a sovereign democracy ties up with the idea of independence: it involves Russia defending its right to make its own decisions and places it as one of a number of poles of power in international relations (Lecture 03/12). The imagination of a multipolar world order is pitted against a unipolar configuration which would entail American hegemony.

> The concept of a unipolar world is a concept oriented towards the US; this was after the end of the Cold War. The position of a unipolar world is somewhat lop-sided. It is not an ideal position. It is a position according to which all countries have to follow the US. ... A multipolar world allows equal opportunities, opportunities of economic and political character. Opportunities of equal cooperation (Anton, 10/6, 4 IR).

Natalija (29/8, 3 PS) similarly thinks that a multipolar world is more just insofar as it allows to adequately take into account the interests of every member. For both students and lecturers at MGIMO it appears to be a matter of fact that the world should be multipolar. In the view of one lecturer, a unilateral hegemony always provokes responses which seek to contain and oppose it and Russia should actively support such responses (Lecture 04/2). The vision a multipolar world is thus construed in such a way as to grant Russia the position it seeks to occupy. It reflects the key tenets of strength and independence which characterise Russian geopolitical identity at MGIMO by mapping out a special position for Russia in world politics.

7.6 Conceptual reflection: Russia as a strong and independent power

The vision of Russia as a strong and independent state is linked to a multitude of ideas about Russia's role and place in world politics and its relations to other states. A strong Russia is a sovereign state; it is neither East nor West but unique in its constitution; it unifies the post-Soviet space; it defends Russian national interests; it means economic prosperity; it upholds national pride; it regains global influence and respect. The idea of a strong Russia is therefore able to unify a seemingly disparate field of different demands, ranging from the economy to nationalist pride and foreign policy. At the same time the idea of a strong Russia becomes essentially amorphous: it does not have any intrinsic meaning but is defined by the demands inscribed on it.

This process of emptying is characteristic for what Laclau (1996: 36) calls empty signifiers – signifiers without a signified. Empty signifiers collapse all differences into chains of equivalence. This unifying effect of a 'strong Russia' is only possible due to its emptiness which makes it possible to insert this signifier into a system of differences. As the meaning of other signifiers becomes partially fixed in relation to the empty signifier, the chain of equivalence begins to structure an ever greater part of the social. This results in the emergence of a discourse in which the flow of differences is arrested around privileged discursive centres that institute definite meanings – empty signifiers that have become nodal points within hegemonic discourses (Laclau and Mouffe 1985: 112). The presence of empty signifiers, and their articulation as nodal points, is thus the very condition for the emergence of hegemonic discourses (Laclau 1996: 43). Hegemony can then be understood as

> the expansion of a discourse ... into a dominant horizon of social orientation and action by means of articulating unfixed elements into partially fixed moments in a context crisscrossed by antagonistic forces (Torfing 1999: 101).

The success of the hegemonic project of a strong Russia is predicated on the ability of various forces to claim to fill the empty signifier of 'strong Russia'. Given the range of different demands projected onto the idea of a strong Russia, the project seems to be rather successful as a unifying force. Even those lecturers and students who are critical of some associations with the idea of strong Russia are hesitant to repudiate it completely. Instead, they suggest different criteria, inscribe different demands, on this signifier. This speaks to the ability of the empty signifier to cancel differences: there is hardly anyone who would reject the project of a strong Russia. Slavophiles interpret it as the reassertion of Russian influence in the Near Abroad; Westernists see it as an attempt to make Russia a full-fledged member of the global group of leading states; supporters of an Asian orientation find cooperation with China the best chance to leverage Russian growth; and those who are primarily concerned with market reform and economic development see it as conducive to bolstering a rising Russia. The concept of a strong Russia is thus a concept everyone can identify with.

Hegemonic projects serve to fill the voids left by structural dislocations such as the collapse of the Soviet Union described in the previous chapter (Laclau 1990). As such, hegemonic projects are characterised by a radical historicity in that they frequently reference the dislocatory experience. This is also a characteristic feature of the strong Russia discourse at MGIMO. The emergence of a strong Russia is almost always imagined as a *re*-emergence. Russia does not acquire a new quality, but returns something that had been lost. This idea of restoration reflects the feeling of loss discussed in the previous chapter and establishes a historical continuity. In this sense, it heals the abrupt social rift, caused by the dislocation of the Soviet collapse, by emphasising the element of stability and continuity: the continuity of the post-Soviet states and Russia belonging together; the continuity of Russia as a great power and the continuity of Russia's independence. In the same vein, notions of other states depending on Russia can be interpreted as the articulation of a reversal of the situation at the beginning of the 1990s, when shame was expressed that Russia was unable to keep its domestic affairs in good order, let alone exert influence on the international stage. While earlier it was Russia which depended on the good will of others, in the hegemonic geopolitical project this relationship is envisioned the other way round: other countries now start to look towards Russia for orientation.

When we talk about the discourse of a strong Russia as a hegemonic project, we should, however, be careful not to equate this with a fully constituted hegemonic identity. For one thing, such an assumption would eclipse that we witness but an emerging hegemony in which the logic of difference has not been completely replaced by the logic of equivalence. In the production of geopolitical identities at MGIMO the logic of equivalence plays a central but not the only role. Cooperation with the West, for example, is not ruled out and even thought of as desirable in many contexts. For another, every hegemony presupposes the existence of antagonistic forces, since no discourse is ever able to fully suture the social. No hegemony is ever complete or unopposed but rather carries within it a perpetual lack, a perpetual blockage of its full realisation. This antagonism is the last and crucial building block in the identification with a strong Russia at MGIMO.

8

Antagonism: danger and exclusion

8.1 Western alienation of the post-Soviet states

Articulations of a strong Russia in the world encompass the loyalty of the post-Soviet states as an important building block of Russian geopolitical identity. A strong and independent Russia must be able to tie the post-Soviet republics to itself, thus reversing or at least compensating the loss of the Near Abroad after the dissolution of the Soviet Union. It is not uncommon for students to see the countries of the Near Abroad as somehow rightfully belonging to Russia. Threatening to severe this close link between Russia and the post-Soviet states, however, is the imminent danger of their dissociation.

> There are no direct threats [to Russia] except for, perhaps, Ukraine now. We have big problems with it. Georgia. The Baltic states, for example. These are our own, our former countries and relations, after all! (Larissa, 15/26, 4 IR)

The dichotomy between aspiration, i.e. the post-Soviet states with Russia, and reality, i.e. many post-Soviet states dissociating themselves from Russia, creates a feeling of alienation. This alienation manifests itself primarily in what is seen as an inadequate, disrespectful behaviour of those states towards Russia.

Ukrainian alienation is probably perceived as the most acute event. Some students have lived in Ukraine, have Ukrainian relatives or even are of Ukrainian nationality. Their assessment of the situation thus carries a markedly personal undertone. Maksim (17/51, 4 IR) went to school in Ukraine and remembers the time when Ukrainian was made compulsory as the language of instruction at all Ukrainian school. This even applied to regions where the vast majority of people was Russian. He recalls how hard it was for him and his school mates to suddenly study and think in a new language which had been imposed on them from outside. To him, the events following the Orange Revolution in

Ukraine are but a continuation of this broader tendency to seek greater distance from Russia.

There is the impression among some students and lecturers at MGIMO that, seeking greater distance, Ukraine has also begun to show disrespectful behaviour towards Russia. Instead of valuing a close, friendly relationship with Russia, Ukraine sows discord and seeks to maximise its own benefit at Russia's expense. Ukrainians are, as Anton (10/59-60, 4 IR) asserts, claiming to free themselves from Russian oppression. They are threatening to take over the lighthouses of the Russian Black Sea Fleet, located on Ukrainian territory, despite long-term lease agreements between Russia and Ukraine and to expel the Black Sea Fleet from its main port of Sevastopol. Ukrainian diversion of Russian gas transiting across Ukrainian territory is another major cause for construing alienation. Again, familial metaphors are used by one lecturer to describe the relationship between Russia and Ukraine. In the narration, a man commissions his friend to sell doors for him, an analogy to Russia commissioning Ukraine to sell its gas. But the friend tries to cheat:

> You know that Ukraine, over many years, has illegally diverted gas. This illegal diversion, depending on the source, is worth between 1.5 and 4 billion dollars. You can imagine the situation: you have gas. You manufacture furniture, doors. But you don't have any time to sell them and you tell your friend: "Sell the doors for me, I don't have any time to do this." And suddenly your friend all the time returns only half of the value of those doors to you. He finds different reasons, for example that the car broke down. For how long will you tolerate such a friend? (Lecture 61/18).

The expected answer to this rhetorical question is, of course, "not for very long!". Ukraine, and in the same vein all other post-Soviet states which follow a similar path, are thus morally ostracised as not deserving of Russian friendship. They are portrayed as constantly trying to play on Russia and only pursuing their own benefit while ignoring the age-old bonds of friendships that tie them to Russia.

The newly created difference between Russia and the post-Soviet states, however, is primarily attributed to the presence of a Western antagonistic force and not to the post-Soviet states themselves.

> Ukraine is not the only example. It is one of many examples of countries which had a tradition of cooperation with Russia, but they saw a great advantage in the US, in the West and changed to their side (Julija, 25/41, 4 PS).

For the vast majority of students at MGIMO it is clear that the driving cause for the Orange Revolution was American and Western European involvement. Nikolaj (22/63, 4 PS) reasons that it was an accurately planned and executed spectacle which Ukrainians would never have been able to engineer themselves. It was Western NGOs which wrote the script and orchestrated the actions. A similar stance is expressed by Tatjana:

> In my opinion, the role of the US is very significant, because the foreign hand is immediately visible in how the campaign was designed, because this would never have dawned upon the Ukrainians themselves. The PR campaign was so meticulously planned that there is already something Western European in it. Maybe German brains played a role, because there was such a precision of execution, such coherent action. There are no revolutionary traditions in Ukraine. Where do the people come from who know how to do what? And there is such an impression that this was not a first time action. This is why I think that the US and Western Europe contributed their parts (*vnesli svoju leptu*) (Tatjana, 08/58, 4 IR).

Having been washed into power through the revolutionary uprising, the Ukrainian government now appears to be acting in a rather clueless fashion. Bereft of immediate Western support, Ukraine is in 'full delirium' (Ljuba, 09/54-56, 4 IR): one government crisis follows the next and economic growth has declined sharply. In Marina's view, it is ill-founded to hope for America or Western Europe to help Ukraine out in such a situation. Russia would have been the more adequate partner but the post-Soviet states turned their backs on it:

> That's the states which now notoriously demand independence. They claim that we impose our interests on them, our policy. But if you use your fuel, our services, you cannot completely abstract yourselves. We were one state, you cannot simply deny your own past, adopt such a stupid policy, hoping on the US, which, by and large, is not interested in them (Marina, 34/19, 4 Other).

The lack of serious Western interest in the Near Abroad is contrasted to Russia's commitment as a sincere partner. Despite this purported absence of earnest Western care about the post-Soviet states, it is nevertheless readily assumed that Western influence played a crucial part in the colour revolutions.

> Nobody has any doubts that this task was posed by Western countries, above all the US, naming it for some reason a revolution, Orange Revolution, Rose Revolution, that is, the establishment of democratic regimes which are controlled by and will conduct their policy together with the policy of the US. Here we have a very obvious influence of the West (Vasilij, 19/57, 4 IR).

The evidence for this 'obvious influence' is constructed as common knowledge. Although the role of the West is difficult to prove, everyone, I am told, knows about it. It is taken to be a well-known matter of public fact in Russia that the West paid protesters to march for Juščenko's party and funded the campaign of the Orange Revolution. This wide-spread belief in the involvement of Western forces in the colour revolutions is also addressed in one lecture in which the professor ridicules the colour revolutions:

> [These people] explain that you only have to look at those botanic revolutions, or at the horticultural revolutions or at the flower revolutions as they call them. Lemon revolution, saffron revolution. All those revolutions cannot do without Western NGOs. The West, in fact, is at work. It is just that in the closed Soviet society we did not know how the West worked against us (Lecture 62/4).

Although he renders this an external point of view which he merely describes, it becomes clear from the context that he has great sympathy for such an interpretation. Natalija (29/19, 3 PS) also professes that she would like to lay the blame for the recent evens in Ukraine on the West but that she will not do it, since this is not 'politically correct'. In any case, Ivan (05/57, 4 IJ) claims, it will not be a big surprise for Russia if countries like Ukraine or Georgia join NATO and, to put it in Ivan's words, 'trade in their Kalašnikovs for M16s', the NATO assault rifle. Such an event would mere formalise the hitherto informal presence of Western influence in the post-Soviet space.

Through supporting the centrifugal tendencies in the post-Soviet states, the West is negotiated into an antagonistic role vis-à-vis Russia. Both factions are vying for influence, they are 'pulling the blanket back and forth between each other' (peretjagivajut drug na druga odejalo) (Julija, 25/16, 4 PS). The expansion of Western, especially American, influence in Eastern Europe and Central Asia is taken to lead to a collision with Russian geopolitical interests: there is a rivalry between Russia and the US over who becomes the main reference point in the post-Soviet states.

> They try to draw away those countries from the Russian sphere of influence. What is more, they do this with completely uncivilised methods, with forceful ones, for example (Mikhail, 11/46, 3 IR).

> All ex-republics of the CIS are rushing to follow the West, joining NATO or joining the EU. There is a constant tendency of dissociation from Russia, of diminishing the Russian influence on these states (Tatjana, 08/3, 4 IR).

According to one lecturer, NATO and the West are unwilling to acknowledge the Collective Security Treaty Organisation (CSTO) as a CIS counterpart to NATO. They prefer to refer to the post-Soviet states as 'Newly Independent States', thus emphasising that these states can look in both directions – both towards Russia and towards the West: 'You must understand. There is a certain rivalry: Who beats whom? (*Kto kogo?*)' (Lecture 41/2). Konstantin says that the post-Soviet states

> do not want to orient themselves towards Russia, because they are offered better conditions, for example by the US. It [the US] invests money there in order to drag them into its sphere of influence. This is not in Russia's interest. This is again linked to the expansion of NATO in Western Europe. I mean Ukraine, Belarus, the Baltic countries. And the new American army bases in Central Asia. All this affects Russia very badly (Konstantin, 16/51, 4 IR).

It is worth noting how, in this statement, a number of geopolitical developments are tied together to generate the general impression of a unitary Western,i.e. NATO or American, force separating the Near Abroad from Russia. The most obvious example of the presence of this force is Georgia. Asking students to explain Georgian president Saakashvili's recent critical statements regarding Russia provoked highly emotional reactions.[21] Many felt offended or hurt by Saakashvili's denouncing Russia as an 'unreliable country', all the more since they felt that Russia had always been true to Georgia and granted Georgia its support when the country was in dire straits.

> He [Saakashvili] cannot possibly find a more reliable partner for his country than Russia. Because it is the most influential country in that region, because it is the biggest and that which has always supported Georgia. If he continues with such statements, he won't achieve anything good. He hopes that the US is going to come and help Georgia and so on. But that won't happen (Ljuba, 09/52, 4 IR).

It is little surprising, then, that Larissa (15/58, 4 IR) regards Saakashvili as an ambassador of the United States and accuses him of being paid for his insults directed at Russia. This move construes the force alienating Georgia from Russia as originating outside of Georgia. It sets up a clash not between the defecting brother states and Russia but between Russia and the West. Western influence in the post-Soviet states therefore not only fuels alienation, but it also acts as an antagonistic force to a strong Russia.

---

21 NB: This was before the war in South Ossetia in August 2008.

Saakashvili's offensive statements are not only seen as indicative of the schism between Russia and Georgia, but they point to the wider confrontation of Russian and US interests, as Nikolaj (22/57, 4 PS) puts it. Luring the post-Soviet states away from Russia is merely a pre-condition for a more comprehensive attempt at containing or countering Russia, perhaps, as one lecturer suggest, even leading up to a new Cold War over Eastern Europe, fought between Russia and Western Europe. For Marina, a clash between Russia and the West in Eastern Europe is obvious:

> There is now a fight between the US and Russia, particularly in Georgia, Ukraine, that is, these countries want to become separate, want to be completely independent, hoping on the support of the US, not understanding that the US is far and we are near. That, if something happens, like it always does, particularly Ukraine and Georgia pursue a very imprudent policy, absolutely not appreciating the real situation and hoping for the US, which in fact exploits them in order to come closer to Russia's borders, in order to control. They are only pawns, marionettes, they can drop them at any time (Marina, 34/14, 4 Other).

This is perhaps the clearest expression of both the idea of alienation of the region that should rightfully belong to Russia and the connection of this alienation to Western antagonism. For Russia, of course, the advance of the West in Eastern Europe needs to be dammed and halted, not least because it threatens to undermine Russian authority in this region.

> Of course, Russia does not want to lose its positions. This is Eastern Europe, after all. Of course, it somehow has to strike an agreement with Ukraine, but I think that it won't play some minor role. Conversely, it will apply some tough measures and try to reclaim what belongs to it and restore its influential role (Anastasija, 20/51, 4 IR).

Some acknowledge, however, that Russia faces difficulties living up to its desired role. It failed to push through its candidate in the Ukrainian presidential elections, which diminished its geopolitical credibility (Aleksandr, 14/59, 3 IR). Especially, US foreign policy in Eastern Europe seems to be more effective than the Russian one:

> What is the difference between Russian and American foreign policy? The Russians are used to do everything with the axe, everything very directly. They started to shout: the facts of violation, what do they do, these Orange Revolutions and so on. They just shouted too much. The Americans calmly, everything very quietly, did not send anyone there to shout. They just gave some 200 billion or million dollars as humanitarian help. Everything quietly, and who won in the end? (Vera, 35/16, 3 IR).

Given this success, Western-driven alienation of what are frequently perceived as Russian brother states poses a subversive potential to Russian geopolitical identity. It threatens to challenge the hegemonic articulation of a strong, independent Russia by exposing its impossibility. If the West is successful in seducing the Near Abroad, the project of a strong Russia will be doomed to fail.

8.2 Threats to Russia

NATO

Potential threats to Russia surface prominently in a number of contexts, not least in the Western alienation of the Near Abroad. This alienation is directly linked to the expansion of NATO as the primary source of threat. Possible NATO membership of Georgia and Ukraine thus increases the level of tension for Russia:

> This will be yet another threat for Russia's security. NATO members have besieged Russia from all sides, so to speak. That cannot not cause discomfort. Because NATO after all is a military block, established against the USSR. Hostile, more or less. Of course this is a threat, a danger. ... A big one (Aleksandr, 14/65, 3 IR).

In this opposition to NATO, Russia implicitly is construed as an heir to the USSR and not as a possible partner or even member of NATO. Because of this imagined opposition, the Orange and Rose Revolutions are at the same time a threat to Russia, since they carry the possibility of the establishment of NATO influence in the immediate vicinity of Russia. With the membership of the Baltic countries, NATO has already accepted those states as members which have always been critical of Russia. If Ukraine and Georgia are accepted, Russia cannot help but get the impression that NATO expansion is somehow directed against Russia:

> NATO expansion in Eastern Europe – this is a separate topic, because NATO administration has declared that the purpose of expansion is not an aggression against Russia. But if, for example, Ukraine, if it also seeks to become a member, just as Georgia, and Ukraine has already transferred its radar stations on the Crimea... And this already means that one part of the Russian Black Sea coast has been left open. The sky over Russia has been left open. Our military potential will mend this gap, but we need resources for this and so on.

> What does the admission of the Baltic (*pribaltijskix*) states mean? Not one of the Baltic states is a member of the Nuclear Non-Proliferation Treaty, which was signed long ago. This means that in theory – unlikely that this will happen in practice – nuclear weapons can be deployed on their territory. That is, just 30 kilometres from St. Petersburg. This not only affects Russia's geopolitical interests, for example a reduction of the sphere of influence of Russia. We would talk about this, if there were bases in the Near East or in Afghanistan, for example. But if they appear on Russia's borders, then we already talk about Russia's immediate security (Tatjana, 08/44, 4 IR).

Here, one of the key features of the constructed polar pair of threat and security comes to the fore: it is based on imagining what threats *might* be possible. In Tatjana's imagination above (note that she uses the Soviet term *pribaltijskij* to refer to the Baltic states and not the official *baltijskij*), threats to Russia's security are multiple: the deployment of nuclear warheads in Estonia or a NATO air raid on the Russian Black Sea coast are conjured up as immediate repercussions of NATO expansion. It is of little significance that the Baltic states are in fact members of the Nuclear Non-Proliferation Treaty and that Ukraine has not transferred its radar stations to anyone. What is important here is the construction of an antagonism through imagining the very possibility of a threat.

The feeling that NATO is somehow out of control both concerning its functioning and its expansion adds to a heightened sense of threat. As one lecturer explains,

> this new function of NATO, the military coercion to peace, is *de facto* without control, that is, they can practically bomb who they want, where they want and for any reason without control. ... Do you like this? I think that citizens of those countries that are not members of NATO should not like this (Lecture 42/37).

For many, NATO lost its *raison d'être* with the dissolution of the Warsaw Pact. The fact that NATO started to expand to include new member states instead of dissolving itself is reason for concern at MGIMO. The rationale for this expansion is considered to be threadbare: NATO can neither explain why it expands nor until what point it expands, one lecturer reasons. In his view, NATO's primary aim is to exert influence on key processes in world politics. He recalls NATO-Russia confrontation over control of Priština airport during the Kosovo war as an example:

> I don't know how much you know about the famous episode 'Clark vs. Jackson', when Russian troops in June 1999 occupied Priština airport. This was our zone of

> responsibility in Kosovo, which they had given us in order to carry out a peace-keeping operation. From the other side at about the same time the new national forces under NATO command arrived on Kosovo territory. Their commander was Jackson. And Clark, as supreme commander of the NATO armed forces, gave Jackson the following order: drive out the Russians from Priština airport! And all that happened on June 12, Russia's national holiday. For the first time, Jackson violated absolutely all fundamental rules (*zapovedi*) and did not obey this command. In so doing, he saved the world from the third world war. ... Try to understand, this is a question about who controls what. NATO people want to control (Lecture 42/37).

The liaison of NATO enlargement and NATO's will to power presents a dangerous concoction to Russia. It does not come as a surprise then that NATO expansion is largely interpreted as a move against Russia. Following Konstantin (16/74, 4 IR), Russia feels somewhat isolated, now that the majority of its former partners in Eastern Europe have become or are about to become members of NATO. Students and lecturers regard NATO behaviour in this context as highly fickle and treacherous. One lecturer complains that NATO broke with its rule not to accept any members with unsettled territorial claims when the Baltic states acceded NATO. This puts additional pressure on Russia, because instead of negotiating on border issues with Estonia as a sovereign state, Russia now always has to take into account NATO as Estonia's 'older brother' (Lecture 42/45). Evgenija (07/63, 4 IR) points out that NATO broke its promise not to expand further after German re-unification. In view of these frequent changes of mind and disappointments on the part of NATO, it is felt that NATO represents a highly unpredictable organisation.

Natalija (29/21, 3 PS) thinks that NATO expansion in Eastern Europe has destroyed the traditional balance of forces and creates the need for Russia to perhaps counterbalance NATO presence in Eastern Europe by espousing CSTO as an alternative to NATO. Not only for Vasilij, such a situation is somewhat reminiscent of the Cold War, since Western confrontation with Russia seems to live on unabated.

> Right now I think that Ukraine and Georgia are like cards which the Western countries, the US among others, play in order to curtail Russia's sphere of influence, overturn its political authority and partly even overturn the country itself. I think that this [NATO membership] is a carrot (*kalač*) with which they entice these countries (Vasilij, 19/59, 4 IR).

Expanding the chain of equivalence that produces threat, Vasilij also sees in NATO an instrument for furthering US influence. Co-articulating NATO and

US threat in such a way is not untypical at MGIMO: NATO expansion is linked with US hegemony to conjure up the imagination of a unipolar world, which is opposed to the vision of multipolarity. Andrej (24/53, 4 PS) argues that the US already sponsor half of NATO's budget and that the organisation will gradually turn into a convenient foreign policy instrument in disguise for the US government. If NATO becomes a global organisation, this would mean that the US could do anything they want in this world.

In light of this reasoning, NATO advance towards Russian borders becomes a somewhat disturbing factor for many at MGIMO. Although Russia would, in principle, be interested in good relations with NATO, it is also afraid of such a powerful military alliance on its eastern borders (Konstantin, 16/38, 4 IR). NATO's territorial and functional expansion becomes increasingly interpreted in terms of threat to Russia and thus as antagonistic to Russian geopolitical identity. Not surprisingly then, in Maksim's (17/68, 4 IR) opinion, Russian response to this threat must be to step up its domestic development. Only as a strong, highly developed country will Russia be able to withstand the threats emanating from NATO expansion.

China

Articulations of threat are not limited to NATO as a representative of the West. With somewhat different content, they equally apply to the rise of China in the east. Rapid economic and population growth make it an emerging second pole in the global geopolitical order, leaving behind the modest ambitions of a regional power. Its stunning growth is set in contrast to Russia's deficient development in the Far East, where it borders on China. Tatjana (08/43, 4 IR) points out that China is almost half the size of Russia but that in contrast to China, Russian territory in the Far East is sparsely populated and weakly developed. She argues that it is difficult to establish control over such a huge territory and govern it efficiently. Because of this, she considers borders in the Russian Far East highly pervious to Chinese population pressure:

> I think that this is a very big threat, considering that the Russian population is currently only slightly higher than the Japanese. But this is Japan here [points at the map to compare the size of the two countries], and this is Russia. That is, Russia currently has a population of 140 million and in Nigeria there are already 120 million. And the Chinese already have 1 billion 300 million. With such a population density, there is already a huge number of illegal immigrants who live on the territory of here –

> Ulan-Udė, Čita – and there is the threat of a gradual colonisation by the Chinese (Tatjana, 08/74, 4 IR).

Students are concerned about Chinese immigration which is taken to be even encouraged by the Chinese state. What is more, Russian businessmen are said to prefer to hire Chinese workers, because they are more industrious and do not tend to drink. If these developments continue, Nikolaj (22/83, 4 PS) predicts a wholesale sinicisation of the Russian Far East. Already, he claims, Russians in the Far East experience cultural alienation and do not orient themselves towards Moscow and European Russia but towards the East. Boris told me how his friends from the Far East experience this situation:

> They say that half of the people there, half of the villages already belong to the Chinese. That is, there aren't any Russians or other nationalities there, only Chinese, right. This is a very big misery for Russia, because it is economically weak, politically weak, socially weak, morally weak. And it cannot effectively control the whole territory of Russia. Certain zones remain outside of military Russia. These zones, of course, like emptiness, when it exists, it is always filled with something. This emptiness is filled by China which is the economically stronger state (Boris, 27/39, 4 IJ).

Eventually, Boris holds, the Russian population could become a minority and the Chinese might demand special rights or perhaps even lobby secession and join China. Such a course of events would fuel Russian territorial disintegration, which is a scenario occasionally envisioned by MGIMO students such as Aleksandr (14/17-20, 3 IR): he sketches a future war between China and the US for the resources in the Russian Far East in which Russia will 'not be a subject, but an object'.

Given the manifold ways in which China encroaches upon Russia, the feeling that there is a very immediate threat is wide-spread:

> The Chinese threat is very real and it is in fact no longer latent but already real. We are faced with the fact that the Russian population is more or less dying out in those areas and is very small there. And the onslaught of this huge nation, this multi-million, multi-billion nation in search of space to live makes the Far East highly vulnerable (Katja, 02/78, 4 IJ).

The notion of threat is construed by portraying China and Russia in contrasting terms. On the one hand, we have a vulnerable and weak Russia which faces territorial disintegration and degradation to a mere resource supplier of China. On the other hand, we are presented with a booming, expanding China which is about to overrun and overpower the Russian Far East. China, as Vera (35/53, 3 IR) puts it, is 'an empire which seeks to expand'. In some variations, this concern is shared by her fellow students.

> I also did some research on China: massive economic growth and as far as the development is concerned, simply a rapid, colossal development, a stunningly able-bodied (*trudosposobnoe*) population. Moreover, they are a lot, the country with the highest population growth, and on top of that they are sensationally able-bodied, they are able to work from morning till night. Consequently, this all manifests itself on the macroeconomic level (Marina, 34/42, 4 Other).

In this account, China's stupendous rise acquires an uncanny quality as the country becomes constructed as highly superior to Russia in almost every respect. In this vein, a near universal, versatile antagonist takes shape that poses a threat to the project of a strong Russia.

What, then, would be appropriate measures to counter this Chinese threat? There is unanimity that giving in to Chinese pressure, perhaps silently allowing a Chinese colonisation of the Russian Far East, is an unacceptable option.

> We will not and never allow that our precious territories, the Far East, will fall to someone else, such a country like China. I don't have anything against China, of course. But it is completely possible that China begins its advance. It has already begun and will continue its advance (Mikhail, 10/72, 3 IR).

The favourite course of action to halt this advance is described by Vasilij (19/73, 4 IR) with the saying 'he who has power/strength, also has power/control' (*u kogo sila, u togo i vlast'*): Russia must become a strong power to be able to resist threats that will result from the rise of China and establish control over its territory. If it does not manage to develop the potential of the Far East more intensively, it is entirely Russia's fault if it gets overpowered by China.

8.3 Exclusion and marginalisation

Western hegemony

Visions of a multipolar world order in which Russia would play the role of one of the centres of power are contrasted to American dominance in a unipolar world. Although, as we have seen, multipolarity is articulated as a moment of the geopolitical identity as a strong Russia and perhaps seen as gradually evolving, unipolarity for many still seems to hold true as an adequate rendition of the present world order.

> I think that there are very few people who do not admit that there has now developed a unipolar world. ... Because according to all indicators, according to military-political, to economic indicators and according to the potential that it has, nobody can, of course, argue with the US. And this gives them the right to dictate their terms in the current world (Ekaterina, 04/5, 4 IR).

A lecturer confirms that as a global hegemon, America is everywhere and American interests need to be taken into account in every situation. There is no problem in international affairs that could be solved without the US (Lecture 04/15). When I asked students to draw the US sphere of influence on a blank map, a significant number located US influence almost everywhere in the world: Latin America is virtually regarded as an American colony, Africa serves as a resource base, the Near and the Middle East are secured by American military presence, Eastern Europe is wooed with military cooperation and financial subsidies and even Western Europe depends at least on American military capacity. American influence does not exempt Russia:

> The US are a hegemon. What can I say about the US? In my understanding, the whole world is under the influence of the US. I think that the US is key and that it decides what, for whom, how. Because we also act like the US wants us to. There is such a good Russian word – kiss-ass (*podxalimaž*): something like that (Galja, 23/21, 4 IR).

American hegemony implies an extension and imposition of the American will on other states. Students and lecturers equally take particular issue with the project of democratisation, which they perceive as an attempt at indoctrinating other states with American ideals. Ukraine, Georgia, Iraq, Afghanistan – all suffer from the American desire to export their system to the whole world. Russia, too, is faced with American coercion in how to best establish democratic institutions in the country.

> The position of America is the following: "We bring democracy to the whole world, we will be everywhere where human rights are infringed". These are all stated principles, this is more or less democratic propaganda. There was not only communist or nationalist propaganda, but there is also democratic propaganda. America hides behind these principles in order to solve the tasks which confront it (Andrej, 24/64, 4 PS).

In this take on American hegemony, talk of democracy and human rights functions merely as rhetorical camouflage for furthering American interests, which it rigorously pursues even at the expense of other states. Marina describes such behaviour as reckless diplomacy:

> It does not mean anything for it [the US] to fire off a couple of rockets. They absolutely do not care about human lives. The country does not care about absolutely anything. Not about any norms (Marina, 34/46, 4 Other).

For Vitalij (28/57, 4 IR), the nuclear programme of Iran is then but a pretext to allow US intervention in order to secure energy resources. If there had not been any conflict about Iran's nuclear capacity, the US would simply have invented another problem that would have guaranteed them influence in this region.

While cooperation in counter-terrorist measures is generally welcomed with reference to Chechnya, the US war on terror is read as a unilateral enterprise and a disguise for furthering American dominance in the world.[22] Andrej (24/67, 4 PS) and Vera (35/62, 3 IR) see in this war just another instrument to push through American interests and provide it with a good pretext to carry out pre-emptive military strikes against any country that does not act according to their will. A lecturer characterises US-Russia cooperation in the war on terror in a very similar vein:

> And they started to argue with us about terrorism, because we said to them: "Let us fight together and in order to do so we need to define what exactly terrorism is". And they say: "We don't need to define, let's fight right away" (Lecture 42/32).

As a consequence, the lecturer argues, Russia felt excluded, for its own concerns about terrorism in Chechnya or Kosovo were brushed aside.

Russian marginalisation and exclusion from world affairs through American hegemony is a more general concern. Andrej (24/27, 4 PS) is convinced that America does not welcome a strong Russia and therefore tries to keep Russia down and out from world politics. Wherever Russia's sphere of influence might grow or be consolidated, the US seems to be eager to contain it.

---

22 A linguistic shortcoming in my question wording revealed this take on the war on terror very clearly: I had intended to ask whether the United States' war on terror influenced Russian geopolitical interests, but my initial question wording (vojna protiv terrorizma SŠA) allowed to interpret this as whether the 'war against US terror' influenced Russian geopolitical interests. Very tellingly, several students asked me to clarify which of the two possible interpretations I was having in mind.

> Why does the US enter Georgia and Ukraine? I think one of the reasons is because it wants to somehow keep Russia in fear, control the process. Because our military production is really completely classified. I also don't know anything, I only know that it exists and that it is at a very high level, perhaps with outdated equipment, but it exists. The US knows this and is afraid of it (Marina, 34/71, 4 Other).

Besides American engineering of NATO expansion in Eastern Europe and the colour revolutions in the post-Soviet states, it is also held responsible for trying to push back Russia's influence in Central Asia. Equally, the US missile shield is interpreted as partly directed against Russia, since it implicates a serious diminution of Russian military power (Lecture 22/18).

Additionally, US behaviour in international conflicts seems to have a tendency to work against Russia. One lecturer recalls her experience from a conference at around the time of the NATO intervention in Kosovo in 1998:

> Over the whole course of 1998 we did not give our approval to a resolution that would allow the bombardment in Yugoslavia. And at that time this formula was created, which at that conference one week before the bombardment one American PhD student said in my presence: "These Russians in the UN Security Council are annoying. Let it be worse for them. 19 are more than 5, so let's make this decision in the North Atlantic Council" (Lecture 42/36).

This statement reflects a perceived disparagement of Russia's role in world politics – not only its exclusion from important decisions but also the imputed desire on the part of the West to give Russia a hard time, to oppose Russia more generally. The West, it is held, does not want Russia to become a serious player in international relations. Russian relations with America, and with the West more generally, are hence often assessed in bleak terms:

> It is evident that in the sphere of economy and politics Russia did not manage to get ... what it aimed to. Neither foreign investment, nor debt cancellation, nor a recognition of Russian interests in the post-Soviet space – nothing of this has happened. Russia does not get any reciprocal steps from the side of the West, but in turn makes concessions to the West. Particularly, when the Bosnian crisis breaks out, Russia's role is reduced to persuading the leadership of the Yugoslavian side, Slobodan Milošević, to accept the terms that the West draws up. Here again, Russia did not play an independent role (Lecture 23/31).

In this statement, Russia is taken to have made significant concessions to the West, but not to have received adequate compensation. Instead of recognising Russia's vested interests, the West even exploited Russia's good relations with Serbia to further its own interests. Russia is kept *down* by not fulfilling the promises the Western countries had given and it is kept *out* by not acknowledging its sovereignty and independent role in international affairs.

While in the articulations of America ideas of dominance and sometimes even confrontation prevail, articulations of Europe tend to stress the element of exclusion.[23] Above all, the feeling of exclusion is linked to European eastward expansion which created new borders and severed old ties, thus pushing Russia further to the brink of Europe. With the entry of states that have long had a rather cool relationship with Russia, the EU has increased the identificatory distance to Russia, while reducing the physical distance. The border of the EU has come closer to Russia, thus creating a certain measure of tension (Nikolaj, 22/40, 4 PS). At the same, it has cut the relationships between Russia and the new member states:

> If earlier there was a number of post-Soviet countries in Eastern Europe, Russia somehow had influence on them. Because, if we remember the past, there were some subsidies, we delivered gas and oil at discounted prices. And that's gone now, it's not ours. We can no longer (Irina, 21/38, 4 PS).

Becoming a member of the European Union or establishing closer ties with Europe, however, is not an option for Russia. For one thing, there are economic drawbacks such closer association would entail:

> Why does Russia not act like Eastern Europe? Just look what it means to become a member of the European Union. Following orders from Brussels in Lithuania they now close 500 firms which produce sugar. Why? Because the European Union doesn't need this. I think that the question that we have to choose is posed artificially for us. I don't think that one can change the current mentality of the Russian elite (Lecture 02/26).

More importantly, perhaps, such integration would of course amount to surrendering a large degree of Russian sovereignty and inviting in Western influence – a scenario that Russia prefers to avoid, according to Julija (25/41, 4 PS). If Russia were to seek rapprochement with Europe, it would also have to admit further European interference with Russian domestic affairs – a condition that is clearly unacceptable.

Ljuba (09/63, 4 IR) paints the vision of an equal partnership between Europe and Russia as the ideal relationship between the two entities. Most students,

---

23 More detailed analyses of the articulation of Europe at MGIMO can be found in Müller (2007b, 2008b). The treatment here is therefore limited to some basic points.

however, are pessimistic about the chances of success in building such a partnership. Judging from an economic point of view, Evgenija (07/73, 4 IR) claims that Europe and Russia are simply 'in different weight classes, just like in boxing'. Due to this difference, Europe is thought not to be interested in cooperating economically with Russia except for the import of oil and gas. It is held to primarily pursue its own benefit, while Russian expectations of a full-fledged partnership are ignored. Even more, with the accession of the Baltic states to the EU, Europe has made rapprochement with Russia still more unlikely and pushed the country further to the margins of Europe.

The West as an illusion

Against the foil of the frequent sobering experiences in Russia's relationship with Western countries, the West is attributed illusive qualities: seductive promises of the benefits of alignment, rapprochement or cooperation with the West are belied by the stark reality. People, one lecturer believes, always look to those countries where they think the situation is better. They are enticed by Pepsi Light and similar icons of American consumer culture, believing that a pro-Western orientation will guarantee wealth and happiness for all. In their naïve enthusiasm, however, they are deceived by the glitzy outward appearance and overlook the underbelly of the West: racial discrimination, unemployment, inequality, market competition:

> Because if we look at it in a sober fashion, nobody more or less needs us in the West. There is competition, there is a market, there are fights and nobody needs new players there (Lecture 61/46).

This illusive quality is found to be especially present in the colour revolutions. They are viewed as short-lived enthusiasm with the façade of Western culture. Although driving alienation between Russia and the post-Soviet states, the West is taken to be unwilling to commit to long-term support and integration of those states. When Ukraine was caught in the gas dispute with Russia, Western Europe backed off instead of supporting Ukraine against Russia. Vera sums up the sobering results of this dispute:

> In principle, this gas crisis showed how seriously the Western countries need Ukraine: nobody supported it! Yes, there were attacks against Russia, there were many accusations of Russia in the mass media, but in reality nobody supported Ukraine in this gas crisis. Nobody pressurised Russia because of this. I think that

> Ukraine will soon return to us. ... Instead of helping Ukraine, they began to worry about their own gas supplies from Russia (Vera, 35/14, 71, 3 IR).

Serious support from the West and serious integration with the West are considered an illusion. One lecturer (03/39) describes the situation when in 2005 Javier Solana, then European Union High Representative for the Common Foreign and Security Policy, declared that Ukraine might perhaps never receive the invitation to join the EU. For Ukraine, he states, this was an unexpected shock but for Russia it merely confirmed what Russia had long known and predicted.

A cognate assessment is applied to the situation in Georgia. In Ljuba's (09/52, 4 IR) view, Georgian president Saakashvili is naïve to believe that America or Europe will support him in his attacks on Russia. They have never had the selfless intention of supporting Georgia against Russia but have rather been pursuing their own interests. Anton similarly declares that

> it is unclear to what extent the Western countries are interested in establishing such a real stronghold on [Georgia's] borders. Perhaps they just play with Mr Saakashvili, perhaps they talk about that they support him, no matter what. But it is unclear how seriously they are prepared to support him (Anton, 10/57, 4 IR).

Repeatedly, students and lecturers voice their concern over what they term the application of double standards by Western countries. Why did the West tolerate the delivery of weapons to the Kosovo Liberation Army, when an arms embargo was in place? Why are elections in Chechnya treated in the same forum as elections in Iraq and Afghanistan, although Chechnya is merely a Russian province and not a sovereign country? Why is one kind of terrorism condemned, while another kind of terrorism is ignored?

Double standards are also found to apply to NATO enlargement. One lecturer explains that NATO officially cannot admit states with unresolved territorial conflicts or with foreign military presence as members. But when it serves Western interests, it is inclined to make exceptions. Mocking NATO he says:

> "Yes, we generally do not admit them, but those we accept." Perhaps they take the Ukrainians [on whose territory the Russian Black Sea Fleet is located]? Azerbaijan also wants to join. Will they also take Nagorno-Karabax? Under whose jurisdiction? Under Armenian or under Azeri? Or will they take Nagorno-Karabax as a problem, which they will then try to unsuccessfully solve after the Treaty of Washington (Lecture 42/45)?

In this reading, international law and legal principles are adduced as a mere cover-up to legitimise political or military actions in the interest of a few. Sometimes, even this masquerade breaks down, as in the case of the US invasion of Iraq. Here, Andrej (24/64, 4 PS) thinks, international law and the international community of nations have failed to punish the US for what he sees as an act of aggression against a sovereign state. By either tolerating or actively supporting the US-led invasion, the validity and equal applicability of international law to all states have *de facto* been nullified. In his view, such exceptions from the rule are only granted to members of the established community of Western states but not to their critics. From the perspective of many students and lecturers at MGIMO, this creates an us/them-distinction, which is a critical feature of the concept of double standards. For Russia, such discriminatory behaviour only widens the chasm and reinforces the antagonistic frontier running between it and the West.

Depreciation of Russia

The topos of exclusion and marginalisation not only appears in articulations of formal foreign policy, but also occupies a prominent position in what is perceived as a general depreciation of Russia and Russians in many other social contexts. On the level of formal diplomacy, Larissa (15/26, 4 IR) argues, many things seem to go smoothly, but once it gets down to everyday politics or to the level of the mass media, Russia still has to play the role of the bad guy. Mikhail (11/71, 3 IR) believes to detect such prejudices in media coverage of Russia. According to him, in the mind of many journalists in the West the stereotypes of the Cold War are still firmly ingrained, prompting them to portray Russian actions in derogatory, imperialist terms. For Aleksandr, Russian gas deliveries to the West are a case in point. Whatever Russia does, he claims, it is always represented negatively in the West:

> We can do what we want: we stay unreliable partners. Here, again, it is tried to create such a negative image of Russia (Aleksandr, 14/57, 3 IR).

Many in the West would still prefer to see Russia revert to imperial sphere-of-influence thinking and thus confirm the stereotypes, Larissa says (15/16, 4 IR). But today, she continues to argue, Russia is no longer interested in subjecting other countries but rather conducts a peaceful, cooperative foreign policy. It is only the West which seems to be unwilling to accept this, being still mired in outdated preconceptions.

This feeling of being constructed as the political and cultural Other also extends into the sphere of everyday life. Natalija reports from her own and her friends' experience in Europe:

> One other thing that I feel sad about is that Russia very often plays the role of a whipping boy (*mal'čik dlja bit'ja*) in international relations, because Russia's prestige, its image in the eyes of other countries is not improving or is only improving very slowly. All of my friends who were in Europe say that Russia is perceived as a monster there. Such negative dispositions! And at all conferences which were especially organised for Russians and Europeans, to jointly study and research certain problems, Russia serves as an example of all the anti-democratic vices you can possibly think of in this world (Natalija, 29/5, 3 PS).

According to Galja (23/72, 4 IR), many Russians feel deeply insulted if Russia is played on or vilified by the supposedly superior West. Russia and Russians do not seem to be taken seriously as equals but are rather looked down on as culturally underdeveloped and backward. For students and lecturers, such a stance is, of course, frustrating:

> In the majority of European countries we stay such a country in which people drink vodka all the time. I just travel a lot in Europe and it hurts me deeply when I hear that we drink the whole day, that we don't know anything, that we are a very backward and poor country. I have been told a story that a [Russian] girl once visited Germany and they gave her shampoo as a present. That is, they think that she doesn't have money to buy herself shampoo. Really horrible stereotypes! I am confronted with them all the time. Both in Europe and in America. This is evidence of a lack of education of people (Marina, 34/62, 4 Other).

By calling people in Europe and America uneducated, Marina repeats the process of Othering from the Russian side, thus reinforcing the boundaries of mutual exclusion. She bemoans the times of the Soviet Union:

> If we just take the USSR. It was a great power (*velikaja deržava*). Nobody would have said this about it. There were a lot of bad things, but still it was a great power (Marina, 34/62, 4 Other).

Once again, the proposed solution to exclusion and Othering is an appeal to the hegemonic project of a strong Russia. For Marina, the assertive Russia under Putin is on its way to reclaim the reputation it has lost and thus to prove the stereotypes of the West finally wrong.

8.4 Lack: aspiration and reality

Unfulfilled potential

One prominent feature of geopolitical identification at MGIMO has gone unaddressed so far: the frequent split between that which Russia aspires to and that which Russia currently is. In numerous statements, there is a markable incongruence between these two conditions which often is couched in terms of unfulfilled potential. Several lecturers are convinced that Russia could live a lot better than it currently does, because in contrast to the other post-Soviet states 'it has everything, it is self-sufficient' (Lecture 03/35). For the first time in history, one lecturer holds, young Russians now have the chance to realise this potential:

> If we are so clever, so talented, if we have such a land, if we have resources everywhere – then why do we live worse? In my time, we only thought about this by ourselves, sitting in the kitchen and drinking tea, but we didn't have the possibilities to change anything. But you can. Because you have the market, you have the economy, the freedom. You really have this. ... You have a sound pragmatism. Why should we live worse than those Europeans? (Lecture 61/45)

This upbeat assessment of the future is shared by many students like in this argument during one lecture:

> This is why I think that if we define the situation of Russia, then Russia has the potential and the ability to play the role of one of the great powers, of one of the first powers on a global level. But at the moment this is not true (Lecture 14/31).

Optimistic ideas about the future are contrasted to the stark reality of the present day. As the weak state Russia presents now, one lecturer reasons, it cannot possibly live up to the geopolitical goals it has set itself (Lecture 13/42-47): it has lost many Slavic partner countries which it wanted to join together and it is unable to spur development in the east of the country, although this is considered one of the primary requirements of Russia's reassertion. Julija (25/47, 4 PS) adds to this the Kaliningrad conflict with the EU in which Russia was unable to push through its demands vis-à-vis the European Union. In her opinion, this is evidence of the fact that Russia cannot completely defend its position. The same reasoning applies to the disintegration of the CIS, which Aleksandr traces back to the fact that Russia was simply too weak to serve as a centre of gravitation which could have kept those states together. He draws the following conclusion:

> We should learn our lessons from all this and gather our strength in order to then solve our tasks. We don't feel hurt that others will play give-away with us (*igrat' v pod-davki*), that they want to settle their accounts with us. As long as we are not strong, nobody is obliged to us in any way (Aleksandr, 14/50, 3 IR).

Again, it is a state's strength that determines whether it plays a leading or a marginalised role in world politics. Russia must develop its potential if it wants to be taken seriously in international arena.

This division into a bitter, stark reality and a more rosy future which is still to come is also characteristic for Russia's ambitions to become a great power. Many reiterate that they would love to see Russia develop into a great power but that Russia still has a long way to go. Although Russia is invited to take part in all conferences and is a member of many international organisations, it mostly plays a pro forma role with little real influence. Marina also complains that with respect to putting its domestic affairs in order, Russia is still far from living up to the the aspired role of a great power. She expresses her hope, however, that this will only be a temporary state of affairs:

> This is my country. Of course I believe that it is a great power. I think this despite a lot of shortcomings. It hurts to watch the news; I often want to turn them off. When you come home, you turn them on and see that in the winter people died of frost because the heat supply did not work. Now we have some landslides, the snow melts, floods. We cannot compare this to anything. Every year the same thing happens over again and every year it appears spontaneous to us. A lot of disasters. But I think that we just begin to develop. I think that everything's going to be okay. We are in a young country and I think that perhaps in a couple of decades, we will rise and we will make it a great power also for others [and not only for ourselves] (Marina, 34/73, 4 Other).

The emergence of a strong, independent Russia, the kernel of the hegemonic geopolitical identification at MGIMO, is thus deferred to the future. For many, it is still lacking but necessary and likely to be realised.

Lack of recognition

Wedded to the notion of unfulfilled potential and contributing to the division between aspiration and reality is the lack of recognition of Russia's desired status in world politics. It is the status of a powerful state equal in the hierarchy to European or Western countries. At the beginning of the 1990s, however, Russia did not act according to its status and therefore lost a considerable part of its influence, as this lecturer describes:

> The failure to understand this factor, the factor of national interests, was crucial for Russia losing its position in the international arena. It started to be perceived as a reliable, faithful satellite of the West, among others in the states of its former influence. Basically, people stopped thinking of Russia as an independent subject of world politics. It said "yes" to all serious suggestions of the West and the few objections it had where not perceived as a serious Russian position by the West. They thought that this were rare whims (*kaprizy*) that did not need to be taken into account or that the Russian partners had to be talked into accepting the Western conceptions nevertheless (Lecture 23/30).

For many, Russia still has not overcome this miserable condition. Vitalij (28/71, 4 IR) thinks that the EU is not interested in having Russia as a full-fledged partner in its neighbourhood. This is also the reason why it does not take seriously Russian concerns about the expansion of the European Union or the Kaliningrad transit regime. In the same vein, one lecturer reasons that the US does not recognise Russia as an equal actor in international relations and brushes Russian interests aside (Lecture 22/18).

According to Katja (02/7, 4 IJ), Russia's eagerness to become a full member of the G8 can be explained as an attempt to overcome Russia's confinement to the role of an underdog and geopolitical object vis-à-vis the West. In many current conflicts, Russia tries not to be an object of Western interests but rather to play an active role in mediating them. Raising relations to the point where both parties can talk at the same level is also declared as the main goal of Russia-Europe relations:

> Our aim is not, by no means, to become a member of the EU but to build full-fledged (*polnopravye*) relations as partners, that is up to that point where the European Union on one side and we on the other side of the scale weigh exactly the same. That is, so that they consider us a full-fledged partner. I think to that point. When we feel that we can talk to the European Union in the same tone, that is on the same level – we can carry our cooperation with them exactly up to that moment (Ljuba, 09/63, 4 IR).

Because such a relationship of mutual recognition currently seems virtually impossible with Western countries, Russia seeks out enhanced cooperation with countries in the East, Larissa (15/9, 4 IR) argues. Organisations such as the Shanghai Cooperation Organisation (SCO) or the Asia-Pacific Economic

Cooperation (APEC) on the Pacific Rim promise to view Russia as a full-grown member and not to belittle it as a junior partner, as the West does.

The main concern here is not, however, with specific disadvantages or unfair behaviour towards Russia in certain cases, but it is with a more general lack of recognition of Russia. This becomes evident in statements which speak out against Russia's role as a supplier of raw materials which condemns it to a mere handmaiden of other states:

> This gives the impression, there appears the stereotype of Russia as a permanent supplier, a permanent dairy cow. If we stay such a dairy cow for the world over a period of many decades, 20 to 30 years, they will continue to perceive us as such even after that time. They won't take us seriously, because they just take from us. If they are engaged in a dialogue with us, then it will be like [a dialogue] with some miserable supplier (Boris, 27/12, 4 IJ).

A similar lack of recognition is voiced in Russia's relationship with the post-Soviet states. For Andrej (24/53, 4 PS), this recognition – or rather the lack thereof – is the main problem in Russian-Ukrainian relations. It is less tragic for Russia that Ukraine might now be looking towards Europe than towards Russia. What hurts, according to Andrej, is that Ukraine does not seem to appreciate Russia's interests as its neighbour and Russia's leading role in the post-Soviet space. According to Ekaterina, it is hard for Russia to now interact with its former brother states not from the position of a superpower but from the position of a relatively young state which does not have firm, long-standing principles for which it is respected:

> Above all, the importance [of the CIS for Russia] is in self-esteem. If we lose our influence in the CIS, in which other countries, in which other regions can we talk about Russia's influence? (Ekaterina, 04/50, 4 IR).

According to this statement, rebuilding Russian influence to make it a great power is not primarily a strategy for increasing Russian military power and imposing the Russian will on others – it is rather the expression of the search for recognition that the country is denied.

8.5 Conceptual reflections: Keeping Russia down and out

The phenomena examined in this chapter share one common characteristic: they are interpreted as keeping Russia down and out, as running counter to

Russia's geopolitical identity, as denying it. Russia wants to be a strong state but there are numerous obstacles to this. These obstacles embody antagonism. Antagonism is the limit of all objectivity and represents the impossibility of any identity to fully constitute itself (Laclau and Mouffe 1985: 122-127). In antagonism, '[t]he hegemonic force ... will construct the excluded identity as one of a series of threatening obstacles to the full realization of chosen meanings and options' (Torfing 1999: 120).

Threat and exclusion are recurrent motifs in articulations of Russian geopolitical identity at MGIMO. Both are antagonistic forces to the hegemonic project of a strong Russia. Threats emanate from the rise of China and from the eastward expansion of NATO – at first glance two very different processes. For Russia, however, both developments challenge the consolidation of Russian influence in world politics. The alienation of the post-Soviet states adds the motif of exclusion to the motif of threat: not only does the breaking away of several post-Soviet republics threaten the emergence of Russia as the key integrator in the post-Soviet space, but it also sharpens the boundaries between the West – into which several post-Soviet states have become subsumed – and Russia. Exclusion, and thus the creation of opposition, also takes place in the marginalisation of Russia in world politics through American hegemony. Exclusion from Europe has been exacerbated by accepting the East European states as new members and thus increasing the opposition to Russia. Exclusion lies at the heart of the construction of the everyday Other, of the construction of the West and Western promises as deceitful illusions. Finally, exclusion can be found in the lack of recognition as an equal partner.

Antagonism blocks the realisation of identity, but at the same time it is the condition of its very possibility (Laclau 1990: 17). David Campbell (1992: 12) therefore concludes that '[t]he constant articulation of danger through foreign policy is ... not a threat to a state's identity or existence; it is its condition of possibility'. The antagonistic forces described in this chapter thus play the paradoxical role of being simultaneously subversive and constitutive of Russian geopolitical identity as a strong country. They are subversive because they threaten or block the emergence of a strong Russia: Due to their presence Russia cannot become what is aspires to. At the same time, the antagonistic forces are constitutive of Russian geopolitical identity, because it is only in their presence that a strong Russia can be thought. Russia must be strong in order to resist and overcome outside threats and marginalisation. Antagonism is thus fought by asserting the hegemonic project, by proposing the solution of strengthening Russia to annihilate the antagonistic forces.

Antagonism always involves the presence of an adversary who negates our identity (Mouffe 1993: 4). In our case, the West frequently takes on the role of this adversary. The West lures the post-Soviet states away from Russia, as in the case of the Orange Revolution. The West wants to keep Russia weak and is acting against it. The West ignores Russia as a subject of world politics and brushes its concerns aside. It is interesting to note how this antagonist is fashioned with agency. By the way it threatens, deludes, disappoints, excludes, pressurises, marginalises etc. Russia we are led to believe that we are faced with a pre-formed actor with a fully constituted identity. For Laclau, however, this agency results from the antagonistic constitution of identities and the emerging hegemonic projects which seek to suture identities (Laclau 1990: 210-211).

> [The structure of discourse] is inhabited by an original lack, by a radical undecidability that needs to be constantly superseded by acts of decision. These acts are precisely what constitutes the subject, who can only exist as a will transcending the structure. Because this will has no place of constitution external to the structure but is the result of the failure of the structure to constitute itself, it can be formed only through acts of identification. If I need to identify with something, it is because I do not have a full identity in the first place. These acts of identification can only be thought of as the result of the lack within the structure and have the permanent trace of the lack (Laclau 1996: 92).

It is a mere effect of the failed structural identity of every subject which compels the subject to act (Laclau 1990: 44). The agency attributed to Russia and the West in world politics is thus a result of the discursive formation of a lack to be overcome. The felt lack of recognition of Russia's position in world politics and the country's unfulfilled potential block the realisation of Russian great power identity, which, in turn, prompts Russia to act in order to fill this lack.

The multiple lack in Russia's geopolitical identity underscores the conceptual link between antagonism and dislocation, emphasised by Laclau (1990: 5-41. This link is most clearly visible in the representation of the alienation in the Near Abroad. The colour revolutions and their negative consequences for Russia are events that cannot be represented in the dominant discourse of a strong Russia integrating the post-Soviet space. The utter surprise and disbelief with which the events are met by some students point to their dislocatory potential. According to Laclau, antagonism is a discursive response to dislocation. Putting the defective post-Soviet states into an equivalential relationship with the West, attributing the centrifugal agency to the West and not to the post-Soviet states themselves establishes this antagonism. The colour revolutions thus function as dislocatory triggers of antagonism.

The antagonism examined in this chapter illustrates to what degree antagonistic elements come to have their differences cancelled and form a homogeneous chain of equivalence.

> Only if the beyond becomes the signifier of the pure threat, of pure negativity, of the simply excluded, can there be limits and system (that is an objective order), but in order to be the signifiers of the excluded ... the various excluded categories have to cancel their differences through the formation of a chain of equivalences to that which the system demonizes in order to signify itself (Laclau 1996: 38-39).

The hegemonic project of Russian geopolitical identity has successfully constructed such a chain of equivalence, adding ever more signifiers into it so that the threat becomes universal. The US, NATO expansion, nuclear missiles, colour revolutions, American military bases, Western cultural hegemony, EU eastward expansion and so on show a tendency to come together to signify a universal constitutive Outside. It is only through this universalisation of antagonism in a chain of equivalence that a discourse can become hegemonic and thus constitutive of identity. While such a thorough universalisation has not occurred at MGIMO, its outlines are foreshadowed in the statements of this chapter. When students state that it is known to all and sundry that the West funded and engineered the Orange Revolution or that Saakashvili is an American marionette, this enlists a not clearly specified public for tacit testimony. In so doing, the universality of the antagonism is underscored by locating it in the public realm, thus purging it from the tarnish of subjectivism. At the same time, this move fashions the geopolitical project of a great power Russia that needs to be strong to stand up to threat and exclusion with societal authority, extending the context of legitimation beyond the immediate institutional setting.

Russian geopolitical identity as a great power is impossible to become fully constituted. The geopolitical subjects at MGIMO are always characterised by a constitutive lack, a failed structural identity that cannot be completely sutured (Laclau 1990: 30, 44). This conceptualisation of the subject as the distance between an undecidable structure and the act of identification, i.e. the decision, draws on Lacan's idea of the subject as a lack (Žižek 1989: 153-200).

> The subject is … penetrated by a constitutive lack. The subject *is* this lack, and the subjectivation of the subject through the identification with different subject positions is merely an attempt to fill it (Torfing 1999: 57).

The presence of this lack at MGIMO has become clear in this chapter: Russia is barred from becoming what it wants to become, Russia cannot realise its potential. The antagonistic forces of threat and exclusion make the act of symbolic representation fail and produce a lack. This rift is filled and bridged by identifying with the hegemonic project of a strong and independent Russia that Russia can never become.

9

Understanding the discursive production of great power identities

In order to understand the discursive production of great power identities at the Moscow State Institute of International Relations (MGIMO) it is necessary to look at two things: first, the institutional context within which identities are produced and, second, the articulation of signifiers in structural relationships. In the specific case of MGIMO, the *institutional context* can be analysed through two conceptual lenses. Drawing on Bourdieu's (1996) study of the reproduction of state nobilities stresses MGIMO's function within Russian society. Its status as an elite school ensures that its graduates occupy high-ranking positions not only in foreign policy, but in the Russian state and the corporate world at large. MGIMO alumni are oligarchs, ministers, heads of state and top business managers. MGIMO acts as a locus of consecration, bestowing societal distinction on a social group that is elected to become the governing elite. Students and lecturers regard MGIMO as an institution that establishes social and professional bonds for a lifetime. It knits them together into a community in which everyone recognises each other and which is recognised as distinct from the outside. With Bourdieu, this internal coherence and external distinction is the characteristic of any elite.

Bourdieu's perspective provides a rationale for the importance of researching MGIMO if one wants to understand the production of Russian elites. But it also does more than that. It alerts us to look in detail at the specific techniques of educating students at elite schools. For the act of consecration is only successful if students and teachers submit to the mechanisms of elite education and become complicit with them. The educational institution then becomes an objective, naturalised structure. It produces subjects who are, however, not aware of their production. It is in the analysis of those mechanisms of subjectivation that Bourdieu's ideas on the state nobility coalesce with those of Foucault (1979) on discipline. But while Bourdieu's interest is directed towards the macro scale, Foucault is more interested in how educational institutions create subjects.

At MGIMO subjectivation happens through a number of small practices of discipline and knowledge. Discipline is an omnipresent element at MGIMO. It is instituted through constant observation and control by teachers and among students. It takes hold through regular tests of knowledge: formal ones like written exams and informal ones like catechising during classes or homework. Students are classified by their academic performance, are rewarded if they outperform and punished if they underperform. With Foucault, classification and normalisation are in themselves an exercise of power and the application of discipline. Less overtly, disciplining also occurs through the partitioning nature of the timetable, dividing time into ever more available slots to be used efficiently, or through the exercise of writing, linked to the control of bodies.

As an educational institution MGIMO produces docile bodies. The drill that performs the creation of such docile bodies also has a second effect: it objectifies knowledge. Through disciplining practices elite schools acquire not only the authority to transmit knowledge but they also transform the nature of knowledge. In the educational process the contingency of knowledge all but disappears. The masses of facts and figures to be consumed and reproduced make knowledge acquisition and accumulation an end in itself. Knowledge can be separated into smaller bits and pieces to be tested by exams and it is clearly either true or false. Students are drilled to 'apply' knowledge in the analysis of foreign policy problems. The mastery of details is represented as the essential part of becoming an expert upon graduating from MGIMO. My primary concern here, therefore, is not that students at MGIMO may be inculcated with certain geopolitical positions. Rather, it is more important that the process of arriving at the support of a certain geopolitical position becomes one of 'objective' analysis. This presumed objectivity, however, clouds the naturalised assumptions underpinning it.

The ideas of Foucault and Bourdieu help us understand the political apparatus of the closure of subject positions. They explain how small practices fashion docile bodies with subject positions that become naturalised in hegemonic discourses and how knowledge can be conferred the status of objectivity. It would be wrong, however, to assume that this political apparatus operates without its break-downs and slippages. If we follow Butler (1990), the constant repetition of practices, which is necessary for the performative constitution of the subject, also offers potential loopholes. One such slippage is the indulgence into consumption that characterises student life at MGIMO. It pits the capacity to consume against the capacity to be a good student and offers a way of escaping from the mechanisms that produce docile bodies. Whoever fails to live up to academic standards can still succeed in becoming a 'good consumer', i.e. in wearing chic clothes or landing a well-paying job. Instead of docile bodies, subjected through the educational institution, students may then become good consumers, subjected through the market.

Consumption and the outward adoption of a Western lifestyle are far from being without political content, though. In contrast, in many cases they are bound up with the articulation of patriotism – the unconditional loyalty to Russia as a state and the commitment to advance it. Because this articulation is enveloped as a self-evident part in everyday situations, the political fixations it entails are not obvious. Patriotism is expressed in the myriad small things like job ads or simple decorations and becomes natural through its fusion with the everyday. Extending Billig's (1995) argument, one could speak of the presence of 'banal patriotism' at MGIMO or even a banalisation of patriotic politics. Insofar as at MGIMO the everyday is conjoined with and woven into high politics, politics becomes as natural and undisputed as the everyday. In a more direct way, official documents and statements also address elite education at MGIMO as doing a service to the country by training people to advance Russia and promote its re-emergence as a great power. The reproduction of elites at MGIMO is therefore closely bound up with the Russian state and framed within a larger patriotic discourse.

For Torfing (1999: 195f.), nationalist and patriotic sentiments are a typical response to discursive dislocation in Eastern Europe. Feelings of loss and crisis are clearly visible as traces of such dislocation at MGIMO. The collapse of the Soviet Union and the ensuing geopolitical, economic and social upheavals occur frequently both in lectures and in the interviews with students. It is a sign of the incisiveness of the dislocatory experience that it is even mourned by students who experienced it as young children. According to Laclau and Mouffe (1985), on the undecidable terrain revealed by the dislocation the subject will identify with one of the emerging hegemonic projects that promise a solution to the crisis of the structure (Torfing 1999: 150). In the terminology of Laclau, a myth emerges.

> The "work" of myth is to suture that dislocated space through the constitution of a new space of representation. Thus, the effectiveness of myth is essentially hege-

> monic: it involves forming a new objectivity by means of the rearticulation of the dislocated elements. Any objectivity, then, is merely a crystallized myth (Laclau 1990: 61).

The myth of a strong Russia represents just such an emerging hegemonic project at MGIMO. It is able to unify the social terrain by providing a universal screen on which all kinds of hopes, demands and aspirations can be inscribed. Whether it is Russian cultural uniqueness, Russian independence and sovereignty in international relations, the concept of multipolarity, the defence of Russian national interests, Russian economic prosperity or Russian influence in the post-Soviet states – all of those come together in a chain of equivalence arranged around the nodal point of a strong Russia to constitute a myth. This project can emerge successfully as hegemonic because of its unparalleled comprehensiveness. Geopolitical discourses like Westernism or right-wing Eurasianism do not manage to structure a comparably large field of the social and therefore fail to draw equally large-scale support.

In accordance with the character of a myth, the position of a strong Russia often appears naturalised. Returning Russian influence in the post-Soviet states, for example, is sometimes regarded as a natural duty in the context of Russia's manifold ethnic, cultural and historical associations with those states. Raising Russian strength largely goes as an unquestioned assumption underlying foreign policy analysis. The loyalty to the Russian state is seldom openly addressed in classes but is implicit in many statements. The degree to which those positions have turned natural becomes especially evident in the emotional reactions attached to them. When Saakashvili's verbal attacks against Russia are met with anger or disappointment, this shows the high subjective investment into the discursive structures. The Russian concern with the recent colour revolutions may then be interpreted not only as a concern about a diminishing Russian sphere of influence but also and perhaps more so as a feeling of dissociation and loss of a brother nation. This distinction is important, since studies sometimes too readily assume that rational geopolitical calculations of protecting its sphere of influence underpin Russia's investment in the post-Soviet states. Recognising the naturalising power of a myth means that what is often perceived as an aggressive, imperialist foreign policy abroad is, from a Russian perspective, but a natural, normal conduct of affairs.

A myth always functions as a metaphor for an absent fullness, i.e. a fullness that cannot be realised. The geopolitical discourse of a strong Russia thus refers not to a fully constituted identity, but to an unachieved fullness. Russia *is not* a strong country but rather *strives to become* a strong country. In this striving for the realisation of one's identity, an antagonistic force always prevents this full realisation. According to Laclau (1990), every identity is characterised by a constitutive lack, by something that prevents it from being. At MGIMO, this antagonistic force is sometimes ascribed to various articulations of 'the West': the West as NATO wants to keep Russia weak; the West as the United States wants to exclude Russia from playing a central role in world affairs; the West as the European Union wants to draw away the post-Soviet states from Russia. In those articulations, the West blocks or perhaps even threatens Russian geopolitical identity.

Due to this failed structural identity, the subject is constituted 'as the locus of a decision how to establish itself as a concrete subjectivity with a fully achieved identity (Torfing 1999: 149). The subject comes to act through the need to fill the lack in the discursive structure. This is important for two reasons. First, because it does not presuppose some essential identity lying at the base of primordial subjects (cf. Kuus 2007b), as almost all of the literature on Russian geopolitical identity does. This literature describes identities as features of subjects, but fails to recognise that subjects are constituted in the very process of forming identities and do not pre-exist them. This failure, second, has a practical implication for explaining Russian foreign policy behaviour: Russia does not behave as it does because it *has* a certain identity but because it wants to *become*, i.e. realise, a certain identity. This difference is not trivial. It means that for coming to act like a strong power, Russia needs an antagonist that blocks this very great power identity. Given this antagonistic role, Western moves directed at opposing a strong Russia are likely to only reinforce the antagonistic divide along a logic of equivalence and thus buttress Russian great power identity, instead of weakening it.

My research at MGIMO also suggests, however, that a strong Russia does not necessarily imply such a logic of equivalence. Both students and lecturers emphasised that Russia may be a separate but nonetheless friendly geopolitical entity in world politics. It is not hostile towards others but also does not want to integrate with others. A strong Russia then would mean a Russia whose opinion is listened to by Western countries and who is treated as an equal partner in mutual relations. Such a constitution of Russian geopolitical identity takes place within a logic of difference that does not construct the West as antagonistic and accepts different subject positions as equally legitimate. Geopolitical identity production at MGIMO is open in the sense that the social field is not completely dominated by either of the two logics of equivalence or difference: in some areas we witness a hegemonic, antagonistic constitution of Russian geopolitical identity, e.g. in the case of NATO expansion and the struggle for influence in the post-Soviet states, in others there are legitimate differences, e.g. in economic development.

With Laclau, every hegemonic project always contains in itself the possibility of its negation and subversion:

> the incomplete and contingent nature of the totality would spring not only from the fact that no hegemonic system can be fully imposed, but also from the intrinsic ambiguities of the project itself (Laclau 1990: 28).

Hegemonic projects are always unstable and constantly challenged by what they exclude. This becomes particularly clear at MGIMO. The hegemonic project of a strong Russia at MGIMO is bound up with fears of a weak Russia – a Russia that fails to realise its ambitious plans, that fails to live up to its potential of a great power. This ambiguity makes for sometimes rather contradictory statements which boast Russian power and lament its marginalisation and exclusion from world politics at the same time. Being the condition of both the possibility and the impossibility of a strong Russia, a weak Russia is always present as a permanent lack in articulations of a strong Russia. Every study of Russian great power identity therefore also needs to be attentive to the articulation of the blockage that underpins this identity.

This instability of hegemonic projects also makes for subject positions to be constantly challenged. The hegemonic project of a strong Russia only works in some situations but breaks down in others. This asks for a differentiation of identity production by context and cautions against the universalisation of identities. As Chantal Mouffe has put it:

> The social agent is constructed by a diversity of discourses among which there is no necessary relation but a constant movement of overdetermination and displacement. The "identity" of such a multiple and contradictory subject is therefore always contingent and precarious, temporarily fixed at the intersection of those subject positions and dependent on specific forms of identification. This plurality does not, however, involve the coexistence, one by one, of a plurality of subject positions, but the constant subversion and overdetermination of one by the others that makes possible the generation of totalizing effects within a field characterized by open and determinate frontiers (Mouffe 1992: 28)

How people become positioned by discourses has been somewhat of a black box in critical geopolitics. Discourses have largely been analysed for what they say, missing the more crucial question of discourse analysis about the mechanisms of subjectivation. It is by bringing together Laclau and Mouffe with ideas of Foucault and Bourdieu that we can understand how discourses acquire the power to make subjects. Such an understanding, however, requires an in-depth analysis of social settings. It is more difficult or perhaps even impossible to gain by analysing textual representations outside the context of their negotiation. Beyond its political thrust, my ethnographic research at MGIMO therefore has an expressly conceptual component. It seeks to go beyond idiographically illustrating local variations of general themes (cf. Hörschelmann and Stenning 2008) and urges us to rethink the conceptual treatment of subject formation towards a different understanding of identities as constituted within discourse through language *and* practice. The power of ethnography then is to gain empirical purchase on social practices as a crucial part of identities.

The conceptual value of Laclau and Mouffe's poststructuralist discourse theory also lies in the structural analysis of discourses it proposes. By structural analysis I here mean the analysis of regularities as expressed in the concepts of crisis, antagonism, lack or chain of equivalence that do not describe the content but rather the configuration of discourses. Such analysis is largely absent from the established literature on Russian geopolitics and foreign policy. Even avowed constructivists or poststructuralists like Tsygankov (1997, 2003a, 2007), Ó Tuathail (O'Loughlin et al. 2004a, b, 2005) or Ingram (2001) often treat discourse analysis as an ordinary summary of the content of different geopolitical storylines. In many cases, a more profound engagement with the discourse theoretical literature and its application to the analysis of empirical material would be desirable for working towards a more theoretically grounded analysis of discourses and identities.

Of course, structure and content can never be completely separated. After all, both work together as constitutive elements of discourse. If I have stressed the necessity of structural analysis, this does not mean that the content of discourses can be dismissed. On the contrary, my empirical analysis has devoted considerable space to this, given the unique source material that would be hard to come by in ordinary research projects. Like the majority of recent studies, I find that there is considerable self-confidence about Russia's role in world politics. Clearly, in the eyes of MGIMO students and lecturers Russia should not be content with the role of a regional state. Rather, it belongs to the world's leading states with an influence that extends over the globe. This position as a great power, however, should not be confused with aggressive imperialism, since the interpretation of what global influence means varies. For most, it means that Russia is accepted as an equal partner in the West and in China, Japan and India – an equal partner whose interests and independence are respected. This respect would also include refraining from trying to pressurise or sway Russia in one direction or the other.

A great power Russia as it is often envisioned at MGIMO can defend its interests, is respected in the world and is a country to be proud of for its citizens. Building up this position is considered one of the key tasks of Russian foreign policy. In almost all cases, this does not entail a confrontation with the West. But it neither means that, in the view of lecturers and students, the West should play the most important role in Russian foreign policy or, even more, that Russia is constructed as somehow Western or European. Looking towards Asian countries in the pursuit of a multivector foreign policy is high on the agenda at MGIMO and underscores Russian distinctiveness as a separate civilisation between East and West. What this concept of Russia does entail, however, is a search for recognition as the strong, respectable state that Russia aspires to be. The lack of this recognition, and thus the impossibility of realising Russia's geopolitical identity as a strong state, constituted a recurrent theme at MGIMO. In the articulation of threat or marginalisation, this lack becomes most prominent. Once again, however, threat and marginalisation are not attributed to a universal, threatening antagonist, but are specific to certain situations such as the economic rise of China or to the expansion of NATO in Eastern Europe.

The majority position on Russia's geopolitical identity at MGIMO shares many similarities with what Smith (1999b) and O'Loughlin et al. (2005) have identified as a democratic statist geopolitical discourse. Russia is considered a great power which is different from the West but nevertheless accepts that cooperation with it is necessary in certain issues or plays the political broker to mediate in conflicts with states like Iran. Just like at MGIMO, democratic statism represents the Near Abroad as somehow belonging to one community with Russia and as crucial to Russian geopolitical interests and its re-assertion as a great power. Both Smith (1999b) and O'Loughlin et al. (2005) find that democratic statism is the dominant discourse among Russia's ruling elites and in the Russian population – a dominance that is also evident at MGIMO. This empirical parallel underscores MGIMO's close involvement in the Russian state apparatus. Reproducing the dominant geopolitical positions from the state level, it fashions a future elite with the authority to perpetuate the hegemonic geopolitical structures.

Yet, my empirical material also exhibits some divergences from the received wisdom on Russian geopolitical orientation. In contrast to other studies, several geopolitical signifiers only rarely appear at MGIMO. Especially Eurasia, the mantra of numerous publications on Russian geopolitics, plays a rather marginal role and is certainly not the 'key term in Russian geopolitical discourse', as Graham Smith (1999b: 492) suggests. One main reason for this divergence probably is the different material on which I have based my analysis. While most other authors have relied on more formal sources like books, political speeches or interviews with politicians, my own research has tapped into a more everyday making of meaning in the professional education of students. In this setting, 'Eurasia' simply does not belong to the professional vocabulary of foreign policy analysis. Much of its meaning is transferred to other terms such as 'great power' or 'Near Abroad' that take over its function in geopolitical discourse. Analysing such less overtly ideological material as it is created in ethnographic research therefore calls for sensitivity to categories different from those found in the overblown rhetoric of high politics.

Moreover, the prominent role of economic signifiers in articulations of Russian geopolitical identity as a great power is often underestimated. At MGIMO, Russia's re-emergence is almost always linked to notions of economic strength. Realising Russia's economic potential is not only a pre-condition for becoming a great power but a constitutive component of it. This importance of economic success is a recurrent theme at MGIMO and applies both to the everyday life of the individual student, who seeks to boost her or his market value, and for Russia at large, which seeks to position itself as a player in the global market. As a generation that has grown up with the market, MGIMO students are intensely wooed as high potentials by companies and command a significant market value. A good part of their everyday lives revolves around becoming successful as a businessman, with the notion of success being closely tied to consumption. The logic of the economy at MGIMO thus weaves together the contexts of everyday life and foreign policy. The primacy of economic rationales in students' lives also plays out in conceptions of a strong and successful Russia in world politics. This observation makes out the empirical case for examining mundane social practices and geopolitical rhetoric together and not separately if geopolitical identity is to be grasped in its fullness.

A situated analysis of the work of discourse at MGIMO finally also asks to recognise that my ethnography can only be partial. It can only be partial in the sense that it has focused on geopolitical articulations at the expense of other aspects of student life that might also have been worth exploring in greater depth. And it can only be partial because of my own discursive mooring from which I deploy my academic representations. This mooring has changed over the course of my research, transforming it from a study in which MGIMO and Russia were the exotic, unknown Other into hopefully a more emic, empathetic account of Russian geopolitical identities. This transformation is not without its consequences. In a public climate in which Russia has increasingly become the aggressive, imperialist scapegoat in world politics it is not easy to write from a position that seeks, primarily, to *understand*. In times when some interpretations of a radical geography advocate joint action against Russia, how can one write *for* Russia, in an empathetic sense? How does one deal with critics at conferences who question your research because you do not sing along the lines of Russian imperialism, revanchism and aggressive behaviour?

Like any other research, my research cannot lay claim to objectivity. There is no point in wanting to paint a somehow 'representative' picture of geopolitical identities at MGIMO. Quite to the contrary, my research is inevitably political insofar as it pits the contextualised making of meaning at MGIMO against the sweeping etic accounts of Russian geopolitical interests pervasive in this field. In so doing, it hopes to challenge and disrupt the picture of the Russian Other that is omnipresent in the formation of European and Western identities (cf. Kuus 2004; Neumann 1999) and underwent a rapid renaissance in the wake of the war in South Ossetia in August 2008. Neoconservative academic and foreign policy circles picked up on the Othering of Russia and under the guise of expert knowledge filled the newspapers with recitations of the old orientalist discourse. Headlines announced that 'The bear is back' (*The Australian*, 18 August 2008), that 'The empire strikes back' (*Time*, 12 August 2008), that the West faces a 'Russia resurgent' (*The Economist*, 16 August 2008) and a 'Russian threat' (*Die Zeit*, 14 August 2008). Even broadsheets like the influential German *Süddeutsche Zeitung* (16/17 August 2008), ran titles like the following: 'Russian foreign policy strategy still knows only one idea: the tank'. Evoking notions of a Russian threat and new geopolitical fault lines ties into the very patterns of reasoning that reinforce hegemonies and that have been dissected by critical geopolitics.

Following in the critical tradition of critical geopolitics I have sought to write an ethnography that perhaps reaches beyond the confines of the local research setting to question larger taken-for-granted conceptions about Russian great power identity. This challenge to the hegemonic discourse is important for two principal reasons. For one thing, its counter-hegemonic thrust works towards the goal of maintaining a plurality of social demands and the co-existence of legitimate differences. The discursive resurrection of the evil empire in the West and, vice versa, of a Western threat in Russia, structures world politics in terms of exclusion and opposition. Exposing this opposition as a contingent construction and not reinforcing it as an allegedly objective given must be part of every emancipatory research that engages with naturalised hegemonies.

For another, as far as my own positionality is concerned, it means that at least to some degree I may have managed to step outside my initial discursive framing – only, of course, to move towards another. Unlike most other studies of Russian foreign policy, this intermediate position means that my research has to do justice to at least two audiences: the imaginary reader at MGIMO and the academic and professional reader outside it. It not only has to make a meaningful contribution to the literature and knowledge about Russian foreign policy and critical geopolitics. But it must also be held accountable for its representation vis-à-vis my research subjects. This double responsibility has made writing difficult and at times asked for compromises. Uncertainty about the 'adequate' representation of my research has accompanied me along the way. But on the other hand these doubts have also made this study more responsible. By collapsing the distance between researcher and researched that characterises so much foreign policy research on Russia, othering one's research subjects becomes considerably more difficult.

10

Where does all this take us?

> Because you not only have to know what happens in every country, who is in power and so on, but you also have to know the situation of the youth, the situation of education in that country. Because this is like a photograph of what we have to expect from that state.
>
> *Lecture at MGIMO, 3 September 2005*

How does Russia view its place in world politics? How does it imagine the political world map? My ethnographic research at Moscow State Institute of International Relations (MGIMO) casts a new light on the questions from which my enquiry has started. Seeking to relate foreign policy and geopolitical identity to the lifeworlds of subjects, it considers the education of the future Russian elite from the inside – to perhaps even get a photograph of what to expect from Russia, as the professor above tells her students. Despite my intention to fashion a micro level analysis of the discursive constitution of Russian geopolitical identities, the implications of my research need not be confined to the research setting.

Even though the social system has changed and career trajectories in post-Soviet Russia are not mapped out as rigidly as they used to be, MGIMO still holds a nodal position in the reproduction of elites in Russia. It creates a highly qualified labour pool of specialists in international affairs and world politics, not only for the Russian Ministry of Foreign Affairs. From this reservoir people are recruited into influential positions in Russia and across the post-Soviet space. It can be surmised, therefore, that the construction and negotiation of geopolitical imaginations and identity at MGIMO is to some extent indicative of the developments not only within Russian and post-Soviet foreign policy circles but, considering the career trajectories of alumni, of the Russian and post-Soviet societies at large, and that perhaps it even allows us a glimpse of the shape of things to come in the future. What, then, can the application of poststructuralist discourse theory and ethnography in this study contribute to the understanding of Russian geopolitical identity and, perhaps, of Russia's role in world politics?

First, it gives us clues as to what might drive Russian behaviour in world politics. Clearly, the vision of a *strong Russia* enjoys most popularity at MGIMO. This is a Russia that is respected as an influential, independent actor in world politics, that has a prospering economy and that plays a leading role in the post-Soviet states. It is a country on a par with Europe, the US and China, but still a distinct centre of power in a multipolar world. What is at the heart of this Russian geopolitical identity at MGIMO is not a somehow innate 'great powerness' (*deržavnost'*) but rather a constitutive lack – an *unfulfilled identity*. Notions of loss and exclusion play a crucial role in articulations of Russian geopolitical identity at MGIMO. Seeking to rebuild Russian influence in the world, rekindling the Russian great power project can then be read as the expression of the search for filling this lack. By acting like it does, Russia is not driven by an identity that is often described by attributes like 'imperialism', 'power politics' or 'aggressive confrontation'. Rather, it tries to overcome this blockage of identity, to achieve a fullness of identity, which, however, is imaginary and can never be achieved. Instead of claiming that Russia *has* a great power identity, it is therefore more appropriate to say that Russia *wants to realise* a great power identity.

In foregrounding Russia's assertive behaviour in foreign policy it is usually overlooked that this behaviour always implicates articulations of a potentially weak Russia. This *ambiguity of the geopolitical identity of a strong Russia* is evident throughout MGIMO in the split between what Russia would like to be and what it currently is, between aspiration and reality. Most accounts of Russian great power fantasies fail to problematise this ambiguity. It is, however, constitutive of the production of Russian geopolitical identity, since a strong Russia is always predicated on what it claims not to be. It would therefore be wrong to assume that the re-emergence of a great power identity somehow resolves the crisis of identity from the 1990s. On the contrary, this re-emergence is crucially predicated on the crisis, because it arises from the attempt to overcome it.

Second, *through actions directed at containing Russia, Western states possibly contribute to the emergence of the very assertive behaviour they seek to discourage.* This conclusion is an immediate consequence of conceptualising Russia's great power identity around a constitutive lack. The idea of Russia as a strong, independent state, and the actions connected to this idea, are always predicated on an antagonist blocking this very identity. The West embodies this antagonist, when it strive to isolate or contain Russia. In the wake of the war between Russia and Georgia in August 2008, calls became ever louder that Russia must be isolated. Especially the US and many Eastern European states moved to endorse and enact policies that were aimed to keep Russia in check: the American missile shield in Eastern Europe was to be built up even faster and to be expanded eastwards to encompass Ukraine. Georgia's and Ukraine's NATO membership became more likely than ever before. The renegotiation of the EU-Russia partnership treaty was called into question.

My research cautions that the more the West seeks to contain Russia, the more Russia will fall back on a geopolitical identity as a great power. Russian agency in world politics is thus not autonomous but predicated on the Western Other. Reinforcing the antagonism of the Western threat to Russian strength contributes to the emergence of a forceful logic of equivalence. In this logic of equivalence, a strong Russia faces a Western opponent. Yet, at MGIMO a strong Russia is not imagined in a way that would necessarily entail an antagonistic confrontation with the West. In contrast, cooperation and partnership feature high on the agenda. Treating Russia as equal and accepting that it will not be part of the West or Europe but rather of a multipolar world could contribute to the recognition of legitimate differences in world politics.

Third and finally, judging from the experience at MGIMO, *Russian economic modernisation and integration into the world economy are unlikely to result in a more Western geopolitical orientation of Russia.* In their consumption and their lifestyle, students at MGIMO are, at first glance, probably the most Western social group in Russia. They are a highly qualified, international elite that regularly travels abroad, that is oriented towards pursuing a successful career with an international outlook and that enjoys all the amenities of a Western lifestyle. All this notwithstanding, the majority of students still remain committed to a geopolitical identity that envisions a strong Russia distinct from Western states. With this identity students are perched, allegorically speaking, *between Pravda and Prada*, positioned at the same time by a patriotic discourse of regaining Russian strength and by a consumerist discourse reminiscent of Western ideals of a good life. In view of these results, the frequently voiced position that economic development will effect a gradual makeover in Russia that gives the country a Western orientation appears highly questionable.

Where does all this take us? Conceptually, it perhaps takes us one step towards recognising the value of a close engagement with poststructuralist discourse theory for critical geopolitics and critical international relations. Methodologically, it perhaps takes us one step towards an ethnography that contributes new insights and conceptual advances to 'the big picture'. Empirically, it perhaps takes us one step towards a different understanding of Russian great power identity. Politically, it would be presumptuous to claim that it perhaps takes us one step towards embracing pluralism and difference as the basis of world politics.

We've looked and looked, but after all where are we?
Do we know any better where we are,
And how it stands between the night to-night
And a man with a smoky lantern chimney?
How different from the way it ever stood?

Robert Frost: *The star-splitter* (1923)

Bibliography

Key Literature

Bourdieu, P. 1996 [1989]. *The state nobility: elite schools in the field of power.* Stanford: Stanford University Press.

Foucault, M. 1979. *Discipline and punish: the birth of the prison.* New York: Vintage.

Hopf, T. 2002. *Social construction of international politics: identities and foreign policies, Moscow, 1955 and 1999.* Ithaca: Cornell University Press.

Laclau, E. 1990. *New reflections on the revolution of our time.* London: Verso.

———. 1996. *Emanicaption(s).* London: Phronesis.

Laclau, E., and C. Mouffe. 1985. *Hegemony and socialist strategy: towards a radical democratic politics.* London: Verso.

Ó Tuathail, G. 1996. *Critical geopolitics: the politics of writing global space.* Minneapolis: University of Minnesota Press.

Ó Tuathail, G., and J. Agnew. 1992. Geopolitics and discourse: practical geopolitical reasoning in American foreign policy. *Political Geography* 11 (2):190-204.

O'Loughlin, J., G. Ó Tuathail, and V. Kolossov. 2005. Russian geopolitical culture and public opinion: the masks of Proteus revisited. *Transactions of the Institute of British Geographers* 30 (3):322-335.

Smith, G. 1999b. The masks of Proteus: Russia, geopolitical shift and the new Eurasianism. *Transactions of the Institute of British Geographers* 24 (4):481-494.

Torfing, J. 1999. *New theories of discourse: Laclau, Mouffe, and Žižek.* Oxford: Blackwell.

Tsygankov, A. P. 2003a. Mastering space in Eurasia: Russia's geopolitical thinking after the Soviet break-up. *Communist and Post Communist Studies* 36:101-127.

———. 2006a. *Russia's foreign policy: change and continuity in national identity.* New York: Rowman & Littlefield.

Full Reference List

Ackleson, J. 2005. Constructing security on the US-Mexico border. *Political Geography* 24 (2):165-184.

Agnew, J. 1998. *Geopolitics: re-visioning world politics.* London: Routledge.

Agnew, J., and S. Corbridge. 1995. *Mastering space: hegemony, territory and international political economy.* London: Routledge.

Allensworth, W. 1998. Derzhavnost': Aleksandr Lebed's vision for Russia. *Problems of Post-Communism* 45 (2):51-58.

Asad, T. ed. 1973. *Anthropology and the colonial encounter.* London: Ithaca Press.

Ašin, G. K. 2002. Ėlitnoe obrazovanie v menjajuščemsja mire [Elite education in a changing world]. In *Elitnoe obrazovanie: mirovoj opyt i model' MGIMO [Elite education: global experience and the model of MGIMO]*, eds. G. K. Ašin and S. A. Kravčenko. Moscow: MGIMO.

Åslund, A. 2002. *Building capitalism: the transformation of the former Soviet bloc.* Cambridge: Cambridge University Press.

———. 2007. *Russia's capitalist revolution: why market reform succeeded and democracy failed.* Washington: Peterson Institute for International Economics.

Atkinson, P. 1990. *The ethnographic imagination: the textual construction of reality.* London: Routledge.

Austin, J. L. 1962. *How to do things with words.* Oxford: Clarendon Press.

Baev, P. 1997. Russia's departure from Empire: self-assertiveness and a new retreat. In *Geopolitics in post-wall Europe: security, territory and identity*, eds. O. Tunander, P. Baev and V. I. Einagel, 174-195. Oslo: International Peace Research Institute.

Bain, A. L., and C. J. Nash. 2006. Undressing the researcher: feminism, embodiment and sexuality at a queer bathhouse event. *Area* 38 (1):99-106.

Ball, S. J. ed. 1990. *Foucault and education: disciplines and knowledge.* London: Routledge.

Baranovsky, V. 2000. Russia: a part of Europe or apart from Europe? *International Affairs* 76 (3):443-458.

Bassin, M. 1991. Russia between Europe and Asia: on the ideological construction of geographical space. *Slavic Review* 50 (1):1-17.

Bassin, M., and K. E. Aksenov. 2006. Mackinder and the heartland theory in post-Soviet geopolitical discourses. *Geopolitics* 11:99-118.

Bech Dyrberg, T. 2004. The political and politics in discourse analysis. In *Laclau: a critical reader*, eds. S. Critchley and O. Marchart, 241-255. London: Routledge.

Berg, E. 2000. Deconstructing border practices in the Estonian-Russian borderlands. *Geopolitics* 5 (3):78-98.

Bevir, M. 1999. Foucault, power and institutions. *Political Studies* 47 (2):345-359.

Bigo, D., and R. B. J. Walker. 2007. International, Political, Sociology. *International Political Sociology* 1 (1):1-5.

Billig, M. 1995. *Banal nationalism.* London: Sage.

Bourdieu, P. 1996 [1989]. *The state nobility: elite schools in the field of power.* Stanford: Stanford University Press.

Bronfenbrenner, U. 1952. Principles of professional ethics. *American Psychologist* 7:452-455.

Brudny, Y. M. 2000. *Reinventing Russia: Russian nationalism and the Soviet state, 1953-1991.* Cambridge, MA: Harvard University Press.

Buszynski, L. 2000. Russia and Northeast Asia: aspirations and reality. *The Pacific Review* 13 (3):399-420.

———. 2004. Russia and the CIS in 2003. *Asia Survey* 44 (1):158-167.

Butler, J. 1990. *Gender trouble: feminism and the subversion of identity.* London: Routledge.

———. 1993. *Bodies that matter: on the discursive limits of 'sex'.* London: Routledge.

———. 1995. For a careful reading. In *Feminist contentions: a philosophical exchange*, 127-144. New York: Routledge.

Butler, J., E. Laclau, and S. Žižek. 2000. *Contingency, hegemony, universality: contemporary dialogues on the Left.* London: Verso.

Campbell, D. 1992. *Writing security: United States foreign policy and the politics of identity.* Minneapolis: University of Minnesota Press.

———. 1996. Political prosaics, transversal politics and the anarchical world. In *Challenging boundaries: global flows, territorial identities*, eds. M. J. Shapiro and H. R. Alker, 7-31. Minneapolis: University of Minnesota Press.

———. 1998. *National deconstruction: violence, identity, and justice in Bosnia.* Minneapolis: University of Minnesota Press.

Chinyaeva, E. 1997. The search for the 'Russian idea'. *Transitions* 4:40-46.

Cladis, M. S. 1999. Durkheim and Foucault on education and punishment. In *Durkheim and Foucault: perspectives on education and punishment*, ed. M. S. Cladis, 3-18. Oxford: Durkheim Press.

Clayton, T. 2002. Politics and nationalism in Scotland: a Clydeside case study of identity construction. *Political Geography* 21 (6):813-843.

Coffey, A., and P. Atkinson. 1996. *Making sense of qualitative data: complementary research strategies*. Thousand Oaks: Sage.

Cook, I., and M. Crang. 1995. *Doing ethnographies*. Norwich: Environmental Publications.

Cymburskij, V. L. 1993. Ostrov Rossija: perspektivy rossiskoj geopolitiki [Island Russia: perspectives of Russian geopolitics]. *Polis* 5:11-17.

D'Anieri, P. J. 1999. *Economic interdependence in Ukrainian-Russian relations*. Albany: SUNY Press.

Dalby, S. 1990a. *Creating the Second World War: the discourse of politics*. New York: Guilford.

———. 1990b. American security discourse: the persistence of geopolitics. *Political Geography Quarterly* 9:171-188.

Deacon, R. 2005. Moral orthopedics: a Foucauldian account of schooling as discipline. *Telos* 130:84-102.

———. 2006. Michel Foucault on education: a preliminary theoretical overview. *South African Journal of Education* 26 (2):177-187.

Deacon, R., and B. Parker. 1995. Education as subjection and refusal: an elaboration on Foucault. *Curriculum Studies* 3 (2):109-122.

Derrida, J. 1976. *Of grammatology*. Baltimore: Johns Hopkins University Press.

Dexter, L. A. 1970. *Elite and specialized interviewing*. Evanston: Northwestern University Press.

Dijkink, G. 1996. *National identity and geopolitical visions: maps of pride and pain*. London: Routledge.

Diligenskij, G. 2000. Zapad v rossijskom obščestvennom soznanii (The West in the Russian societal perception). *Obščestvennye Nauki i Sovremennost'* 5:41-53.

Dittmer, J. 2005. NATO, the EU and Central Europe: differing symbolic shapes in newspaper accounts of enlargement. *Geopolitics* 10 (1):76-98.

Dodds, K. 1994. Geopolitics in the Foreign Office: British representations of Argentina 1945-1961. *Transactions of the Institute of British Geographers* 19:273-290.

Dowler, L., and J. P. Sharp. 2001. A feminist geopolitics? *Space & Polity* 5 (3):165-176.

Dugin, A. 2000. *Osnovy geopolitiki: geopolitičeskoe buduščee Rossii. Myslit' prostranstvom (The foundations of geopolitics: the geopolitical future of Russia. Thinking spatially*. Fourth ed. Moscow: Arktogeja-Centr.

Dunlop, J. B. 1997. Russia: in search of an identity? In *New states, new politics: building the post-Soviet nations*, eds. I. Bremmer and R. Taras, 29-95. Cambridge: Cambridge University Press.

Ellis, C., and A. P. Bochner. 2000. Autoethnography, personal narrative, reflexivity: researcher as subject. In *The handbook of qualitative research*, eds. N. Denzin and Y. S. Lincoln, 733-768. Thousand Oaks: Sage.

Elwood, S. A., and D. G. Martin. 2000. "Placing" interviews: location and scales of power in qualitative research. *The Professional Geographer* 52 (4):649-657.

Emerson, R. M., R. I. Fretz, and L. L. Shaw. 1995. *Writing ethnographic fieldnotes*. Chicago: University of Chicago Press.

Fine, G. A. 1994. Ten lies of ethnography: Moral dilemmas of field research. *Journal of Contemporary Ethnography* 22 (3):267-294.

Fischer, S. 2006. *Die EU und Russland: Konflikte und Potentiale einer schwierigen Partnerschaft [The EU and Russia: conflicts and potentials of a difficult partnership]*. Berlin: Stiftung Wissenschaft und Politik.

———. 2007. The EU and Russia: stumbling from summit to summit. In *Russia's foreign policy: key regions and issues*, eds. R. Orttung, J. Perovic, H. Pleines and H.-H. Schröder, 15-17. Bremen: Forschungsstelle Osteuropa.

Forsberg, T. 2005. Russia's relationship with NATO: a qualitative change or old wine in new bottles? *Journal of Communist Studies and Transition Politics* 21 (3):332-353.

Foucault, M. 1971. J. K. Simon: a conversation with Michel Foucault. *Partisan Review* 38:192-201.

———. 1972. *The archaeology of knowledge*. London: Tavistock.

———. 1977 [1971]. Revolutionary action: "until now". In *Language, counter-memory, practice: selected essays and interviews by Michel Foucault*, ed. D. F. Bouchard, 218-234. Ithaca: Cornell University Press.

———. 1979 [1975]. *Discipline and punish: the birth of the prison*. New York: Vintage.

———. 1982. The subject and power. In *Michel Foucault: beyond structuralism and hermeneutics*, eds. H. L. Dreyfus and P. Rabinow, 208-226. Chicago: University of Chicago Press.

———. 1991. Questions of method. In *The Foucault effect: studies in governmentality*, eds. G. Burchell, C. Gordon and P. Miller, 73-86. Chicago: University of Chicago Press.

Fox, R. C. 2004. Observations and reflections of a perpetual fieldworker. *Annals of the American Academy of Political and Social Science* 595:309-326.

Fuller, D. 1999. Part of the action or 'going native'? Learning to cope with the 'politics of integration'. *Area* 31 (3):221-227.

Gadžiev, K. S. 2003. *Vvedenie v geopolitiku (Introduction to geopolitics)*. Moscow: Logos.

Gilbert, M. 1994. The politics of location: doing feminist research at "home". *The Professional Geographer* 46:90-96.

Glasze, G. 2007a. Vorschläge zur Operationalisierung der Diskurstheorie von Laclau und Mouffe in einer Triangulation von lexikometrischen und interpretativen Methoden. *Forum Qualitative Social Research* 8 (2).

———. 2007b. The discursive constitution of a world-spanning region and the role of empty signifiers: the case of Francophonia. *Geopolitics* 12 (4):656-679.

Glesne, C., and A. Peshkin. 1999. *Becoming qualitative researchers*. Reading: Addison-Wesley.

Goldman, M. I. 2008. *Petrostate: Putin, power and the new Russia*. Oxford: Oxford University Press.

Graham, T. E. 2000. The fate of the Russian state. *Demokratizatsiya* 8 (3):354-375.

Gregson, N., and G. Rose. 2000. Taking Butler elsewhere: performativities; spatialities and subjectivities. *Environment and Planning D: Society & Space* 18 (4):433-452.

Gvosdev, N. K. 2007. Russia: 'European but not Western?'. *Orbis* 51 (1):129-140.

Hall, K. 2003. Exceptional speakers: contested and problematised gender identities. In *The handbook of language and gender*, eds. J. Holmes and M. Meyerhoff, 353-380. Oxford: Blackwell.

Hall, S. 1997. *Representation: cultural representations and signifying practices.* London: Sage.

Hammersley, M., and P. Atkinson. 1995. *Ethnography: principles and practices.* New York: Routledge.

Haraway, D. 1991. *Simians cyborgs and women: the reinvention of nature.* Routledge: London.

Harrington, B. 2002. Obtrusiveness as strategy in ethnographic research. *Qualitative Sociology* 25 (1):49-61.

Hauner, M. 1990. *What is Asia to us? Russia's heartland yesterday and today.* Boston: Unwin Hyman.

Heffernan, M. 1998. *The meaning of Europe: geography and geopolitics.* London: Arnold.

Herbert, S. 2000. For ethnography. *Progress in Human Geography* 24 (4):550-568.

Herrera, C. D. 1999. Two arguments for 'covert methods' in social research. *British Journal of Sociology* 50 (2):331-343.

———. 2003. A clash of methodology and ethics in 'undercover' social sciences. *Philosophy of the Social Sciences* 33 (3):351-362.

Herspring, D. R., and P. Rutland. 2005. Putin and Russian foreign policy. In *Putin's Russia: past imperfect, future uncertain*, ed. D. R. Herspring, 259-292. Oxford: Rowman & Littlefield.

Hilbert, R. A. 1980. Covert participant observation: on its nature and practice. *Urban Life* 9 (1):51-78.

Höllwerth, A. 2007. *Das sakrale eurasische Imperium des Aleksandr Dugin: eine Diskursanalyse zum postsowjetischen russischen Rechtsextremismus [Aleksandr Dugin's sacral Eurasian empire: a discourse analysis of post-Soviet Russian right-wing extremism].* Stuttgart: ibidem.

Hopf, T. 2002. *Social construction of international politics: identities and foreign policies, Moscow, 1955 and 1999.* Ithaca: Cornell University Press.

———. 2005. Identity, legitimacy, and the use of military force: Russia's great power identities and military intervention in Abkhazia. *Review of International Studies* 31:225-243.

Hörschelmann, K., and A. Stenning. 2008. Ethnographies of postsocialist change. *Progress in Human Geography* 32 (3):339-361.

Howarth, D. 2000. *Discourse.* Buckingham: Open University Press.

———. 2004. Applying discourse theory: the method of articulation. In *Discourse theory in European politics: identity, policy and governance*, eds. D. Howarth and J. Torfing, 316-349. Basingstoke: Palgrave Macmillan.

Howarth, D., Y. Stavrakakis, and A. J. Norval eds. 2000. *Discourse theory and political analysis: identities, hegemonies and social change.* Manchester: Manchester University Press.

Howarth, D., and J. Torfing eds. 2004. *Discourse theory in European politics.* Basingstoke: Palgrave Macmillan.

Humphrey, C. 2002. "Eurasianismus": Ideologie und politische Vorstellungen in der russischen Provinz ['Eurasianism': ideology and political imaginations of the Russian province]. In *Postsozialismus: Transformationsprozesse in Europa und Asien aus ethnologischer Perspektive [Post-socialism: processes of transformation in Europe and Asia in ethnological perspective]*, ed. C. Hann, 373-400. Frankfurt Campus.

Humphreys, L. 1970. *Tearoom trade: A study of homosexual encounters in public places.* London: Duckworth.

Ingram, A. 2001. Alexander Dugin: Geopolitics and neo-fascism in post-Soviet Russia. *Political Geography* 20:1029-1051.

Ivanova-Galitsina, A. 2000. A training ground for tomorrow's elite: MGIMO. *Financial Times*, 10 May 2000:8.

Jameson, F. 1984. Foreword to Lyotard's "The postmodern condition", vii-xxii. Minneapolis: University of Minnesota Press.

Jørgensen, M. W., and L. Phillips. 2002. *Discourse analysis as theory and method.* London: Sage.

Kagan, R. 2008. Putin makes his move. *The Washington Post*, 11 August 2008:A15.

Kanet, R. E. ed. 2007. *Russia: re-emerging great power.* Basingstoke: Palgrave Macmillan.

Katz, C. 1994. Playing the field: questions of fieldwork in geography. *The Professional Geographer* 46 (1):67-72.

Keller, R. 2004. *Diskursforschung: Eine Einführung für Sozialwissenschaftler [Discourse research: an introduction for social scientists]*. Opladen: Leske + Budrich.

Kerr, D. 1995. The new Eurasianism: the rise of geopolitics in Russia's foreign policy. *Europe-Asia Studies* 47 (6):977-988.

Kimura, H., S. Li, and I.-D. Koh. 1999. 'Frontiers are the razor's edge: Russia's borders with its eastern neighbors. In *Russia and East Asia: the 21st century security environment*, eds. G. Rozman, M. G. Nosov and K. Watanabe, 150-176. Armonk: M.E. Sharpe.

Kleine-Brockhoff, T. 2008. Russland will nicht mehr nach Westen [Russia no longer wants into the West]. *Süddeutsche Zeitung*, 26 August 2008:2.

Kolossov, V. ed. 2000. *Geopolitičeskoe položenie Rossii: predstavlenija i realnost' (The geographical location of Russia: representations and reality)*. Moscow: Art-Kur'er.

———. 2003. 'High' and 'low' geopolitics: images of foreign countries in the eyes of Russian citizens. *Geopolitics* 8 (1):121-148.

Kolossov, V., and R. Turovsky. 2001. Russian geopolitics at the fin-de-siècle. *Geopolitics* 6 (1):141-164.

Kolossov, V. A., and N. S. Mironenko. 2001. *Geopolitika i političeskaya geografija [Geopolitics and political geography]*. Moscow: Aspekt Press.

Kolstø, P. 2004. Nation-building in Russia: a value-oriented strategy. In *Nation-building and common values in Russia*, eds. P. Kolstø and H. Blakkisrud, 1-28. Lanham, MD: Rowman & Littlefield.

Kuus, M. 2004. Europe's eastern expansion and the reinscription of otherness in East-Central Europe. *Progress in Human Geography* 28 (4):472-489.

———. 2007a. *Geopolitics reframed: security and identity in Europe's Eastern Enlargement.* New York: Palgrave Macmillan

———. 2007b. Ubiquitous identities, elusive subjects: puzzles from Central Europe. *Transactions of the Institute of British Geographers* 32 (1):90-101.

Kuzio, T. 2003. National identities and virtual foreign policies among the eastern Slavs. *Nationalities Papers* 31 (4):431-452.

Laclau, E. 1990. *New reflections on the revolution of our time.* London: Verso.

——— ed. 1994. *The making of political identities.* London: Verso.

———. 1995. Subject of politics, politics of the subject. *Differences* 7 (1):145-164.

———. 1996. *Emanicaption(s)*. London: Phronesis.

———. 2006. Ideology and post-Marxism. *Journal of Political Ideologies* 11 (2):103-114.

Laclau, E., and C. Mouffe. 1985. *Hegemony and socialist strategy: towards a radical democratic politics*. London: Verso.

———. 1990 [1987]. Post-Marxism without apologies. In *New reflections on the revolution of our time*, ed. E. Laclau, 97-132. London: Verso.

Laruelle, M. 2004. The two faces of contemporary Eurasianism: an imperial version of Russian nationalism. *Nationalities Papers* 32 (1):115-136.

Lazuech, G. 1998. Le processus d'internationalisation des Grandes Écoles françaises [Internationalization of the French "grandes ecoles"]. *Actes De La Recherche En Sciences Sociales* (121-22):66-76.

Ledeneva, A. V. 1998. *Russia's economy of favors: blat, networking and informal exchange*. Cambridge: Cambridge University Press.

Leech, B. L. 2002. Asking questions: techniques for semi-structured interviews. *PS: Political Science and Politics* 35 (4):665-668.

Livia, A., and K. Hall. 1997. "It's a girl!" Bringing performativity back to linguistics. In *Queerly phrased: language, gender, and sexuality*, eds. A. Livia and K. Hall, 3-20. Oxford: Oxford University Press.

Lo, B. 2002. *Russian foreign policy in the post-Soviet era*. Basingstoke: Palgrave.

Lofland, J., and L. Lofland. 1995. *Analyzing social settings*. Belmont: Wadsworth.

Lossau, J. 2000. Anders Denken. Postkolonialismus, Geopolitik und Politische Geographie [Think different. Postcolonialism, geopolitics and political geography]. *Erdkunde* 54 (2):157-168.

———. 2002. Politische Geographie und Geopolitik: Bemerkungen zu einem (un-)bestimmbaren Verhältnis [Political geography and geopolitics: remarks on an (in-)definable relationship]. *Erdkunde* 56 (1):73-81.

Lucas, E. 2008. *The new Cold War: Putin's Russia and the threat to the West*. Basingstoke: Palgrave Macmillan.

Lynn, N. J., and V. Bogorov. 1999. Reimagining the Russian idea. In *Nested identities: nationalism, territory, and scale*, eds. G. H. Herb and D. H. Kaplan, 101-120. Lanham: Rowman & Littlefield.

Mäkinen, S. 2003. On the geopolitical discourses of the Russian Yabloko association, 1993-2001. *Geopolitics* 8 (1):149-180.

Mattissek, A., and P. Reuber. 2004. Die Diskursanalyse als Methode in der Geographie: Ansätze und Potentiale [Discourse analysis as a method in geographical research: approaches and potential]. *Geographische Zeitschrift* 92 (4):227-242.

Mayne, J. 1990. *The woman at the keyhole: feminism and women's cinema.* Bloomington Indiana University Press.

McCracken, G. 1988. *The long interview.* Newbury Park: Sage.

McNicol Jardine, G. 2005. *Foucault & education.* New York: Peter Lang.

Megoran, N. 2002. The borders of eternal friendship? The politics and pain of nationalism and identity along the Uzbekistan-Kyrgyzstan Ferghana Valley boundary, 1999-2000. PhD dissertation, Department of Geography, University of Cambridge, Cambridge.

———. 2004. The critical geopolitics of the Uzbekistan-Kyrgyzstan Ferghana Valley boundary dispute, 1999-2000. *Political Geography* 23 (6):731-764.

———. 2005. The critical geopolitics of danger in Uzbekistan and Kyrgyzstan. *Environment and Planning D: Society and Space* 23 (4):555-580.

———. 2006. For ethnography in political geography: experiencing and re-imagining Ferghana Valley boundary closures. *Political Geography* 25:622-640.

Menon, R., Y. E. Fedorov, and G. Nodia eds. 1999. *Russia, the Caucasus, and Central Asia: the 21st century security environment.* Armonk: Sharpe.

MGIMO. 2005. Programma strategičeskogo razvitija MGIMO MID Rossii (2005-2012 gg.) [MGIMO strategic development programme (2005 2012)]. Moscow: MGIMO.

———. 2008. *Jurij Kofner: "Ja verju v vozmožnosti Rossii" (I believe in Russia's potential)* 2008 [cited 11 August 2008]. Available from www.mgimo.ru/study/dean/news/n13403.phtml.

Min'jar-Beloručev, K. V. 2006. *Mirovaja geopolitika: učebno-metodičeskaja razrabotka po kursu lekcij.* Moscow: Prospekt-AP.

Minh-ha, T. T. 1989. *Woman, native, other: writing postcoloniality and feminism.* Bloomington: Indiana University Press.

Molchanov, M. A. 2002. *Political culture and national identity in Russian-Ukrainian relations.* College Station, TX: Texas A&M University Press.

Morozov, V. 2003. Auf der Suche nach Europa: Der politische Diskurs in Russland [In search of Europe: political discourse in Russia]. *Osteuropa* 53 (9-10):1501-1514.

———. 2008. Sovereignty and democracy in contemporary Russia: a modern subject faces the post-modern world. *Journal of International Relations and Development* 11 (2):152-180.

Morris-Suzuki, T. 1999. Lines in the snow: imagining the Russo-Japanese frontier. *Pacific Affairs* 72 (1(Spring)):57-77.

Moser, S. 2008. Personality: a new positionality? *Area* 40 (3):383-392.

Mouffe, C. 1992. Citizenship and identity. *October* 61 (Summer):28-32.

———. 1995. Post-Marxism: democracy and identity. *Environment and Planning D: Society and Space* 13:259-266.

———. 2000. *The democratic paradox*. London: Verso.

Mouzelis, N. P. 1988. Marxism or post-Marxism? *New Left Review* 167:107-125.

———. 1990. *Post-Marxist alternatives: the construction of social orders*. Basingstoke: Macmillan.

Müller, M. 2007a. What's in a word? Problematising translation between languages. *Area* 39 (2):206-213.

———. 2007b. Zusammen, aber doch getrennt? Vorstellungen von Russlands Platz in Europa an einer russischen Elitehochschule [Together but separate: Imaginations of Russia's place in Europe at a Russian elite university]. *Europa Regional* 15 (4):199-208.

———. 2008a. Reconsidering the concept of discourse in the field of critical geopolitics: towards discourse as language and practice. *Political Geography* 27 (3):322-338.

———. 2008b. Situating identities: enacting and studying Europe at a Russian elite university. *Millennium: Journal of International Studies* 37 (1):3-25.

Müller, M., and P. Reuber. 2008. Empirical verve, conceptual doubts: looking from the outside in at critical geopolitics. *Geopolitics* 13 (3):458-472.

Nartov, N. A. 2004. *Geopolitika: učebnik dlja vuzov*. Third ed. Moscow: Unity-Dana.

Neumann, I. B. 1996. *Russia and the idea of Europe: a study in identity and international relations*. London: Routledge.

———. 1997. The geopolitics of delineating 'Russia' and 'Europe': the creation of the 'Other' in European and Russian tradition. In *Geopolitics in post-wall Europe: security, territory and identity*, eds. O. Tunander, P. Baev and V. I. Einagel, 147-173. Oslo: International Peace Research Institute.

———. 2002a. Returning practice to the linguistic turn: the case of diplomacy. *Millennium: Journal of International Studies* 31 (3):627-651.

———. 2002b. From the USSR to Gorbachev to Putin: perestroika as a failed excursion from 'the West' to 'Europe' in Russian discourse. In *The meaning of Europe: variety and contention within and among nations*, eds. M. af Malmborg and B. Stråth. Oxford: Berg.

———. 2008. Russia as a great power, 1815-2007. *Journal of International Relations and Development* 11 (2):128-151.

Nonhoff, M. 2006. *Politischer Diskurs und Hegemonie: das Projekt "Soziale Marktwirtschaft" [Political discourse and hegemony: the project of a "social market economy"]*. Bielefeld: transcript.

Ó Tuathail, G. 1994a. (Dis)placing geopolitics: writing on the maps of global politics. *Environment and Planning D: Society and Space* 12 (5):525-546.

———. 1994b. The critical reading/writing of geopolitics: re-reading/writing Wittfogel, Bowman and Lacoste. *Progress in Human Geography* 18 (3):313-332.

———. 1996. *Critical geopolitics: the politics of writing global space*. Minneapolis: University of Minnesota Press.

———. 2002. Theorizing practical geopolitical reasoning: the case of the United States' response to the war in Bosnia. *Political Geography* 21 (5):601-628.

———. 2006. Geopolitical discourses: Paddy Ashdown and the tenth anniversary of the Dayton peace accords. *Geopolitics* 11:141-158.

Ó Tuathail, G., and J. Agnew. 1992. Geopolitics and discourse: practical geopolitical reasoning in American foreign policy. *Political Geography* 11 (2):190-204.

O'Loughlin, J. 2001. Geopolitical fantasies, national strategies and ordinary Russians in the post-communist era. *Geopolitics* 6 (3):17-48.

O'Loughlin, J., G. Ó Tuathail, and V. Kolossov. 2004a. A 'risky westward turn'? Putin's 9-11 script and ordinary Russians. *Europe-Asia Studies* 56 (1):3-34.

———. 2004b. Russian geopolitical storylines and ordinary Russians in the wake of 9-11. *Communist and Post-Communist Studies* 37:281-318.

———. 2005. Russian geopolitical culture and public opinion: the masks of Proteus revisited. *Transactions of the Institute of British Geographers* 30 (3):322-335.

O'Loughlin, J., and P. F. Talbot. 2005. Where in the world is Russia? Geopolitical preferences and perceptions of ordinary Russians. *Eurasian Geography and Economics* 46 (1):23-50.

Oushakine, S. A. 2000. The quantity of style: imaginary consumption in the New Russia. *Theory, Culture & Society* 17:97-120.

Paasi, A. 1996. *Territories, boundaries, and consciousness: the changing geographies of the Finnish-Russian border.* Chicester: Wiley.

Parr, H. 1998. Mental health, ethnography and the body. *Area* 30 (1):28-37.

———. 2000. Interpreting the 'hidden social geographies' of mental health: ethnographies of inclusion and exclusion in semi-institutional places. *Health and Place* 6:225-237.

Patico, J. 2003. Consuming the West but becoming Third World: food imports and the experience of Russianness. *The Anthropology of East Europe Review* 21 (1).

Pavliatenko, V. N. 1999. Russian security in the Asia-Pacific region: the dangers of isolation. In *Russia and East Asia: the 21st century security environment*, eds. G. Rozman, M. G. Nosov and K. Watanabe, 13-44. Armonk, NY: Sharpe.

Pels, P., and O. Salemnik. 1994. Five theses on ethnography as colonial practice. *History and Anthropology* 8 (1-4):1-34.

Pouliot, V. 2007. "Sobjectivism": toward a constructivist methodology. *International Studies Quarterly* 51 (2):350-384.

Prozorov, S. 2006. *Understanding conflict between Russia and the EU: the limits of integration.* New York: Palgrave Macmillan.

———. 2007. The narratives of exclusion and self-exclusion in the Russian conflict discourse on EU-Russian relations. *Political Geography* 26 (3):309-329.

Rahr, A. 2008. *Russland gibt Gas: die Rückkehr einer Weltmacht.* München: Hanser.

Rangsimaporn, P. 2006. Interpretations of Eurasianism: justifying Russia's role in East Asia. *Europe-Asia Studies* 58 (3):371-390.

Rausing, S. 2002. Re-constructing the "Normal": identity and the consumption of Western goods in Estonia. In *Markets and moralities: ethnographies of postsocialism*, eds. R. Mandel and C. Humphrey, 127-142. Oxford: Berg.

Redepenning, M. 2006. *Wozu Raum? Systemtheorie, critical geopolitics und raumbezogene Semantiken [What's the purpose of space? Systems theory, critical geopolitics and spatial semantics]*. Leipzig: Leibniz-Institut für Länderkunde.

Reuber, P. 2000. Die Politische Geographie als handlungsorientierte und konstruktivistische Teildisziplin: angloamerikanische Theoriekonzepte und aktuelle Forschungsfelder [Postmodern and action-based approaches in political geography: Anglo-American concepts and recent fields of research]. *Geographische Zeitschrift* 88 (1):36-52.

Ries, N. 2000. Foreword: Ethnography and postsocialism. In *Fieldwork dilemmas: anthropologists in postsocialist states*, eds. H. G. DeSoto and N. Dudwick, ix-xi. Madison: University of Wisconsin Press.

Rose, G. 1997. Situating knowledges: positionality, reflexivities and other tactics. *Progress in Human Geography* 21 (3):305-320.

Rose, R., and N. Munro. 2008. Do Russians see their future in Europe or the CIS? *Europe-Asia Studies* 60 (1):49-66.

Roth, J. 1992. Of what help is he? A review of "Foucault and Education". *American Educational Research Journal* 29 (4):683-694.

Routledge, P. 2001. Within the river: collaboration and methodology. *Geographical Review* 91 (1/2):113 121.

———. 2002. Travelling East as Walter Kurtz: identity, performance, and collaboration in Goa, India. *Environment and Planning D: Society and Space* 20:477-498.

———. 2003. River of resistance: critical collaboration and the dilemma of power and ethics. *Ethics, Place and Environment* 6 (1):66-73.

Rožkov, I. 2007. *Interview* 2007 [cited 15 May 2007]. Available from faces.mgimo.ru.

Rozman, G. ed. 2000. *Japan and Russia: the tortuous path to normalization, 1949-1999*. New York: St. Martin's Press.

———. 2002. A chance for a breakthrough in Russo-Japanese relations: will the logic of great-power relations prevail? *The Pacific Review* 15 (3):325-357.

Sakwa, R. 2008. 'New Cold War' or twenty years' crisis? Russia and international politics. *International Affairs* 84 (2):241-267.

Schiellerup, P. 2008. Stop making sense: the trials and tribulations of qualitative data analysis. *Area* 40 (2):163-171.

Schlindwein, S. 2008. Russlands edle Kaderschmieden: Luxus mit einem Hauch Sowjetmief [Russia's noble cadre academies: luxury with a touch of Soviet fug]. *Der Spiegel/Unispiegel*, 28 July 2008.

Schwalbe, M. 1996. *Unlocking the iron cage: the men's movement, gender politics, and American culture.* New York: Oxford University Press.

Sergunin, A. A. 2004. Discussions of international relations in post-communism Russia. *Communist and Post-Communist Studies* 37:19-35.

Shapiro, M. J. 1992. *Reading the postmodern polity: political theory as textual practice.* Minneapolis: University of Minnesota Press.

Sharp, J. P. 2000a. *Condensing the Cold War: Reader's Digest and American identity.* Minneapolis: University of Minnesota Press.

———. 2000b. Remasculinising critical geopolitics? Comments on Gearoid O Tuathail's Critical Geopolitics. *Political Geography* 19:361-364.

Shevchenko, O. 2002. 'In case of fire emergency': consumption, security and the meaning of durables in a transforming society. *Journal of Consumer Culture* 2:147-170.

Shlapentokh, D. 1997. Eurasianism: past and present. *Communist and Post-Communist Studies* 30:129-151.

Sidorov, D. 2006. Post-imperial Third Romes: Resurrections of a Russian Orthodox geopolitical metaphor. *Geopolitics* 11:317-347.

Silverman, D. 1985. *Qualitative methodology and sociology.* Aldershot: Gower.

———. 1989. Six rules of qualitative research: a post-romantic argument. *Symbolic Interaction* 12 (2):25-40.

———. 1993. *Interpreting qualitative data.* London: Sage.

Simonsen, S. G. 2001. Nationalism and the Russian political spectrum: locating and evaluating the extremes. *Journal of Political Ideologies* 6 (3):263-288.

Smith, A. M. 1998. *Laclau and Mouffe: the radical democratic imaginary*. London: Routledge.

Smith, G. 1999a. *The post-Soviet states: mapping the politics of transition*. London: Arnold.

———. 1999b. The masks of Proteus: Russia, geopolitical shift and the new Eurasianism. *Transactions of the Institute of British Geographers* 24 (4):481-494.

Smith, G., V. Law, A. Wilson, A. Bohr, and E. Allworth. 1998. *Nation-building in the post-Soviet borderlands: the politics of national identities*. Cambridge: Cambridge University Press.

Smith, M. A., and G. Timmins. 2001. Russia, NATO and the EU in an era of enlargement: vulnerability or opportunity? *Geopolitics* 6 (1):69-90.

Smith, N. 2000. Is critical geopolitics possible? Foucault, class and the vision thing. *Political Geography* 19 (3):365-371.

Spivak, G. C. 1988. Can the subaltern speak? In *Marxism and the interpretation of culture*, eds. C. Nelson and L. Grossberg, 271-313. Chicago: University of Illinois Press.

Splidsboel-Hansen, F. 2002. Russia's relations with the European Union: A constructivist cut. *International Politics* 39:399-421.

Staeheli, L., E. Kofman, and L. Peake eds. 2004. *Mapping gender, making politics: feminist perspectives on Political Geography*. New York: Routledge.

Stäheli, U. 1999. Die politische Theorie der Hegemonie: Ernesto Laclau und Chantal Mouffe [The political theory of hegemony: Ernesto Laclau and Chantal Mouffe]. In *Politische Theorien der Gegenwart: eine Einführung [Contemporary political theories: an introduction]*, eds. A. Brodocz and G. S. Schaal, 143-166. Opladen: Leske + Budrich.

———. 2000. *Poststrukturalistische Soziologien [Poststructural sociologies]*. Bielefeld: transcript.

Stewart, A. 1998. *The ethnographer's method*. Thousand Oaks: Sage.

Stoddart, K. 1986. The presentation of everyday life: some textual strategies for "adequate ethnography". *Urban Life* 15:103-121.

Strüver, A. 2005. *Stories of the 'boring border': the Dutch-German borderscape in people's minds*. Münster: LIT.

Sturm, T. 2008. Critical methodological geopolitics: discourse analysis/ethnography. *Geopolitics* 13 (3):600-609.

Temnickij, A. L. 2002. Sociologičeskij monitoring processa polučenija elitnogo obrazovanija (na primere studentov MGIMO) [Sociological monitoring of the process of elite education (in the case of students at MGIMO)]. In *Elitnoe obrazovanie: mirovoj opyt i model' MGIMO [Elite education: global experience and the model of MGIMO]*, eds. G. K. Ašin and S. A. Kravčenko, 189-223. Moscow: MGIMO.

Thomassen, L. 2005. Reading radical democracy: a commentary on Clive Barnett. *Political Geography* 24 (5):631-639.

Thompson, H. S. 1967. *Hell's Angels: a strange and terrible saga.* New York: Random House.

Thrift, N. 2000. It's the little things. In *Geopolitical traditions: a century of geopolitical thought*, eds. K. Dodds and D. Atkinson, 380-387. London: Routledge.

Titscher, S., M. Meyer, R. Wodak, and E. Vetter. 2000. *Methods of text and discourse analysis: in search of meaning.* London: Sage.

Torfing, J. 1999. *New theories of discourse: Laclau, Mouffe, and Žižek.* Oxford: Blackwell.

———. 2004. Discourse theory: achievements, arguments, and challenges. In *Discourse theory in European politics: identity, policy and governance*, eds. D. Howarth and J. Torfing, 1-32. Basingstoke: Palgrave Macmillan.

Torkunov, A. V. 2004. *MGIMO-Universitet: tradicii i sovremennost': 1944-2004. (MGIMO-university: traditions and present: 1944-2004).* Moscow: Moskovskie učebniki i kartolitografia.

Trenin, D. 2002. From pragmatism to strategic choice. In *Russia after the fall*, ed. A. Kuchins, 187-204. Washington D.C.: Carnegie Endowment for International Peace.

———. 2005. *Russland: Die gestrandete Weltmacht.* Hamburg: Murmann.

———. 2006. Russia leaves the West. *Foreign Affairs* 85 (4):87-96.

———. 2007. Russia redefines itself and its relations with the West. *The Washington Quarterly* 30 (2):95-105.

Tsygankov, A. P. 1997. From international institutionalism to revolutionary expansionism: the foreign policy discourse of contemporary Russia. *Mershon International Studies Review* 41 (2):247-268.

———. 2001. *Pathways after empire: national identity and foreign economic policy in the post-Soviet world.* Lanham: Rowman & Littlefield.

———. 2002a. The culture of economic security: national identity and politico-economic ideas in the post-Soviet world. *International Politics* 39:153-173.

———. 2002b. Rediscovering national interests after the "End of History": Fukuyama, Russian intellectuals, and a post-cold war order. *International Politics* 39:423-446.

———. 2003a. Mastering space in Eurasia: Russia's geopolitical thinking after the Soviet break-up. *Communist and Post-Communist Studies* 36 (1):101-127.

———. 2003b. The irony of western ideas in a multicultural world: Russians' intellectual engagement with the "End of History" and "Clash of Civilizations". *International Studies Review* 5:53-76.

———. 2005. Vladimir Putin's vision of Russia as a normal great power. *Post-Soviet Affairs* 21 (2):132-158.

———. 2006a. *Russia's foreign policy: change and continuity in national identity.* New York: Rowman & Littlefield.

———. 2006b. New challenges for Putin's foreign policy. *Orbis* 50 (1):153-165.

———. 2007. Finding a civilisational idea: "West," Eurasia," and "Euro-East" in Russia's foreign policy. *Geopolitics* 12 (3):375-399.

———. 2008. Russia's international assertiveness: what does it mean for the West? *Problems of Post-Communism* 55 (2):38-55.

Tsygankov, A. P., and P. A. Tsygankov. 1999. Pluralism or isolation of civilisations? Russia's foreign policy discourse and the reception of Huntington's paradigm of the post-Cold War world. *Geopolitics* 4:47-72.

———. 2004. New directions in Russian international studies: Pluralization, Westernization and isolationism. *Communist and Post-Communist Studies* 37:1-17.

Tuminez, A. S. 2000. *Russian nationalism since 1856: ideology and the making of foreign policy.* Rowman & Littlefield: New York.

Turner, S., and S. E. Coen. 2008. Member checking in human geography: interpreting divergent understanding of performativity in a student space. *Area* 40 (2):184-193.

Valentine, J. 2001. The hegemony of hegemony. *History of the Human Sciences* 14 (1):88-104.

Van Dijk, T. A. 2008. *What do we mean by "discourse analysis"?* [cited 18 August 2008]. Available from www.discourses.org/whatisda.htm.

Vasilenko, I. A. 2007. *Geopolitika sovremennogo mira [Geopolitics of the current world].* Moscow: Gardariki.

Verkhovsky, A. 2007. The rise of nationalism in Putin's Russia. *Helsinki Monitor* 18 (2):125-137.

Wedel, J. R. 2001. *Collision and collusion: the strange case of Western aid to Eastern Europe.* New York: Palgrave Macmillan.

White, S., I. McAllister, M. Light, and J. Löwenhardt. 2002. A European or a Slavic choice? Foreign policy and public attitudes in post-Soviet Europe. *Europe-Asia Studies* 54 (2):181-202.

Wolcott, H. F. 1995. Making a study "more ethnographic". In *Representation in ethnography,* ed. J. van Maanen. Thousand Oaks: Sage.

———. 1999. *Ethnography: a way of seeing.* Walnut Creek: Altamira Press.

Yulikova, M. 2008. *An inconvertible education* August 2008 [cited 11 August 2008]. Available from http://www.russiaprofile.org/page.php?pageid =Culture+%26+Living&articleid=a1218126277.

Yurchak, A. 2006. *Everything was forever, until it was no more.* Princeton: Princeton University Press.

Zagorski, A. V. 1999. Traditional security interests in the Caucasus and Central Asia: perceptions and realities. In *Russia, the Caucasus, and Central Asia: the 21st century security environment,* eds. R. Menon, Y. E. Fedorov and G. Nodia, 61-86. Armonk: Sharpe.

Zevelev, I. 2002. Russian and American national identity, foreign policy, and bilateral relations. *International Politics* 39:447-465.

Zimmerman, W. 2002. *The Russian people and foreign policy: Russian elite and mass perspectives, 1993-2000.* Princeton: Princeton University Press.

———. 2005. Slavophiles and Westernizers redux: contemporary Russian elite perspectives. *Post-Soviet Affairs* 21 (3):183-209.

Žirinovskij, V. V. 1993. *Poslednij brosok na Jug [Last push south].* Moscow: LDPR.

Žižek, S. 1989. *The sublime object of ideology.* London: Verso.

Zjuganov, G. 1998. *Geografija pobedy: osnovy rossijskoj geopolitiki [The geography of victory: fundamentals of Russian geopolitics].* Moscow..

About the author

Martin Müller is Assistant Professor in the School of Humanities and Social Sciences at the University of St. Gallen in Switzerland. He studied Economic Geography at the University of Munich and subsequently read for a Master of Philosophy in Development Studies at the University of Cambridge. In 2008 he was awarded a PhD in Human Geography (*summa cum laude)* from the University of Frankfurt. Among other distinctions, he is a former fellow of the Studienstiftung des deutschen Volkes and the Stiftung Maximilianeum.

His current research interests fall into the fields of *Politics and Space* and *Economy, Society and Nature* with a regional focus on Germany and Eastern Europe. Papers of his have appeared in *Political Geography*, *Millennium: Journal of International Studies*, *Area*, *Geopolitics*, *Geographische Zeitschrift* and *Osteuropa* as well as in *Biological Conservation* and *Environmental Management.*

martin.muller@cantab.net

www.martin-muller.net

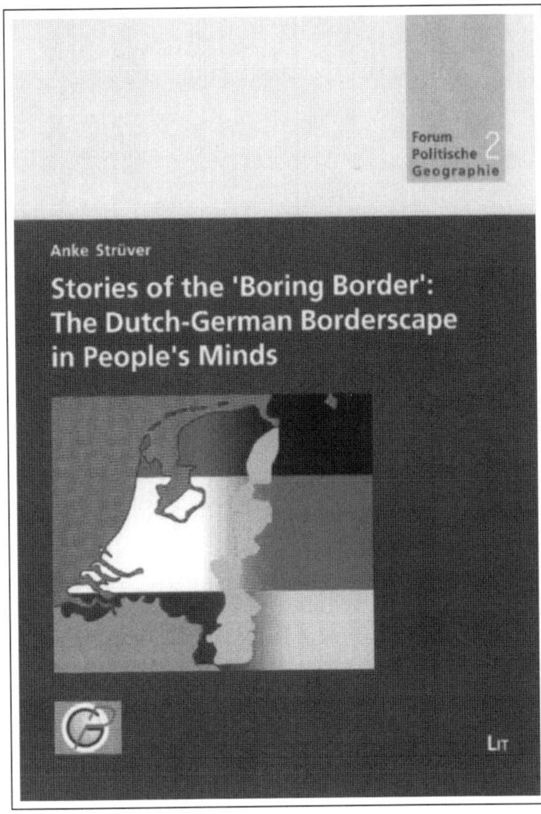

Anke Strüver

Stories of the 'Boring Border': The Dutch-German Borderscape in People's Minds

This book examines the 'open' Dutch-German border and people's everyday practices in relation to this border within the context of Dutch-German relations and the process of European integration. It concentrates on people's perceptions of the 'open' Dutch-German border and people's practices of crossing it - or not. The work also introduces new methodologies and forms of border research, e.g. on borders in people's minds, which are concerned with the construction of bordered spaces and the performed manners of nationalised daily routines. In this context, borders are framed as constructed by narratives and images, but also as representations themselves - as part of popular imaginations.

Bd. 2, 2005, 184 S., 19,90 €, br., ISBN 3-8258-8890-8

LIT Verlag Berlin – Münster – Wien – Zürich – London

Auslieferung Deutschland / Österreich / Schweiz: siehe Impressumsseite